MILESTONE VISUAL DOCUMENTS IN AMERICAN HISTORY

THE IMAGES, CARTOONS, AND OTHER VISUAL SOURCES THAT SHAPED AMERICA

Milestone Visual Documents in American History

The Images, Cartoons, and Other Visual Sources
That Shaped America

Volume 2: 1859–1940

Craig Kaplowitz
Editor in Chief

Dallas, TX

**MILESTONE VISUAL DOCUMENTS IN AMERICAN HISTORY:
THE IMAGES, CARTOONS, AND OTHER VISUAL SOURCES THAT SHAPED AMERICA**

Copyright © 2023 by Schlager Group Inc.

All rights reserved. No part of this book may be reproduced or utilized in any form or by any means, electronic or mechanical, including photocopying, recording, or by any information storage or retrieval systems, without permission in writing from the publisher. For information, contact:

Schlager Group Inc.
10228 E. Northwest HWY, STE 1151
Dallas, TX 75238
USA
(888) 416-5727
info@schlagergroup.com

You can find Schlager Group online at https://www.schlagergroup.com

For Schlager Group:
Vice President, Editorial: Sarah Robertson
Vice President, Operations and Strategy: Benjamin Painter
Founder and President: Neil Schlager

Printed in the United States of America 10 9 8 7 6 5 4 3 2 1
Print ISBN: 9781935306726
eBook: 9781935306733

Library of Congress Control Number: 2022943991

CONTENTS

Reader's Guide..viii
Contributors..ix
Acknowledgments...x
Introduction..xi

Volume 1

Smallpox Epidemic among the Aztec Illustration...2
John White: Village of Secotan Illustration...8
Nova totius Map of the World..14
Nova Britannia Recruiting to the Colonies Flyer...20
Brockett's Map of New Haven..26
The Castello Plan: New Amsterdam Map...30
John Foster's Gravestone...36
Cherokee Delegation to England Portrait..42
"A View of Savannah" Map...48
Robert Feke: Portrait of Isaac Royall and Family..54
Dockside at Virginia Tobacco Warehouse Illustration..60
Benjamin Franklin: "Join, or Die" Cartoon...66
Slaves for Sale Advertisement...72
William Bradford: "Expiring: In Hopes of a Resurrection to Life Again" Newspaper Protest................78
Thomas Jefferson: Advertisement for a Runaway Slave..84
Paul Revere: *The Bloody Massacre* Flyer...90
Philip Dawe: "Tarring & Feathering" Satirical Print...96
Philip Dawe: *Edenton Tea Party* Satirical Print..102
The Old Plantation Painting..108
"The Times, a Political Portrait" Cartoon...114
Colonial Cloth Makers Illustration..120
Painting of a Newly Cleared Small Farm Site..126
Elkanah Tisdale: "The Gerry-mander" Cartoon..132
The Plantation Painting...138
Carl Rakeman: "The Iron Horse Wins—1830" Painting..142
"Camp-Meeting" Lithograph..148
"King Andrew the First" Cartoon...154
William Henry Bartlett: Erie Canal, Lockport Illustration..160
Robert Cruikshank: "President's Levee" Illustration..166
Lowell Offering Masthead..172
Nathaniel Currier: "The Drunkard's Progress" Cartoon..178
Richard Doyle: "The Land of Liberty" Cartoon...184
Nathaniel Currier "The Way They Go to California" Cartoon..190
Currier & Ives: "Congressional Scales" Cartoon...196
McCormick's Patent Virginia Reaper Flyer...202
"Emerson School for Girls" Photograph...208
John H. Goater: "Irish Whiskey and Lager Bier" Cartoon...214
George Caleb Bingham: *The County Election* Painting..220
John L. Magee: "Forcing Slavery Down the Throat of a Freesoiler" Cartoon...226
"Picking Cotton, Georgia, 1858" Illustration..232

Volume 2

Cartoon Mocking Women's Rights Conventions..238
Louis Maurer: "Progressive Democracy—Prospect of a Smash Up" Cartoon...244
Photograph of Powder Monkey on USS *New Hampshire*...250

Andrew J. Russell: Ruins of Richmond Photograph...............256
Photograph of the 107th U.S. Colored Infantry...............262
James E. Taylor: "Selling a Freedman to Pay His Fine" Engraving...............268
Alfred Rudolph Waud: "The First Vote" Illustration...............274
"Reconstruction" Cartoon...............280
Thomas Nast: "This Is a White Man's Government" Cartoon...............286
Thomas Nast: "The American River Ganges: The Priests and the Children" Cartoon...............292
John Gast: *American Progress* Painting...............298
Photograph of Nicodemus, Kansas...............304
Joseph Keppler: "The Modern Colossus of (Rail) Roads" Cartoon...............310
Haymarket Mass Meeting Flyer...............316
Photograph of Carlisle Indian School Students...............322
Jacob Riis: "Bayard Street Tenement" Photograph...............328
Louis Dalrymple: "School Begins" Cartoon...............334
Photograph of Freed Slaves at a County Almshouse...............340
Buffalo Bill's Wild West Flyer...............346
William McKinley Campaign Poster...............352
"Dreamland at Night" Photograph of Coney Island...............358
Edgar Thomson Steel Works Photograph...............362
Louis Wickes Hines: Photograph of Boys Working in Arcade Bowling Alley...............368
Photograph of Congested Chicago Intersection...............374
Photograph of Garment Workers Strike...............380
"Indian Land for Sale" Poster...............386
Photograph of Health Inspection of New Immigrants, Ellis Island...............392
Woman's Party Campaign Billboard...............398
"Gee! I Wish I Were a Man": Navy Recruiting Poster...............404
Photograph of Harlem Hellfighters Regiment...............410
Photograph after Raid on IWW Headquarters...............416
"The Only Way to Handle It" Cartoon...............420
Assembly Line Photograph...............426
Judge Magazine Cover: The Roaring Twenties...............432
Edward Hopper: *Automat* Painting...............438
Fazil Movie Poster...............444
Photograph of Bread Line, New York City...............448
John T. McCutcheon: "A Wise Economist Asks a Question" Cartoon...............454
NAACP: "A Man Was Lynched Yesterday" Photograph...............460
Photograph of Cab Calloway and Dancing Couples...............466
Jacob Lawrence: *The Great Migration* Painting...............472

Volume 3
Civilian Conservation Corps Poster...............478
"We Can Do It!" Rosie the Riveter Poster...............484
Photograph of B-17 Formation over Schweinfurt, Germany...............490
Ansel Adams: "Manzanar Relocation Center" Photograph...............496
Photograph of Navajo Code Talkers...............502
"Kultur-terror" Pro-German, Anti-American Propaganda Poster...............508
Alfred T. Palmer: "Detroit Arsenal Tank Plant (Chrysler)" Photograph...............514
Rube Goldberg: "Peace Today" Cartoon...............520
Photograph of Joseph McCarthy...............526
Photograph of the 101st Airborne Division outside Little Rock Central High School...............532
Thomas J. O'Halloran: "Kitchen" Debate Photograph of Richard Nixon and Nikita Khrushchev...............538
Photograph of Levittown, Pennsylvania...............544
Photograph of Interstate 10 under Construction in California...............550
Fred Blackwell: Woolworths Lunch Counter Sit-In Photograph...............556

Hélène Roger-Viollet: Drive-in Restaurant Photograph..562
Herbert Block: "I Got One of 'em" Cartoon about Selma, Alabama..568
Photograph of Black Panther Party Demonstration..574
American Indians Occupy Alcatraz Photograph...580
United Farm Workers Strike Photograph...586
Photograph of Vietnam War Destruction...590
Herbert Block: "National Security Blanket" Cartoon...596
"Remember Wounded Knee" Patch..602
Marty Lederhandler: Photograph of Gasoline Rationing..608
Photograph of Anti-Busing Rally in Boston...614
Warren K. Leffler: Photograph of Phyllis Schlafly at White House Demonstration.....................620
Herbert Block: "Strange How Some Choose to Live Like That" Cartoon..626
Pat Oliphant: "There He Goes Again" Cartoon..632
"Silence = Death" Flyer..638
Photograph of Berlin Wall Teardown...644
Tom Olin: "Wheels of Justice" March Photograph...648
Greg Gibson: Photograph of Anita Hill Testifying before the Senate Judiciary Committee........654
Steve Greenberg: "Bill Clinton's Foreign Policy Vehicle" Cartoon...660
Steve Greenberg: "Contract with America" Cartoon...666
Oklahoma City Bombing Photograph..672
Bush v. Gore Election Photograph..678
Photograph of World Trade Center Towers after 9/11 Terrorist Attack..684
J. Scott Applewhite: "Mission Accomplished" Photograph..690
"We the People Are Greater Than Fear" Flyer...696
Mihoko Owada: Photograph of Rioters Breaching the U.S. Capitol..702
Steve Helber: Photograph of Robert E. Lee Statue Removal..708

List of Documents by Category..713
Index..717

MILESTONE VISUAL DOCUMENTS IN AMERICAN HISTORY

THE IMAGES, CARTOONS, AND OTHER VISUAL SOURCES
THAT SHAPED AMERICA

Cartoon Mocking Women's Rights Conventions

Author/Creator
Harper's Weekly

Date
1859

Image Type
Cartoons

Significance
A wood engraving published in a prominent periodical that appears to mock women's rights conventions, which often met with an unsympathetic response in the press

Overview

On May 12, 1859, the Ninth National Woman's Rights Convention was held at Mozart Hall in New York City. With women's rights activist and social reformer Lucretia Mott presiding, Caroline Dall, a feminist author, journalist, lecturer, and champion of women's rights, read the convention's resolutions, all of which were adopted. Among the resolutions was one to send a "memorial" to the legislature in every state, demanding new laws that would guarantee women the right to a trial by jury of female peers, the right to vote for representatives, the right to retain their own wages, and the "right to person, property, children, and home."

The resolution read, in part: "All republican constitutions set forth the great truth that every human being is endowed with certain inalienable rights—such as life liberty and the pursuit of happiness. . . . We demand . . . that you shall, by your future legislation, secure to women all those rights and privileges and immunities which in equity belong to every citizen of a republic."

The convention, which was marked by rowdiness and heckling that often made the speakers hard to hear, included speeches made by Dall; Mott, an abolitionist who, along with Elizabeth Cady Stanton, essentially organized the women's rights movement in the United States; Antoinette Brown Blackwell, the first U.S. woman to be ordained a minister in a mainstream Protestant religious denomination (the Congregationalist church) and who melded her feminist activism with her religious vocation; and Ernestine Rose, a leader in the movement known as the "Queen of the Platform," despite being an atheist and a Polish Jew by birth. Also speaking at the convention was Wendell Phillips, an ardent abolitionist who had gained considerable experience dealing with hostile audiences at anti-slavery conventions and who, at the Ninth Convention, was said to have "held that mocking crowd in the hollow of his hand."

About the Artist

The name of the individual who actually created the engraving is unknown. The engraving was published in *Harper's Weekly*, one of the most prestigious periodicals in the United States at the time. The Harper Brothers publishing house was founded in 1825 by

Document Image

The "Denouncing Ye Lords of Creation" cartoon
(Library of Congress)

brothers James, John, Wesley, and Fletcher Harper in New York City. In 1850 Harper Brothers inaugurated *Harper's Monthly Magazine*, an illustrated literary journal that followed the example set by *The London Illustrated News*. The journal was among the earliest ones to include illustrations, which were coming to be regarded as an essential element of a successful periodical. The monthly published the work of Charles Dickens, William Makepeace Thackeray, and other established authors, giving it the financial resources to later become a weekly publication. After Frank Leslie launched *Frank Leslie's Illustrated Newspaper* in 1855, Harper Brothers concluded that the company had to follow suit with *Harper's Weekly*, which hit the newsstands in 1857 and by 1860 had reached a circulation of 200,000. While Leslie's publication focused on news, *Harper's Weekly* carried somewhat less news and more literary material, including fiction, essays on a wide range of subjects, and humor. Found in its pages was the work of some of the most prominent illustrators of the time, including Winslow Homer, Granville Perkins, Porte Crayon, and Livingston Hopkins. In the years that followed, the weekly provided extensive coverage of the Civil War, and it became widely known for the political cartoons of Thomas Nast, often regarded as the "father" of American political cartooning.

Context

The context of this illustration can be thought of as extending back to the women's rights convention held at Seneca Falls, New York, on July 19–20, 1848. This convention, organized by Elizabeth Cady Stanton and Lucretia Mott, is often regarded as the start of the women's rights movement in the United States, a movement that would gather steam throughout the century and lead, ultimately, to the ratification of the Nineteenth Amendment to the U.S. Constitution, affirming the right of women to vote.

The convention's origins stretched back to 1840, when Mott and Stanton met in London during the World Anti-Slavery Convention—where, ironically, Mott and Stanton, because they were women, were excluded from the floor of delegates. The two women used their time to discuss the possibility of calling a convention on the status of women in the United States. Their goal became a reality in 1848, when Mott was visiting the Seneca Falls region, where the Stanton family had its home. There, the two women met again, and with the help of Mott's sister and other women, they planned a

convention, which was held with only a week of preparation. The organizers ran an advertisement in the *Seneca Country Courier* that stated: "A Convention to discuss the social, civil and religious condition and rights of women, will be held in the Wesleyan Chapel, at Seneca Falls, New York, on Wednesday and Thursday, the nineteenth and twentieth of July, current; commencing at 10 o'clock a.m." The first day would be held exclusively for women, but the second day would be open to the public. Prior to the convention, Mott and Stanton (primarily Stanton) drafted a Declaration of Sentiments and Resolution, which became a seminal document in the struggle for women's rights. It articulated the rationale and goals of the women's rights movement and set the agenda for feminist leaders for decades to come. Three hundred people, mostly locals, attended the convention.

In the aftermath of such a successful local gathering, it was felt that a national women's rights convention had to be held, and that such a convention should be an annual one. The first of the annual conventions was held in Worcester, Massachusetts, in October 1850. Nearly a thousand men and women from eleven states attended the convention in Worcester's Brinley Hall. The participants called for equal pay, equal education, employment of women in all professions, the freedom to choose to combine a career with a family, the ability to hold public office, and the right to vote. Among the speakers at this convention was a "who's who" in the nineteenth-century women's rights movement: Lucy Stone; Sojourner Truth, an African American who, according to the *New York Herald*, asserted her right "to vote, to hold office, to practice medicine and the law, and to wear the breeches with the best white man that walks upon God's earth"; Abby Kelley Foster, whose incendiary addressed included assertion of the right to "cut the tyrant's throats"; Paulina Kellogg Wright Davis, who presided over the convention; Frederick Douglass, who urged women to "take their rights"; Ernestine Rose; Susan B. Anthony; and Lucretia Mott, who rejected the notion that others were "giving us our rights, permitting us to receive them."

The response of the press to this first convention was mixed. In the *New York Daily Tribune*, Horace Greeley wrote that whether the right to vote "would improve the lot of Women may be doubtful, but we are willing to give the Democratic theory a full and fair trial." The *New York Herald*, however, was openly contemptuous, anticipating the reaction of the men at the 1859 convention language so vitriolic as to be almost comical:

"That motley gathering of fanatical mongrels, of old grannies, male and female, of fugitive slaves and fugitive lunatics, called the Woman's Rights Convention, after two day's discussion of the most horrible trash, has put forth its platform and adjourned. The sentiments and doctrines avowed, and the social revolution projected, involve all the most monstrous and disgusting principles of socialism, abolition, amalgamation, and infidelity. The full consummation of their diabolical projects would reduce society to the most beastly and promiscuous confusion—the most disgusting barbarism that could be devised; and the most revolting familiarities of equality and licentiousness between whites and blacks, of both sexes, that lunatics and demons could invent."

Interestingly, after the convention, two thousand petitions were submitted to the Massachusetts legislature, but the legislative committee that oversaw voter qualifications reasoned that in a state with 200,000 adult women, it could infer that most women in the state did not want the right to vote.

The women's rights convention became an annual event. A second convention was held in Worcester in 1851. Subsequent conventions were held in Syracuse, New York; Cleveland, Ohio; Philadelphia, Pennsylvania; Cincinnati, Ohio; and three in New York City, including the 1859 convention. The last convention was held in 1860; the outbreak of the Civil War in 1861 put an end to the conventions. The Women's Rights National Historical Park in Seneca Falls, New York, commemorates the national conventions and, more broadly, the struggle for women's rights in the nineteenth century.

Explanation and Analysis of the Document

This widely reproduced image, a wood engraving, is simple. Taking up an entire page of the June 11, 1859, issue of *Harper's Weekly*, it depicts a lecture hall with large windows in the background and two chandeliers hanging from the ceiling. The hall includes an upper gallery to the right and to the left. A woman in a voluminous dress is on her feet at the dais speaking to the audience of men and women, presumably supporters, who are seated around her. In the galleries, however, are numerous men who are disrupting the speaker by heckling her, gesturing in a mocking way with their hands and arms, and with their hats. Many of the women in the foreground have expressions on their faces expressing dismay at the reactions of the men in the galleries. The image's caption reads: "Ye May session of ye woman's rights convention—ye orator of ye day denouncing ye lords of creation." ("Ye," of course, is nothing more than an antique spelling of "the.") The "lords of creation" was a widely used expression to refer, usually in a satiric way, to men who held economic, political, and social power, suggesting that they had set themselves up as gods over the nation—and over women.

It is difficult to determine what the intention of the cartoon is. In one sense, it can be interpreted as a form of simple reporting, in effect doing nothing more than depicting what took place at the convention. It can also be interpreted as a satire directed against the men in the galleries, who often greeted women's rights crusaders with derision that they expressed in a disruptive way. Alternatively, the target of satire might be the women themselves, who were thought—by the creator of the image and others—to have brought this kind of reaction on themselves for daring to question the established societal order.

—Michael J. O'Neal

Questions for Further Study

1. What may have been the purpose of *Harper's Weekly* in producing this cartoon?

2. Is the cartoon satirical? What or who is the target of the satire?

3. How might the readers of *Harper's Weekly*, a genteel literary publication, have responded to the cartoon?

4. Why were so many people, like the men in the galleries, derisive of advocates for women's rights?

Further Reading

Books

Donovan, Josephine. *Feminist Theory: The Intellectual Traditions of American Feminism*. New York: Frederick Ungar, 1985.

Du Bois, Ellen Carol. *Women Suffrage and Women's Rights*. New York: New York University Press, 1998.

McClymer, John F. *This High and Holy Moment: The First National Women's Rights Convention, Worcester, 1850*. San Diego, CA: Harcourt Brace, 1999.

Schneir, Miriam, ed. *Feminism: The Essential Historical Writings*. New York: Vintage Books, 1972.

Websites

Lewis, Jone Johnson. "National Women's Rights Conventions: 1850–1859." ThoughtCo., March 17, 2018. https://www.thoughtco.com/national-womans-rights-conventions-3530485.

Navasky, Victor S. "Why Are Political Cartoons Incendiary?" *New York Times*, November 12, 2011. https://www.ny-times.com/2011/11/13/opinion/sunday/why-are-political-cartoons-incendiary.html.

"Proceedings of the Ninth National Woman's Rights Convention Held in New York City, Thursday, May 12, 1859: With a Phonographic Report of the Speech of Wendell Phillips." Library of Congress. https://www.loc.gov/item/93838290/.

"The Women's Rights Movement, 1848–1917." History, Art & Archives, U.S. House of Representatives. https://history.house.gov/Exhibitions-and-Publications/WIC/Historical-Essays/No-Lady/Womens-Rights/.

Documentaries

The Story of Elizabeth Cady Stanton & Susan B. Anthony: "Not for Ourselves Alone." Ken Burns and Paul Barnes, producers. PBS, 1999.

LOUIS MAURER: "PROGRESSIVE DEMOCRACY—PROSPECT OF A SMASH UP" CARTOON

AUTHOR/CREATOR
Louis Maurer

DATE
1860

IMAGE TYPE
CARTOONS

SIGNIFICANCE
A commentary on the internal dissensions that derailed the Democratic Party in the run-up to the 1860 election of Abraham Lincoln as president of the United States

Overview

This 1860 cartoon highlighted the divisive presidential election taking place that year. The 1860 election was one of the most contentious in American history, in large part because of divisions in the country over the issue of slavery. The ultimate winner, Abraham Lincoln, was the nation's first Republican president, but he won with less than 40 percent of the popular vote—and he was not even on the ballot in ten Southern slave states. The remainder of the vote was divided among three other candidates. Two were Democrats, but the Democratic Party was split between "Northern Democrats," or Democrats from those states where slavery was largely opposed, and "Southern Democrats," or those from states where slavery was an entrenched institution.

The candidate of the Northern Democrats was Illinois senator Stephen A. Douglas, running on a ticket with Herschel V. Johnson. The candidate nominated by the Southern Democrats was John C. Breckinridge, whose running mate was Joseph Lane ("Jack" and "Joe" in the cartoon). A fourth candidate, John Bell, was nominated by the Constitutional Union Party. One of the specific issues dividing the Democratic Party was the extension of slavery into the new western territories. The Compromise of 1850, an effort to avert a crisis between North and South, permitted slavery in new states established south of the boundary established by the Missouri Compromise of 1820 but rendered slavery illegal in new states north of the line. The 1854 Kansas-Nebraska Act, legislation drafted by Douglas, repealed the Missouri Compromise and allowed the voters in those two territories to determine whether slavery would be allowed, establishing the principle of popular sovereignty in connection with slavery. During the 1850s sectional divisions over the issue deepened, and those tensions would ultimately lead to Southern secession and the Civil War of 1861–1865.

About the Artist

The cartoon was most likely produced by Louis Maurer, an American lithographer born in Biebrich, Germany, on February 21, 1832. Before immigrating to the United States in 1851, he studied anatomy, mechanical drawing, and lithography in Mainz, Germany, and he also worked with his father as a cabinet maker. In the United States, he went to work as a wood carver, but a friend convinced him that he could earn more

Document Image

The Louis Maurer cartoon from 1860
(Library of Congress)

as a lithographer, so after applying at several shops, he was hired in 1852 by the lithography firm of T.W. Strong. Later that year, after he showed some of his work to Nathaniel Currier, he was hired away by Currier & Ives, the well-known printmaking firm based in New York City, at a salary of $5 a week. He worked for Currier & Ives until 1860, although after that date he continued to work for the firm on a commission basis. At the time of his death, Maurer was thought to be the last surviving artist known to have worked for Currier & Ives.

Maurer was best known for his prints of sporting subjects and of horses. He produced more than a hundred prints depicting these subjects, including a series of prints titled *The Life of a Fireman* and another series titled *Preparing for the Market*. He developed a system that involved several artists working on a single print, with each artist doing a portion of the print that was his specialty. He often collaborated with Arthur Fitzwilliam Tait in producing prints of Native American and western subjects. He worked briefly for the lithography firm Major & Knapp (earning $25 a week), then, from 1872 until his retirement in 1884, he was a partner in the lithography firm Heppenheimer & Maurer. He died in New York City on July 19, 1832, at the age of 100.

Context

The purpose of the editorial cartoon was to illustrate the fundamental split in the Democratic Party over the issue of slavery during the 1860 presidential campaign. Democrats that year actually had multiple nominating conventions. The first was held from April 23 to May 3 in Charleston, South Carolina, but after fifty-seven ballots, the convention failed to nominate a candidate. The leading candidate at the convention was Douglas, but Southern Democrats opposed Douglas's stances on slavery and whether new states had the right to submit the issue of slavery to a popular vote. The Democrats reconvened in Baltimore, Maryland, on June 18, but a number of Southern delegates boycotted the convention, and others walked out when the party pledged to abide by the rulings of the U.S. Supreme Court on the issue of slavery. It was at this convention that Douglas and his running mate, Herschel Johnson, were nominated.

The boycotting Democrats, along with those who had walked out, formed what amounted to a separate party and held a separate convention in Baltimore. Their nominee was John C. Breckinridge for president and Joseph Lane for vice president. The pro-slavery platform of the Southern Democrats stated:

"2. Inasmuch as difference of opinion exists in the Democratic party as to the nature and extent of the powers of a Territorial Legislature, and as to the powers and duties of Congress, under the Constitution of the United States, over the institution of slavery within the Territories, . . .

"6. Resolved, That the enactments of the State Legislatures to defeat the faithful execution of the Fugitive Slave Law, are hostile in character, subversive of the Constitution, and revolutionary in their effect."

This split was the culmination of a decade of sectional tensions that rendered the future of the Union uncertain. Among other provisions, the Compromise of 1850 enacted a strict Fugitive Slave law, but opponents of slavery in the North had little interest in aiding in the capture of fugitive slaves, and a number of northern states, including Connecticut, Massachusetts, Michigan, Maine, New Hampshire, Ohio, Pennsylvania, Wisconsin, and Vermont, passed "personal liberty laws" that prevented state authorities from cooperating in the capture and return of fugitive slaves. The Kansas-Nebraska Act of 1954 repealed the Compromise of 1850, but it led to "Bleeding Kansas," the term used to refer to outbreaks of guerrilla warfare between pro-slavery and anti-slavery forces in Kansas and western Missouri after the creation of Kansas and Nebraska Territories in 1854. The congressional act that created the territories gave each the right to submit the issue of slavery to a popular vote. Two particularly noteworthy events took place during this violent period. In 1856, pro-slavery "border ruffians" sacked the town of Lawrence, Kansas. This in turn prompted abolitionist John Brown (who later would become famous for leading the raid on Harpers Ferry, Virginia, now in West Virginia) to lead a party of seven men, including four of his sons, who dragged five men from their homes along Pottawatomie Creek in Kansas and murdered them. The infamous decision by the U.S. Supreme Court in *Dred Scott v. Sandford* (1857), which declared in effect that slaves were not citizens, added to the tension. Although President Franklin Pierce (1853–1857) and his successor, James Buchanan (1857–1861), were Northern Democrats, their sympathies lay with the South, adding another ingredient to the simmering tensions.

In the 1860 nominating convention in Chicago, the Republican Party, formed in 1856 to replace the old Whig Party, nominated Abraham Lincoln, who ran on a platform that stated that a Republican president would not interfere with slavery in the South but would oppose the extension of slavery into new western territories. Meanwhile, the tensions that divided North and South led to internal dissensions in the Democratic Party. The ultimate candidate of the Northern Democrats, Stephen A. Douglas, ran on a platform of popular sovereignty (note the play on this word in the cartoon, "Sovereing," which embeds the word "rein"), meaning that the settlers in each territory would be allowed to vote on the question of whether to allow slavery—a position that enraged many Southern Democrats and led them, with Buchanan's support, to hold a breakaway nominating convention.

The irony is that the dissensions within the Democratic Party, as depicted in the cartoon by the two teams of horses pulling in different directions, split the vote. Douglas won 1,380,202 popular votes (29.46 percent), and Breckinridge won 848,019 (18.10 percent). Together they won 2,228,221 popular votes to Lincoln's 1,865,908. (Bell won nearly 600,000 popular votes, or more than 12 percent). Lincoln, however, carried all of the more populous Northern states with their troves of electoral votes, so he handily won in the Electoral College, with 180 electoral votes to Breckinridge's 72, Douglas's 12, and Bell's 39.

The election of Lincoln was the proximate cause of declarations of secession in the Southern states of South Carolina, Mississippi, Florida, Alabama, Georgia, Louisiana, and Texas, which formed the Confederate States of America. Secession was also considered in Missouri and in four states that later joined the Confederacy: Virginia, Tennessee, Arkansas, and North Carolina. Lincoln refused to cede federal property to the seceding states. Hope for some sort of compromise to avert hostilities ended with the Southern bombardment of Fort Sumter in South Carolina on April 12, 1861—the event that began the Civil War.

Explanation and Analysis of the Document

The document is a political cartoon originally published as a lithograph by Currier & Ives. It depicts Republican presidential candidate Abraham Lincoln, accompanied by his running mate, Hannibal Hamlin, about to bring ruin to the Democratic Party, which is paralyzed by internal dissension. The Republicans are riding a locomotive named "Equal Rights." The locomotive is approaching a crossing where a wagon called "Democratic Platform" is being drawn by two opposing teams of horses but is stalled across the track because the two teams are pulling in opposing directions. One team, with the heads of Northern Democratic candidate Stephen A. Douglas and his vice presidential running mate, Herschel V. Johnson, identified by a flag, is pulling to the left. The heads on the other team of horses are those of Southern Democratic candidate John C. Breckinridge and his running mate, Joseph Lane, who are pulling to the right. Driving the wagon is a Native American who is cracking a whip and who is identified as "A squatter Sovereing," possibly a tongue-in-cheek reference to the position of Douglas and others that popular sovereignty, or "squatter sovereignty," should determine the issue of slavery in the western territories. The "bubble" from the Indian contains the words "Now then little Dug! put in and pull, while I cry 'Tammany to the rescue' for I hear a rushing sound that bodes us no good." The reference is to Tammany Hall, the political machine that essentially ran New York City and could deliver the state's electoral votes to a favored candidate. On the right in the wagon is incumbent president James Buchanan, who supported the candidacy of Breckinridge. He too is cracking a whip and exclaiming, "Come Jack, and Joe [referring to Breckinridge and Lane], pull up! and don't let the other team stir the wagon. I'd rather the Machine would be smashed than have them run away with it." Lincoln is shouting "Clear the track!" while Hamlin is shouting "Look out for the Engine, when the bell rings!"

—Michael J. O'Neal

Questions for Further Study

1. What is the primary message of this cartoon?

2. Who is the intended audience of the cartoon?

3. How effective might the cartoon have been in influencing a voter's views of the candidates?

4. How does the artist use satire to underscore the point of the cartoon?

Further Reading

Books

Baker, Jean H. *Affairs of Party: The Political Culture of Northern Democrats in the Mid-Nineteenth Century.* Ithaca, NY: Cornell University Press, 1983.

Egerton, Douglas. *Year of Meteors: Stephen Douglas, Abraham Lincoln, and the Election That Brought on the Civil War.* New York: Bloomsbury, 2010.

Fuller, A. James, ed. *The Election of 1860 Reconsidered.* Kent, Ohio: Kent State University Press, 2011.

Holt, Michael F. *The Election of 1860: A Campaign Fraught with Consequences.* Lawrence: University Press of Kansas, 2017.

Peters, Harry Twyford. *Currier & Ives, Printmakers to the American People.* Garden City, NY: Doubleday, 1942.

Websites

"A Fractured Election." National Museum of American History. https://americanhistory.si.edu/lincoln/fractured-election.

"Northern Democratic Party." Ohio History Central. https://ohiohistorycentral.org/w/Northern_Democratic_Party.

Documentaries

Mavretic, Michael, and Brian Rose. *Fighting for Lincoln: The Wide Awakes.* Wide Awake Films, 2020.

Photograph Of Powder Monkey On USS *New Hampshire*

Author/Creator Unknown	**Image Type** Photographs
Date 1864–65	**Significance** Contrasts the youth and stature of the young sailor with the power and lethality of the ship's cannon

Overview

During the American Civil War (1861–65), both the Union and the Confederacy used children as young as ten as soldiers and sailors. The photograph is of a young sailor serving as a powder monkey, a naval term for someone assigned to bring gunpowder from a ship's magazine to its cannons. The picture is from the later years of the Civil War and features the deck of the USS *New Hampshire* (some sources identify the ship as the USS *Pawnee*, a much smaller vessel). The *New Hampshire* was launched in May 1864 and served as part of the naval blockade of the coast of South Carolina until the war ended the following year.

The blockade was one of the most important components of the Union strategy during the war. The Union deployed its navy off the Confederate coastline in an effort to choke off trade between the rebel states and other countries. The blockade was highly successful and cut foreign trade by more than 90 percent by the end of the conflict. The U.S. Navy also used its fleet to capture key Confederate ports such as Mobile, Alabama, and New Orleans, Louisiana. The seizure of New Orleans was especially important as it also meant control over the Mississippi River and the division of the Confederacy between the states east and west of the river. Union ships also patrolled for Confederate commerce raiders. These were ships that endeavored to penetrate the blockade and attack Union merchant vessels.

Naval warfare changed significantly during the Civil War. The ship in the photograph was a sailing ship, propelled by the wind, but by the time of the war, ships were increasingly powered by steam engines that used paddles or propellers. The ship was also a wooden warship, but by the later years of the war, both the Union and Confederate navies were deploying ships made of iron. During the war, the first battle in history was fought between two iron ships. Dubbed the Battle of Hampton Roads and fought on March 8–9, 1862, between the United States Ship (USS) *Monitor* and the Confederate States Ship (CSS) *Virginia*, the encounter was a draw as neither ship was able to inflict serious damage on the other. However, the battle changed the course of naval warfare as navies around the world abandoned wooden ships and began to build iron ones.

About the Artist

The photographer is unknown. The Civil War was one of the first military conflicts to be widely pho-

Document Image

***The Powder Monkey* photograph**
(Library of Congress)

tographed, but little is known about many of the surviving images from the conflict. This picture is from a collection of photographs that were copied by the Library of Congress during the 1950s and 1960s from private collections.

Context

When the American Civil War broke out in 1861, both the Union and Confederate navies quickly expanded. The Union Navy grew from approximately ninety ships, only about half of which were in service, to more than 650. The number of personnel had to grow dramatically as well to provide crews for the additional ships. More than 80,000 men served in the Union Navy during the War. A small number of Union naval officers, around 300, resigned their positions to join the Confederate Navy. However, the South's naval forces remained a fraction of the size of their Northern counterparts since the Confederacy had to build its navy essentially from scratch, without the shipyards or resources of the Union.

When the war commenced in 1861, the Union implemented a strategy to defeat the Confederacy known as the Anaconda Plan. The initiative was designed to reduce or "strangle" the Southern economy, as a snake strangles its prey, by preventing goods from being imported or exported through a blockade. At the time, the majority of the South's trade was with Europe and consisted of shipments of agricultural products, led by cotton and tobacco. Key to the Anaconda Plan was a naval blockade of major Confederate ports. The Union Navy stationed ships off of the South's major harbors to intercept any commercial vessels traveling to or from them. The Union ships had to remain on station for long periods of time, and they were often a long away from friendly ports. To supply the vessels, the U.S. Navy deployed store ships such as the *New Hampshire*, which carried large amounts of food, nautical supplies, and other materials.

Most of the major U.S. shipbuilding facilities were in the North. Therefore, instead of attempting to build a large navy, the Confederacy endeavored to use new technology to overcome the numerical superiority of the Union. For instance, the South developed and deployed a submarine, the CSS *Hunley*, which became the first undersea vessel to sink another ship in combat. It sank the USS *Housatonic* on August 29, 1862, as the Union ship was blockading Charleston, South

Carolina. The Confederacy also built the first ironclad warship, the CSS *Virginia*. The *Virginia* was constructed using the hull of the USS *Merrimack*, which had been scuttled on May 11, 1862, to prevent its capture by the Confederates. The first iron warship commissioned by the Union Navy was the *Monitor*, which entered service on February 25, 1862. Because of its superior shipbuilding capabilities, the Union ultimately built sixty iron warships during the Civil War, while the Confederacy constructed twenty.

On March 8, 1862, the *Virginia* attacked a Union fleet blockading Hampton Roads, Virginia. The Southern ironclad sank two wooden Union vessels, the USS *Congress* and the USS *Cumberland*. The *Virginia* and the *Monitor* then fought an inconclusive battle the next day. However, the success of the *Virginia* spelled the beginning of the end of wooden warships. The iron hulls offered a far higher degree of protection from enemy shells. Also, the iron ships were powered by steam and therefore did not rely on the wind, which made them more maneuverable and often faster than their wooden counterparts. Finally, iron ships were far less susceptible to fire.

Although individual Southern ships were able to break through the Union blockade, the Northern strategy was ultimately successful in suppressing Southern trade. This contributed to shortages of military and commercial items throughout the Confederacy and significantly hurt the South's economy. The size and strength of the Union Navy was one of the deciding factors of the war.

Explanation and Analysis of the Document

The photograph is of a young sailor in front of a cannon on the deck of a wooden warship, the USS *New Hampshire* (or perhaps the *Pawnee*), while the ship is on blockade duty off the coast of South Carolina. In the background of the picture is a ship's boat in the upper left and rows of cutlasses to the right rear. In the upper midsection of the photograph are lines, known as ratlines, that allowed sailors to climb the masts of the ships and set, adjust, or furl the sails.

Many of the sailors in both the Union and Confederate navies were younger than eighteen. Boys as young as ten were used in a variety of positions in naval service at the time. Powder monkeys were younger sailors who were assigned to pick up gunpowder charges from the ship's magazine. The magazine was located deep within the hull of the ship, to protect it from enemy fire. The powder monkeys would carry the charges, which might weigh more than ten pounds, to the cannon and then race back for another. Boys were used since they were small and could easily travel through the cramped spaces of the ship. When not in combat, the powder monkeys had a number of other duties. They cleaned the ship, helped perform basic maintenance and repairs, and sometimes acted as servants for the ship's officers. Other youth, known as cabin boys or ship's boys, primarily worked as servants or messengers for the officers. Some youth as young as thirteen or fourteen were trained to be officers and were known as midshipmen.

The *New Hampshire* was not in service at the beginning of the war. Construction on the warship had begun in 1819, but budget reductions meant that the vessel was not launched. Instead it remained in storage until the Civil War. However, it was outdated. Originally designed to carry seventy-four cannons, when it was launched in May 1864 it was repurposed as a supply ship. It had just ten cannons, serviced by gunners and powder monkeys.

The artillery piece in the photograph was most likely a 100-pounder cannon. It was known as a 100-pounder because it fired a shell that weighed up to 100 pounds (45.4 kilograms). The cannon had muzzle that was 6.4 inches (16.3 centimeters) in diameter and had a range of more than a mile. Powder monkeys had to carry a gunpowder charge that weighed 10 pounds (4.5 kilograms). The cannon was aimed by adjusting the screw mechanism at the back of the gun. It took seventeen sailors to position and fire the 100-pounder, not including the powder monkey.

The cutlasses mounted in the background were used by sailors in hand-to-hand combat when their vessel was boarded by the crew of an enemy ship. Sailors also used muskets, pistols, boarding axes, and pikes. The ship's boat in the photograph was used to bring supplies aboard or to take crew members ashore or to another ship. It could also serve as a lifeboat or a scouting vessel, depending on the need.

The ratlines pictured would become obsolete as steamships replaced those powered by sail and as iron ships supplanted those with wooden hulls. Powder monkeys would also become outmoded because of advances in naval artillery, including the use of increasingly large shells and automatic loading systems. By the late 1800s, the public became opposed to the use of younger boys as soldiers and sailors.

The Civil War was the deadliest conflict in U.S. history. More than 620,000 Americans were killed in the fighting. It is not known how many of those killed were under the age of eighteen, but an estimated one million soldiers and sailors were seventeen or younger.

—Tom Lansford

Questions for Further Study

1. What were the duties of powder monkeys on board naval ships during the Civil War? Why were young boys chosen to fulfill those responsibilities?

2. What impact did the use of ironclad warships have on naval warfare during the conflict?

3. Why did the Union adopt the blockade strategy against the Confederacy? Was the strategy successful?

4. How did the rise of ironclad vessels change naval warfare? What made these ships superior to ones like that in the photograph?

Further Reading

Books

Bisbee, Saxon. *Engines of Rebellion: Confederate Ironclads and Steam Engineering in the American Civil War.* Tuscaloosa: University of Alabama Press, 2018.

Coddington, Ronald S. *Faces of the Civil War Navies: An Album of Union Sailors.* Baltimore, MD: Johns Hopkins University Press, 2016.

Roberts, William H. *Civil War Ironclads: The U.S. Navy and Industrial Mobilization.* Baltimore, MD: Johns Hopkins University Press, 2002.

Simson, Jay W. *Naval Strategies in the Civil War: Confederate Innovations and Federal Opportunism.* Nashville, TN: Cumberland House, 2001.

Tucker, Spencer C. *Blue & Gray Navies: The Civil War Afloat.* Annapolis, MD: Naval Institute Press, 2006.

Andrew J. Russell: Ruins Of Richmond Photograph

Author/Creator Andrew J. Russell	**Image Type** Photographs
Date 1865	**Significance** Documents the destruction of Richmond, Virginia, the capital of the Confederate States of America, at the end of the Civil War

Overview

At the outbreak of the Civil War, the city of Montgomery, Alabama, was chosen as the capital of the Confederacy, but in May 1861 the decision was made to move the capital to Richmond, Virginia. The move was made for a number of reasons. One was that Richmond, as one of the largest cities in the Confederacy, was a manufacturing center and in fact had more industrial capacity than the rest of the Confederacy combined. Among its industries were the Tredegar Iron Works, which provided most of the Confederacy's munitions, and the largest flour mill in the South. Aiding the city's industrial development was the James River, which provided the city's industries with a considerable amount of hydropower.

It was also felt that moving the capital to Richmond would strengthen the hold of the Confederacy on Virginia and neighboring states. Virginia had wavered in its commitment to the Confederacy. In April 1861 its legislature initially voted against secession, although it later reversed itself, but the decision to secede was subject to approval by the state's voters. The state then entered into a temporary alliance with the Confederacy before finally accepting the invitation of the Confederate congress to join. Further, many of the nation's most prominent generals, graduates of West Point and veterans of such campaigns as the U.S. War with Mexico (1846–48), were from Virginia. Virginia also had considerable symbolic value, for many of the nation's Founding Fathers, including George Washington, Thomas Jefferson, James Madison, and George Mason, were from Virginia. It has also been facetiously suggested that the capital was moved to escape the heat and mosquitoes of the Deep South.

With the exception of the Battle of Gettysburg in Pennsylvania, the Battle of Antietam in Sharpsburg, Maryland, and minor battles in Missouri, Vermont, and elsewhere, virtually the entirety of the Civil War was fought on southern territory. Virginia in particular was an ongoing battleground, with 120 battles fought in the state. Much of the effort of Union armies was directed at capturing Richmond, for the fall of the capital would have sapped the Confederacy's will to fight on and most likely would have meant the fall of the Confederacy—which it essentially did. After numerous campaigns, Union troops entered Richmond in early April 1865 to witness scenes of destruction such as that depicted in the photograph.

Document Image

Andrew J. Russell's 1865 photograph of Richmond in ruins
(Library of Congress)

About the Artist

The photographer who took this photo, Andrew Joseph Russell, was born in Walpole, New Hampshire, in 1829, but he was raised in upstate New York. His early training was as a portrait artist, and he gained a local reputation as painter of political portraits and landscapes. He opened an art studio in New York City, where he painted stage sets. When the Civil War broke out, he produced a battle diorama that was used as a backdrop at Union enlistment rallies. In August 1862, he returned to his home in Steuben County, New York, to recruit a company of infantry, Company F, 141st New York Infantry, to which he was elected captain.

In early 1863 the 141st was assigned to defend Washington, D.C. There, Russell met Egbert G. Fowx, a photographer for the U.S. Military Railroad, a unit created to operate rail lines seized during the war. Russell became Fowx's assistant and learned from him the principles of wet-plate photography (the process of covering a photographic plate with a light-sensitive emulsion). Brigadier General Daniel C. McCallum, who was assigned to oversee U.S. Military Railroad operations in Virginia, depended on Russell, Fowx, and others to document the construction of bridges, rail facilities, defenses, quartermaster facilities, wharves, and other Union undertakings.

Russell was the only official military photographer in uniform during the war. He was behind the camera for a famous photograph, "Confederate Dead behind the Stone Wall," taken during the Chancellorsville campaign. The Library of Congress has nearly 350 Civil War photos taken by Russell, who went on after the war to document the construction of the Transcontinental Railroad for the Union Pacific Railroad, including the driving of the "golden spike" at Promontory Summit, Utah Territory, on May 10, 1869. In the early 1890s he worked as an illustrator for *Frank Leslie's Illustrated Newspaper*. He died in 1902.

Context

The Confederate capital of Richmond, Virginia, located just 110 miles from Washington, D.C., was under constant threat from Union forces during the Civil War. Numerous battles in Virginia were fought virtually within earshot of the city, and the city's residents grew accustomed to the rumble of artillery fire and the pall of smoke of battle in the air. The city was had

been threatened during the Peninsular Campaign of 1862, which culminated in what were called the Seven Days' Battles. The campaign was led by Union general George B. McClellan, whose forces at one point advanced to within six miles of the capital. The battle pitting McClellan's forces against Confederate forces led by General Joseph E. Johnston was a stalemate, but it had two important outcomes. One was that it made McClellan overly cautious, prompting President Abraham Lincoln to contact him, saying in effect that if he, McClellan, was not using his army, perhaps he would not mind if he, the president, borrowed it. The other was that because of an injury, Johnston was sidelined and General Robert E. Lee was put in charge of Richmond's defense.

Union war planners believed that the key to capturing Richmond was first to capture the city of Petersburg, about twenty-five miles to the south. Petersburg was a major rail hub, and large amounts of provisions and war matériel passed through the city on the way to Richmond and elsewhere. The Union believed that if Petersburg could be choked off, Richmond could in essence be starved into submission. In June 1864, Union forces laid siege to Petersburg, a siege that lasted nearly ten months at a cost of more than 11,000 casualties on both sides. One of the most dramatic events of the siege was the Battle of the Crater, depicted in 2003 in the major motion picture *Cold Mountain*. The battle took place after Union forces detonated four tons of gunpowder in a tunnel they had dug under the Confederate position—the largest manmade explosion in history to that point. The explosion created an immense crater that became the scene of bloody fighting. By the end of March 1865, General Lee's forces were depleted by disease, desertions, and lack of supplies, and the forces of Union general Ulysses S. Grant, who had replaced McClellan, outnumbered Lee's by more than two to one. After Lee's starving army suffered a devastating defeat at Five Forks, Union forces broke through the Confederate lines on April 2 and captured Petersburg.

On April 1 Davis received a telegram from Lee urging Davis to make preparations for abandoning the city. On April 2, as he was attending a Sunday morning service at St. Paul's Episcopal Church, Davis received a second telegram from Lee, stating: "I think it is absolutely necessary that we should abandon our position tonight. I have given all the necessary orders on the subject to the troops, and the operation, though difficult, I hope will be performed successfully. I have directed General Stevens to send an officer to Your Excellency to explain the routes to you by which the troops will be moved to Amelia Courthouse, and furnish you with a guide and any assistance that you may require for yourself."

In response, Davis issued orders for the government's evacuation of the city. Officials began burning potentially sensitive documents in the streets. Stores of whiskey were poured into gutters to prevent them from falling into the hands of Union troops. Davis and his family boarded a train and left at 11:00 p.m. The intention was to remove the government to the city of Danville, Virginia.

Chaos reigned in the city. Angry citizens looted warehouses and found caches of food—smoked meats, flour, sugar, and coffee—that had been stored by speculators while the citizenry had starved. They scooped up the whiskey that was running in the gutters and gulped it down. The city's military governor, Lieutenant General Richard Ewell, was under orders to destroy all tobacco, cotton, and foodstuffs to keep them out of the hands of the enemy. To that end, Ewell had tobacco warehouses set ablaze. These fires, along with fires started by looters, were spread by winds, and soon a full third of the city was engulfed in flames. One of the buildings that caught on fire was the Tredegar Iron Works, where loaded artillery shells exploded. The Richmond Arsenal exploded, blowing out windows in homes as far as two miles away. On the James River, ships were packed with munitions and set on fire, again with a view to preventing the Yankees from seizing them, causing massive explosions that rocked the city and could be heard miles away. Ironically, fearful Richmonders, huddled in their homes, were convinced that marauding Yankee troops were pillaging their city, when in fact the noise, smoke, and chaos was caused by the Confederates themselves as they tried to tie up loose ends.

On the morning of April 3, Union troops, meeting with only token resistance, marched into the city and hoisted the Union flag over the Capitol building. Their first task was to put out the fires that had partially or completely destroyed more than 800 buildings. On that date, Richmond resident Sally Putnam provided a vivid account of the fall of Richmond in her memoirs:

"As the sun rose on Richmond, such a spectacle was presented as can never be forgotten by those who witnessed it. . . . All the horrors of the final conflagration,

when the earth shall be wrapped in flames and melt with fervent heat, were, it seemed to us, prefigured in our capital. The roaring, crackling and hissing of the flames, the bursting of shells at the Confederate Arsenal, the sounds of the Instruments of martial music, the neighing of the horses, the shoutings of the multitudes . . . gave an idea of all the horrors of Pandemonium. Above all this scene of terror, hung a black shroud of smoke through which the sun shone with a lurid angry glare like an immense ball of blood that emitted sullen rays of light, as if loath to shine over a scene so appalling. . . . [Then] a cry was raised: 'The Yankees! The Yankees are coming!'"

That morning, too, the city's mayor, Joseph C. Mayo, had this message delivered to the Union forces poised just outside the city: "The Army of the Confederate Government having abandoned the City of Richmond, I respectfully request that you will take possession of it with organized force, to preserve order and protect women and children and property."

President Lincoln had been following developments from a Union command post at City Point, about twenty miles away along the James River. He arrived in Richmond on April 4 and toured the destruction with Major General Godfrey Weitzel, who was in command of the city. When Weitzel asked the president for guidance on how to treat the people of Richmond, Lincoln responded: "If I were in your place, I'd let 'em up easy, let 'em up easy."

Explanation and Analysis of the Document

The photograph invites little analysis and explanation. It captures what remained of the bleak cityscape of the Confederate capital at the end of the Civil War. In the foreground is a mass of rubble, mostly bricks. The scene is that of the grounds of the Richmond Arsenal, as evidenced by the surviving archway and the cannon balls that remain stacked in pyramids on the grounds. Two soldiers seem to be examining the destruction, with what appear to be two children in their wake. In the background are the skeletal remains of a number of partially destroyed buildings. Most of the destruction took place in the city's commercial and industrial center rather than in residential areas.

—Michael J. O'Neal

Questions for Further Study

1. What emotions do pictures of the destruction caused by war, such as this one, elicit in the viewer?

2. What might the reactions of Richmond's citizens have been in seeing photos such as this?

3. How might the citizens of the North have responded to photos of this nature?

Further Reading

Books

Ash, Stephen V. *Rebel Richmond: Life and Death in the Confederate Capital*. Chapel Hill: University of North Carolina Press, 2019.

Bowery, Charles R., Jr., and Ethan S. Rafuse, eds. *Guide to the Richmond-Petersburg Campaign*. Lawrence: University Press of Kansas, 2014.

Dunkerly, Robert M., and Doug Crenshaw. *Embattled Capital: A Guide to Richmond during the Civil War*. El Dorado Hills, CA: Savas Beatie, 2021.

Lankford, Nelson. *Richmond Burning: The Last Days of the Confederate Capital*. New York: Penguin, 2002.

Newsome, Hampton. *Richmond Must Fall: The Richmond-Petersburg Campaign, October 1864*. Kent, OH: Kent State University Press, 2013.

Putnam, Sallie Brock. *Richmond during the War: Four Years of Personal Observation*. Lincoln, NE: Bison Books, 1996.

Articles

Williams, Susan E. "Richmond Taken Again." *Virginia Magazine of History and Biography* 110, no. 4 (2002): 427–60.

Websites

"Reactions to the Fall of Richmond." American Battlefield Trust. https://www.battlefields.org/learn/articles/reaction-fall-richmond.

DeCredico, Mary, and Jaime Amanda Martinez. "Richmond during the Civil War." *Encyclopedia Virginia*. https://encyclopediavirginia.org/entries/richmond-during-the-civil-war/.

Documentaries

The Fall of Richmond. Digital Scholarship Lab. https://dsl.richmond.edu/april1865/.

Photograph Of The 107th U.S. Colored Infantry

Author/Creator
William Morris Smith

Date
1865

Image Type
Photographs

Significance
Documents the participation of African Americans in the U.S. military during and after the U.S. Civil War

Overview

This photograph of fifteen members of the 107th U.S. Colored Infantry at Fort Corcoran in northern Virginia, each one armed with a rifle, might very well have unsettled many white viewers at the time it was taken. Civil War casualties were high, totaling some 620,000; that figure, if it were extrapolated to the U.S. population in the 2020s, would amount to about six million dead. As the war ground on, both sides in the conflict found themselves starved for troops, although the problem was more pressing in the less populous South than it was in the North. The question then arose whether "colored" men should be allowed to fight. Eventually, they were. Modern moviegoers are likely to be familiar with the film Glory, which tells the story of the 54th Massachusetts Infantry Regiment, under the command of Colonel Robert Shaw, and its heroic attack on Fort Wagner, South Carolina. For many Americans, this movie might have been their first insight into the fact that significant numbers of African Americans served the Union cause with distinction during the war. Nearly 180,000 Black men, or 10 percent of the Union Army, served as soldiers during the war (some estimates run as high as 200,000); 19,000 served in the U.S. Navy. More than 93,000 who served were former slaves. Some 40,000 Black servicemen died, about three quarters of those from infection and disease. The issue of arming Black men to fight, however, was a controversial one, and for that reason this photo might have been surprising to some, even in the anti-slavery North.

About the Artist

It is uncertain who specifically took this photograph, but it is highly likely that it was taken by William Morris Smith, who took other photos of Black soldiers at Fort Corcoran at this time. Smith (1819–1891) was born in England, and during the Civil War he worked under famed Civil War photographer Alexander Gardner. Gardner, born in 1821, was a Scotsman by birth. At age fourteen, he began a seven-year apprenticeship to a jeweler. He was a socialist, and as an adult he wanted to create a cooperative community in the United States, specifically in Iowa, although he never lived in the community that was formed there by like-minded people. Meanwhile, he became the owner and editor of the Glasgow Sentinel in 1851. When he visited the 1851 Great Exhibition in London, he saw the work of American photographer Matthew Brady, sparking his interest in the field of photography. In 1856 he and his family immigrated to the United States, settling in New York. Gardner served as Brady's assistant until 1862.

Document Image

The 107th U.S. Colored Infantry at Fort Corcoran in Virginia
(Library of Congress)

By 1858 Gardner was in charge of Brady's gallery in Washington, D.C. After Abraham Lincoln was elected president and war clouds began to gather over the country, Gardner was in a position to photograph soldiers who were on their way to war. Brady had the idea that Gardner should photograph the events and people of the Civil War. His idea had to be pitched to Lincoln, which was done with the help of Allan Pinkerton, the chief of the agency that would become the secret service. It was Pinkerton who recommended that Gardner be given the position of chief photographer under the jurisdiction of the U.S. Topographical Engineers. Later, Gardner was the staff photographer under Union General George B. McClellan. In this role he was given the honorary rank of captain. Gardner died at his home in Washington, D.C., in 1882.

Context

After the guns of war erupted at Fort Sumter, South Carolina, in April 1861 and news that war was underway reached the North, large numbers of free Black men, eager to fight and win freedom for their brethren in the South, rushed to join military units. (At that time various companies of soldiers were formed locally in each of the states; the state governor would merge ten of these companies into a regiment, placed under the command of a colonel. These regiments, in turn, were placed under the control of the federal government, which organized them into "armies" under the command of a general.) These men were refused admittance, however, because a federal law, the Militia Act of 1792, barred Black men from bearing arms for the U.S. Army—even though Blacks had served in both the Revolutionary War and the War of 1812. During this era, it was feared that armed Blacks could pose a threat of insurrection and of uprisings of enslaved people. A number of these men met in Boston and adopted a resolution petitioning the government to change the law to allow them to enlist.

The administration of President Abraham Lincoln struggled with the question of forming Black regiments, a step that even many anti-slavery citizens would oppose. The president and his advisors were concerned that admitting Black troops would result in the secession of the so-called border states: Kentucky, Missouri, Maryland, and Delaware. Some generals were on board with the notion of Black enlistment. Among them were General John C. Frémont in Missouri and General David Hunter in South Carolina.

These generals emancipated enslaved men in their military districts and allowed them to enlist. Their superiors, however, revoked those orders. By the middle of 1862, however, the government began to rethink its position because the number of formerly enslaved Blacks was large and growing, the number of white volunteers was declining, and needs of the Union Army for fresh troops was urgent. Large numbers of troops were dying from disease, particularly dysentery, and the early naive promise of a war in which right would triumph at the hands of heroes was being replaced by bitter disappointment and cynicism. If the North was to effectively prosecute the war, it needed men, and Black men were likely more accustomed to privation and hardship than were many white soldiers.

Accordingly, on July 17, 1862, Congress passed the Second Confiscation and Militia Act. This act freed enslaved African Americans whose owners were in the Confederate army. The act stated in part: "And be it further enacted, That the President be, and he is hereby, authorized to receive into the service of the United States, for the purpose of constructing intrenchments, or performing camp service or any other labor, or any military or naval service for which they may be found competent, persons of African descent, and such persons shall be enrolled and organized under such regulations, not inconsistent with the Constitution and laws, as the President may prescribe." Two days later, on July 19, slavery was abolished in the U.S. territories, and three days after that, on July 22, the president submitted a draft of the Emancipation Proclamation to his Cabinet. The ground was being cleared for African American enlistment.

After the Union Army turned back General Robert E. Lee's invasion of the North at Antietam, Maryland, in September 1862 and the Emancipation Proclamation was issued on January 1, 1863, the recruitment of African American accelerated. Black volunteers from South Carolina, Tennessee, and Massachusetts filled the first Black regiments. Recruitment, however, was sluggish until Frederick Douglass urged Black men to enlist as a step to eventually achieving full citizenship. On April 6, 1863, he stated: "Once let the black man get upon his person the brass letter, U.S., let him get an eagle on his button, and a musket on his shoulder and bullets in his pocket, there is no power on earth that can deny that he has earned the right to citizenship." At that point Black enlistment ballooned, prompting the government, in May 1863, to create the Bureau of Colored Troops to manage the influx.

During the war, Black soldiers served in a variety of capacities. Some served in the infantry or artillery. Many others served in noncombat positions as cooks, ostlers, steamboat pilots, laborers, scout, spies, carpenters—any position that would aid the cause of the war and free up others for service in combat units. Nearly eighty African American men were commissioned officers. Although Black women could not join the army, many, including Harriet Tubman, served as scouts, while others served as nurses. Generally, however, Black units were not deployed in combat roles, although they took part in a number of major battles at Milliken's Bend and Port Hudson, Louisiana; Petersburg, Virginia; and Nashville, Tennessee. During the assault on Fort Wagner, South Carolina, in 1863, the 54th Massachusetts Infantry Regiment lost two-thirds of its officers and half of its troops. By the end of the war, twenty-six Black soldiers and sailors had been awarded the Medal of Honor.

Black soldiers faced a number of obstacles. Although the units comprised Black soldiers, the officers were always white. Further, Black soldiers were paid less than white soldiers—$10 a month compared to $13 a month. Worse, $3 were deducted from the Black soldiers' wages to pay for clothing; no such deduction was made from the pay of white soldiers. This discrepancy was rectified in June 1864 when Congress mandated that "U.S. Colored Troops" be paid the same as white troops. Another peril faced by Black troops was capture by the Confederate army. After the Confederate Congress pledged to punish officers of Black troops and to enslave Black soldiers, President Lincoln issued General Order 232, which threatened reprisals in response to Confederate plans: "For every soldier of the United States killed in violation of the laws of war, a rebel soldier shall be executed. For every one enslaved by the enemy or sold into slavery, a rebel soldier shall be placed at hard labor on the public works, and continued at such labor until the other shall be released and receive the treatment due to a prisoner of war."

Explanation and Analysis of the Document

The photograph requires little explanation. It depicts a squad of fifteen African American soldiers, each holding a rifle by the muzzle end, although the man at the far left appears to be holding just a sword. Bayonets project above the muzzles of the rifles. The men are in Union uniforms and are standing before a small, light-colored building, likely a barracks. They are not standing stiffly at attention, but they are standing erect and alert. The photo provides evidence that African Americans served as soldiers during the Civil War era (although the photo was taken about six months after the end of the war) and were willing to fight for a better life for themselves and others.

In the wake of the war, African American veterans had to fight against disenfranchisement and Jim Crow laws that would deny them their civil rights. These men, however, because of the pride instilled in them by military service, were perhaps better able to wage the fight than were many other African Americans in the Reconstruction era, in large part because of the respect they had earned in their own communities.

—Michael J. O'Neal

Questions for Further Study

1. What would likely have been the reaction of the average white Northerner to this photo? The average Black Northerner?

2. How would the average white Southerner have responded to this photo? The average Black Southerner?

3. What might have been the photographer's purpose in taking a photo such as this?

Further Reading

Books

Dobak, William A. *Freedom by the Sword: The U.S. Colored Troops, 1862–1867*. Washington, D.C: Center of Military History, 2011.

McPherson, James M. *The Negro's Civil War: How American Blacks Felt and Acted during the War for the Union*. New York: Pantheon, 1965; reprinted, New York: Vintage, 2003.

Mendez, James G. *A Great Sacrifice: Northern Black Soldiers, Their Families, and the Experience of Civil War*. New York: Fordham University Press, 2019.

Shaffer, Donald R. *After the Glory: The Struggles of Black Civil War Veterans*. Lawrence: University Press of Kansas, 2004.

Smith, John David, ed. *Black Soldiers in Blue: African American Troops in the Civil War Era*. Chapel Hill: University of North Carolina Press, 2002.

Willis, Deborah. *The Black Civil War Soldier: A Visual History of Conflict and Citizenship*. New York: NYU Press, 2021.Articles

Articles

Cohen, William. "Negro Involuntary Servitude in the South, 1865–1940: A Preliminary Analysis." *Journal of Southern History* 42, no. 1 (February 1976): 31–60.

Freeman, Elsie, Wynell Burroughs Schamel, and Jean West. "The Fight for Equal Rights: A Recruiting Poster for Black Soldiers in the Civil War." *Social Education* 56, no. 2 (February 1992): 118–20.

Hauser, Christine. "A Call to Remember the 200,000 Black Troops Who Helped Save the Union." *New York Times*, February 26, 2022. https://www.nytimes.com/2022/02/26/us/civil-war-black-troops.html.

Richardson, Joe M. "Florida Black Codes." *Florida Historical Quarterly* 47, no. 4 (April 1969): 365–79.

Websites

African American Civil War Memorial Museum website. https://www.afroamcivilwar.org/.

"African-American Soldiers during the Civil War." Library of Congress. https://www.loc.gov/classroom-materials/united-states-history-primary-source-timeline/civil-war-and-reconstruction-1861-1877/african-american-soldiers-during-the-civil-war/.

"African Americans in the Civil War." American Experience, PBS. https://www.pbs.org/wgbh/americanexperience/features/lincolns-soldiers/.

Grimsley, Mark. "The Social Dimension of the U.S. Civil War." Foreign Policy Research Institute, June 10, 2007. https://www.fpri.org/article/2007/06/the-social-dimensions-of-the-u-s-civil-war/.

"United States Colored Troops in the American Civil War." National Museum, U.S. Army. https://www.thenmusa.org/articles/united-states-colored-troops-in-the-american-civil-war/.

Documentaries

Fight for Freedom: The Inspiring Story of African American Soldiers in the Civil War. Joe Geraghty, producer and director. https://www.youtube.com/watch?v=6vWsMAwHgd4.

James E. Taylor: "Selling A Freedman To Pay His Fine" Engraving

Author/Creator
James E. Taylor

Date
1867

Image Type
Illustrations

Significance
Signified that even though slavery as an institution had ended by 1867, African American freedmen, or former slaves, continued to face oppression at the hands of white governments and landowners

Overview

In connection with the publication of this illustration, developed from a sketch by James E. Taylor and published in the January 19, 1867, issue of *Frank Leslie's Illustrated Newspaper*, the publisher included this statement, which summarizes what the reader of the newspaper was looking at: "Our artist sends us the following account of his sketch: 'It is customary, when a white or Black man commits some petty crime or misdemeanor, to fine him; and if unable to pay, whatever the sum may be, the equivalent is required in labor. The culprit is taken to the County Court-House and sold to the highest bidder. The purchaser then takes possession of the culprit, who is put to work, and serves his time. A fine of $100 is equivalent to three months' labor.'"

Taylor added: "I sketched this scene on the spot. The sheriff led the victim to the place of sale having hold of one end of a leathern thong; the other end secured the negro by the wrists." The illustration, then, provides a dramatic indication of the precarious position occupied by impoverished, formerly enslaved Blacks in the years following the Civil War.

About the Artist

James E. Taylor was born in Cincinnati, Ohio, in 1839. At age sixteen, he graduated from the University of Notre Dame, and already by age eighteen, he had painted a Revolutionary War panorama. In 1861, after the outbreak of the Civil War, he enlisted in the 10th New York Infantry, also known as the National Zouaves. (The colorfully uniformed Zouaves were of French origin; various Zouave regiments fought in the Civil War.) During his enlistment, he sent battlefield drawings he had made to *Frank Leslie's Illustrated Newspaper*. When he left the army in 1863, he was hired by *Leslie's* as a "special artist," and for the rest of the war he traveled with the Union Army through Virginia, West Virginia, South Carolina, and North Carolina. Much of his work consisted of panoramas of battles and war settings. Sixty-one of his drawings were published by *Leslie's*. After the war, Taylor joined the Indian Peace Commission in the West; in 1867 his drawings of the Medicine Lodge Council of the Peace Commission appeared in *Leslie's*. (The Medicine Lodge Treaties were three treaties the commission signed with the Cheyenne, Arapahoe, Comanche, Kiowa, and Kiowa-Apache.) *Leslie's* also published his "Branding Cattle on the Prairies in Texas," the first illustration of the western cattle industry to appear in the national

Document Image

The 1867 engraving based on James E. Taylor's sketch
(Library of Congress)

press. Taylor later produced a number of drawings of the Great Chicago Fire of 1871. In 1883, Taylor left *Leslie's* to become a freelance illustrator. He died in New York City in 1901.

Context

During the U.S. Civil War, three to four million African Americans continued to be enslaved, nearly all of them in the South. They had hope for freedom, however. In January 1863, President Abraham Lincoln issued the Emancipation Proclamation, which declared that "all persons held as slaves" within the Confederate states "are, and henceforward shall be free." Their status, however, was both uncertain and precarious. Further hope was provided on December 6, 1865, when the twenty-seventh state (Georgia) ratified the Thirteenth Amendment to the Constitution. (Twenty-seven out of the thirty-six states had to ratify the amendment for it to take effect.) The amendment stated simply: "Neither slavery nor involuntary servitude, except as a punishment for crime whereof the party shall have been duly convicted, shall exist within the United States, or any place subject to their jurisdiction." This was a red-letter day, for it meant that the aspirations of abolitionists and the enslaved were realized: slavery was no longer legal in the United States.

"Freedom" from bondage was all well and good, but virtually all of those who had been enslaved were destitute, without land or any money to support themselves and with little to no education that would equip them for meaningful work. Most were illiterate, for the states that would form the Confederacy had passed laws making it illegal to teach enslaved people to read. In response to this need, the U.S. government in 1865 established the Freedmen's Bureau, or more formally, the Bureau of Refugees, Freedmen, and Abandoned Lands. Its purpose, according to the congressional bill that created it, was to provide "provisions, clothing, and fuel . . . for the immediate and temporary shelter and supply of destitute and suffering refugees and freedmen and their wives and children." Until its mandate ended in 1872, the Freedmen's Bureau also created schools and provided medical care for the formerly enslaved; by 1870 some quarter of a million Black children and adults had attended one of four thousand schools established for freedmen throughout the South. The Freedmen's Bureau's efforts extended to the workplace. The bureau tried to ensure that former slaves received fair wages and that they could freely choose whom to work for. The bureau created tribunals to adjudicate disputes between African American workers and white employers, and it was empowered to intervene in any case where the rights of freedmen were under assault.

The postwar effort to extend economic opportunity and equality before the law to freedmen was vigorously opposed by many white Southerners, who were embittered by Reconstruction policies that installed military governors who had power over the states of the former Confederacy. They were equally embittered by the sweeping authority of the Freedmen's Bureau. In an effort to restore self-rule, a number of the former Confederate states held conventions to form new state governments, but as might have been expected, they did not extend the right to vote to freedmen. By the end of 1865, most of the Southern states had held elections, in many cases returning former Confederate leaders to state government offices and the U.S. Congress. These state legislatures also began to enact "Black Codes," or laws that severely restricted the freedom of former slaves. None could vote, serve on juries, travel without impediment, or work in occupations that they chose. Even many marriages were rendered illegal. The Macon, Georgia, *Daily Telegraph* wrote: "There is such a radical difference in the mental and moral [nature] of the white and black race, that it would be impossible to secure order in a mixed community." Additionally, plantation owners feared that if freedmen did not continue to work for white landowners, the plantation economy of the South would collapse. Then a rumor spread among freedmen that the government was going to give each formerly enslaved person forty acres of land and a mule to work it. "Forty acres and a mule" was just that, a rumor, but the rumor was powerful enough to prevent many former slaves from signing contracts with white landowners in anticipation of receiving a grant of land from the federal government.

This illustration is indicative of the precarious position occupied by freedmen in the years following the Civil War. Although slavery had ended, many Southern Blacks continued to work and live in a kind of economic slavery, where they had little control over their lives. A Black person who was guilty of any kind of offense, even a minor one such as vagrancy, could be auctioned into bondage, requiring him to provide labor for a period of months. The continued oppression of Blacks was particularly severe in Florida (as well as in Mississippi and South Carolina). For example, ac-

270   MILESTONE VISUAL DOCUMENTS IN AMERICAN HISTORY

cording to Florida law at the time, vagrancy, which was selectively enforced against Blacks, could result in a sentence of as much as one year of labor. The children of a convicted vagrant could be hired out as apprentices. Black workers could be punished for disrespecting white employers. Blacks who broke labor contracts could be whipped, pilloried, and sold and required to provide a year's labor.

Explanation and Analysis of the Document

The meaning of this widely reproduced image might not be clear at first glance. It is only through the caption, "Selling a freedman to pay his fine, at Monticello, Florida," that the observer understands what is taking place. At the center of the illustration are two men standing on the steps of the county courthouse. One, a sheriff, is white, the other is Black. The Black man is bound by the wrists and tethered to the sheriff with a thong. The sheriff is gesturing. Behind them and to their left is the "Planters Hotel." Assembled in front of the men is a group of men and boys, most of whom appear from their dress to be working class. Two of the men in the crowd are on horseback. To the right of the two men, a Black person is sitting on a low brick wall. At the far left of the image stands a Black man with a crutch and a wooden leg. The observer infers that the white man on the steps is offering the Black man, who appears to be reasonably well dressed, for auction to anyone in the crowd willing to "buy" him. It was only in this way that the Black man would be able to pay off a fine that had been levied against him. The image makes clear that even though slavery had been ended by the ratification of the Thirteenth Amendment to the Constitution in 1865, freedmen, lacking money and property, continued to suffer the oppressions they had endured during slavery. In the view of many historians, the condition of African Americans in the Reconstruction period was simply slavery by another name.

—Michael J. O'Neal

Questions for Further Study

1. What does this illustration suggest about the condition of freedmen after the Civil War?

2. What might have been Taylor's purpose in creating and publishing the illustration?

3. How effective might the illustration have been in influencing public opinion about post–Civil War Reconstruction?

Further Reading

Books

Blackmon, Douglas A. *Slavery by Another Name: The Re-enslavement of Black Americans from the Civil War to World War II.* New York: Anchor, 2009.

Cimbala, Paul A. *The Freedmen's Bureau: Reconstructing the American South after the Civil War.* Malabar, FL: Krieger Publishing, 2005.

Guelzo, Allen C. *Reconstruction: A Concise History.* New York: Oxford University Press, 2018.

Novak, Daniel A. *The Wheel of Servitude: Black Forced Labor after Slavery.* University Press of Kentucky, 1978.

Oubre, Claude F., and Katherine C. Mooney. *Forty Acres and a Mule: The Freedmen's Bureau and Black Land Ownership.* Baton Rouge, LA: LSU Press, 2012.

Taylor, James E. *With Sheridan Up the Shenandoah Valley in 1864: Leaves from a Special Artist's Sketchbook and Diary.* Cleveland, Ohio: Western Reserve Historical Society, 1989.

Weinfeld, Daniel R. *The Jackson County War: Reconstruction and Resistance in Post–Civil War Florida.* Tuscaloosa: University of Alabama Press, 2012.

Wilson, Theodore Brantner. *The Black Codes of the South.* University of Alabama Press, 1965.

Articles

Cohen, William. "Negro Involuntary Servitude in the South, 1865–1940: A Preliminary Analysis." *Journal of Southern History* 42, no. 1 (February 1976): 31–60.

Richardson, Joe M. "Florida Black Codes." *Florida Historical Quarterly* 47, no. 4 (April 1969): 365–79.

Websites

"Freedmen's Bureau Acts of 1865 and 1866." U.S. Senate. https://www.senate.gov/artandhistory/history/common/generic/FreedmensBureau.htm#:~:text=On%20March%203%2C%201865%2C%20Congress,including%20newly%20freed%20African%20Americans.

"Documentary Media" (includes links to numerous resources related to the Civil War, freedmen, and the post–Civil War South). Reconstruction 360. https://reconstruction360.org/forty-acres-and-a-mule/media/.

Schermerhorn, Calvin. "The Not-So-Lost Cause." *We're History: Americans Then for Americans Now*, December 18, 2015. http://werehistory.org/not-so-lost-cause/.

"The Southern 'Black Codes' of 1865–66." Constitutional Rights Foundation. https://www.crf-usa.org/brown-v-board-50th-anniversary/southern-black-codes.html.

Alfred Rudolph Waud: "The First Vote" Illustration

Author/Creator
Alfred Rudolph Waud

Date
1867

Image Type
Illustrations

Significance
Symbolic of the promise of democracy during the Reconstruction era for Black men, whose ability to exercise the right to vote was a key feature of their new standing in America and a reflection of their interest in full participation in government

Overview

This document is a cover image for *Harper's Weekly*, a widely circulated periodical of the late nineteenth century. In this image, a Black man in Virginia is casting a ballot while three others stand in line behind him. This took place during first election in Virginia after the Civil War and was enabled by the Reconstruction Acts of 1867.

Created by Alfred Rudolph Waud, an artist known for capturing crucial moments in U.S. history, this image introduces *Harper's Weekly*'s coverage of the historic election. At this time, many formerly enslaved people cast their first ballots for Republican officials across the South, posing a significant political threat to the white Democrats who controlled the seats of government in southern states before secession from the United States and the creation of the Confederacy.

The text inside the pages of the publication noted the serious demeanor of the men as well as the diversity of their dress. The image is significant because it projects a powerful representation of Black pride and civic engagement in a widely circulated northern periodical.

About the Artist

This image was created by Alfred Rudolph Waud, who was born in London in 1828. He attended the Government School at Somerset House, London, to train as a marine painter. Instead, he found himself drawn to theater and immigrated to the United States in 1850 to work with John Brougham, a playwright and theater manager in New York City. Waud took on jobs as an illustrator. He married Mary Jewell, and together they raised four children in Orange, New Jersey.

Waud became well known during the Civil War. He could quickly illustrate a scene using charcoal and paper, and this skill helped him to record major events in battle. In 1860 he took a position as "special artist" with the *New York Illustrated News* and was assigned to cover the activity of the Army of the Potomac, starting with the Battle of Bull Run in July 1861. Waud remained with Army of the Potomac until the Siege of Petersburg in 1865. In the middle of the war, he took a new position with *Harper's*. He is believed to have created the only eyewitness illustration of Pickett's Charge. Though his sketches were rapidly produced, they were detailed and often transformed into woodcut prints.

Document Image

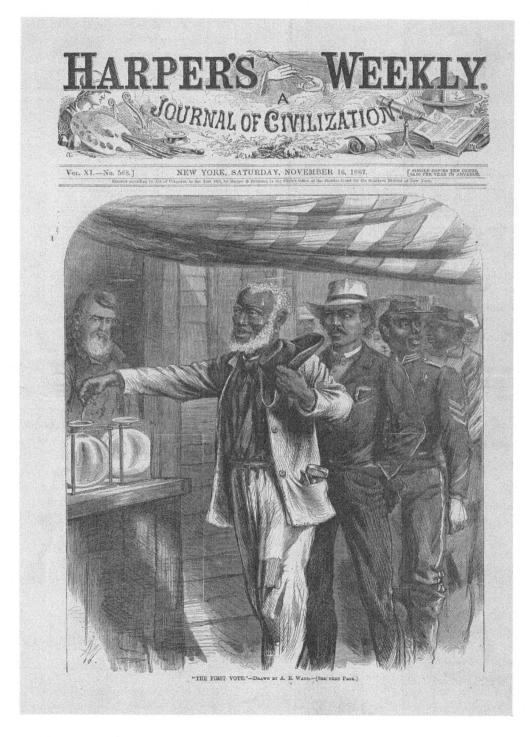

Alfred Rudolph Waud's cover of Harper's Weekly, November 16, 1867
(Library of Congress)

After the war, Waud documented various aspects of U.S. life during Reconstruction, capturing scenes of commerce, the South, and life on the frontier. He worked as a freelance artist and contributed many images to William Cullen Bryant's two-volume compilation *Picturesque America; or, The Land We Live In* (1872–74), which featured landscapes, natural scenery, and urban street scenes from across the United States. Waud died April 6, 1891, in Marietta, Georgia.

Context

After the Civil War ended in 1865, four million formerly enslaved people in the United States charted lives as free people. This included civic participation and exercising the rights and benefits of full citizenship. Casting a ballot in an election was an important part of the experience of freedom after emancipation.

The period after the Civil War known as Reconstruction (1865–1877) was a time of great tension in which the U.S. government tried to reconstruct a unified government after fellow Americans had taken up arms against one another. In 1867, the Reconstruction Acts set requirements for southern states to meet before they could be readmitted into the Union. This included ratifying the Fourteenth Amendment to the U.S. Constitution, which declared Black people to be citizens and included the Equal Protection Clause, requiring the law to be applied the same way to all citizens.

Throughout the South, formerly enslaved people rushed to polling places to cast their first votes. Over 1,500 Black people were elected to public office during Reconstruction, including Senators Hiram Rhodes Revels and Bruce Kelso Blanche. The voting power of Black Americans was significant. In South Carolina, for example, Black voters outnumbered white voters. Black Americans tended to vote for Republicans, as the Republican Party had supported emancipation and Black enfranchisement.

White southern Democrats, threatened by the demonstrated impact of Black enfranchisement, used intimidation, violence, and murder to dissuade Black men from voting. Southern states passed Black Codes to suppress the political power of African Americans and restrict employment opportunities for Black workers. Mobs of white people targeted Black business owners, landowners, and voters. Many white suprema-

cist organizations emerged, including the Ku Klux Klan, founded in 1865, and whose express purpose was the maintain white Democratic political dominance in the South. White Democrats not only threatened but murdered would-be Republican voters across the South. For example, a violent massacre of 200 Black Republicans in the parish of St. Landry, Louisiana, in September 1868 effectively intimidated the Black voting population. Despite a strong political presence earlier in the year, not a single Republican vote was counted in the election that November. Actual violence, or even threats of violence, kept Black voters away from the polls.

Black women, yet unable to vote, worked to secure the franchise for women. Gaining political power in the face of white supremacy required a multifaceted approach, so many Black suffragists worked for labor rights, education access, and protection from sexual violence alongside the pursuit for the right to vote.

The debates over the future of the United States, and of Black freedom in particular, took place in the press. White newspapers in the South depicted Black elected officials as corrupt and incompetent to undermine their authority. Johnathan Pike toured South Carolina and published many articles that eventually became a single volume, *The Prostrate State*, in 1874. In it, he degraded the South Carolinian government and Black elected officials generally. These racist stereotypes were folded into other media forms as well. Traveling minstrel shows featured white actors in blackface who played up racist stereotypes for the entertainment of white audiences. Notably, *The Birth of a Nation*, the first film ever screened at the White House, showed Black Republicans to be dangerous and Klansmen to be the redeemers of democracy. President Woodrow Wilson praised the film as an accurate portrayal of the Reconstruction era, and despite calls from Black activists to ban the film, it became one of the most popular films in U.S. history.

Explanation and Analysis of the Document

Harper's Weekly was a northern Republican periodical first published in 1850. It quickly became widely popular, with 50,000 copies in circulation after just six months. Technological innovation of the mid-nineteenth century fueled the expansion of the press; the Taylor Cylinder Presses used to print *Harper's* could produce 1,200 sheets in an hour. Its pages contained fiction and news for a general audience. Notable authors featured in the magazine included Horatio Alger and Mark Twain. It reported on major news stories and technological innovations. Because the magazine used a higher image quality than newspapers, its pictures proved a stand-out feature of the publication.

The image of "The First Vote" was featured on the cover of *Harper's* on November 16, 1867, to honor the Black voters who cast their first votes after the Reconstruction Act. The men standing in line to cast their ballots represent a cross-section of the African American experience. The clothing of each man offers clues about his work and role in the community.

The first man is white-haired and wears patched clothing. Tools hang from a pocket in his jacket, suggesting he is a manual laborer who may have been formerly enslaved. Four million formerly enslaved people after the Civil War sought to start their lives anew in freedom. Their priority was to reconnect with lost family members sold away under slavery. They also aimed to secure land on which they could build homes and farms and participate in government as free and equal citizens.

The man behind him is sharply dressed and clean shaven, suggesting he works in business and may have been free for some time. Free Blacks, as African Americans who were free before the Civil War were known, formed vibrant religious, economic, and social communities in the South, despite the specter of slavery. They spoke out against slavery and produced *Freedom's Journal* in 1827, which was the first Black newspaper in the United States. Free Blacks also facilitated the Underground Railroad.

The third man in line is wearing a Union soldier's uniform, displaying his loyalty to the U.S. government and suggesting he served as part of a Black regiment. About 179,000 Black men served in the Union army, comprising about 10 percent of the army's total forces. At first, President Abraham Lincoln refused to admit Black men into the army during the Civil War, but as self-emancipated Black men rushed into Union territory even as the Union army needed more men, Lincoln decided to admit Black troops in 1862. In May 1863 the U.S. government established the Bureau of Colored Troops. Black men believed their military service should guarantee them the basic rights and freedoms of citizenship, even as these were denied to them. In fact, Black men in uniform became targets of white lynch mobs because they represented a power and authority that threatened white supremacy.

The final man in line appears to be farmer. A large portion of the newly free Black population in the South worked as farmers after the Civil War. Black people purchased as much land as they could during Reconstruction. For some, farm work was the best way to achieve autonomy—working one's own land and living off the fruits of one's own labor had long been a central tenet of the antebellum version of the American dream.

There are several figures behind these four men, suggesting a crowd waiting to cast their ballot and perhaps to bear witness to this historic event. A white man oversees the ballot collection, perhaps foreshadowing the ways in which the infrastructure of white supremacy would soon mobilize to suppress Black voting power. However, as W. E. B. Du Bois famously said, Reconstruction, and the civic pride and power exhibited in this image, was but "a brief moment in the sun" for Black Americans.

—Mallory Szymanski

Questions for Further Study

1. What do you notice about the facial expression, body language, and clothing of the voters? What can you conclude about their lives and their views about voting from these cues?

2. Given the political divides between Republicans and Democrats in the Reconstruction era, and considering the role of the media in shaping debates about race and politics, what messages about race, power, and politics do you think this image would have conveyed to audiences at the time?

3. If someone at the polls wanted to prevent men from casting their ballot, what measures could they have taken? If they wanted to skew the votes after ballots have been cast, how could they go about that?

4. What emotions might this image elicit in readers picking up this paper in 1867? How would the reaction have been different for Republicans compared to Democrats?

Further Reading

Books

Du Bois, W. E. B. *Black Reconstruction in America: An Essay toward a History of the Part Which Black Folk Played in the Attempt to Reconstruct Democracy in America, 1860–1880*. New York: Russell, 1935.

Foner, Eric. *Reconstruction: America's Unfinished Revolution, 1863–1877*. New York: Harper and Row, 1988.

Ortiz, Paul. *Emancipation Betrayed: The Hidden History of Black Organizing and White Violence in Florida from Reconstruction to the Bloody Election of 1920*. Berkeley: University of California Press, 2006.

Websites

"Reconstruction and Rights." Library of Congress. https://www.loc.gov/classroom-materials/united-states-history-primary-source-timeline/civil-war-and-reconstruction-1861-1877/reconstruction-and-rights/.

Documentaries

Reconstruction: America after the Civil War. Julia Marchesi, director. Inkwell Films and McGee Media, 2019.

"Reconstruction" Cartoon

AUTHOR/CREATOR J. L. Giles/F Ratellier	IMAGE TYPE ILLUSTRATIONS; CARTOONS
DATE c. 1867	SIGNIFICANCE An allegorical representation expressing hope for reconciliation of the North and the South during the Reconstruction period following the U.S. Civil War

Overview

If the Civil War was the most turbulent period in U.S. history, the Reconstruction era, spanning the years 1865 to 1877, might deserve consideration as a close second. After the war, attention turned to stitching the torn country back together, extending civil rights to African Americans, particularly newly freed slaves, and ending the lingering bitterness between North and South. This engraving, produced soon after the guns of war fell silent, presents a highly idealized hope for the future of Reconstruction, when many Americans entertained the belief that the nation could bind up its wounds.

About the Artist

Virtually nothing is known about John Lawrence ("J. L.") Giles, the artist who created the lithograph from which the engraving was made, other than the fact that he worked in New York City as an artist and lithographer in the post–Civil War era. Similarly, little is known about Francis ("F") Ratellier, who printed the work and who operated out of premises on Broadway in New York City. The engraving was subsequently published by New York publisher Horatio Bateman.

Context

America's bloodiest conflict, fought almost entirely in the South, left much of the Confederacy in ruins. After the surrender of Confederate General Robert E. Lee in April 1965, the nation faced the arduous task of restoring the rebellious states to the Union and ending the evils of slavery. The Reconstruction period briefly provided African Americans with a measure of social and political power, but it was ultimately undermined by squabbling and a political backlash that ushered in the Jim Crow era, when Blacks were routinely and often violently denied their rights.

President Abraham Lincoln intended to strive for peaceful reconciliation—"with malice toward none, with charity for all," as he would put it in his second inaugural address. His goal was to make it easy for the Southern states to rejoin the Union, and he rejected harsh, retributive measures that would only add to the bitterness of the war. In 1863 he issued a proclamation that ensured readmission to any state that met certain conditions, including adherence to the Emancipation Proclamation he had issued earlier that year.

Document Image

The "Reconstruction" cartoon based on a sketch by J. L. Giles
(Library of Congress)

Under his plan, pardons would be granted to anyone who took an oath of allegiance to the Union, and the states would be allowed to draft new constitutions and hold elections.

Lincoln's proposals, however, were resisted by a group of congressmen, the so-called Radical Republicans, who thought them too lenient. They argued that although those proposals extended freedom to former slaves, they did not go far enough in ensuring their civil rights, so they offered an alternative plan: the 1864 Wade-Davis bill. Lincoln believed the provisions of the congressional bill were too punitive, so he refused to sign it. Then in 1865, Congress passed the Thirteenth Amendment to the Constitution, abolishing slavery; any Southern state that sought readmission to the Union would be required to ratify the amendment. That year, too, Congress created the Freedmen's Bureau, a federal agency whose purpose was to provide education, food, and assistance to newly emancipated African Americans and to oversee the distribution among them of land seized during the war.

Tragically, of course, Lincoln was assassinated on April 15, 1865, before he could put most of his plans into effect. It was widely assumed that his vice president, Andrew Johnson, would continue his policies. Johnson, however, was a Tennessean and a former slave owner, and his sympathies lay with the South. His plans included blanket pardons for former Confederates, including high-level officials, and he made no effort to extend access to Southern legislatures to African Americans. He allowed the states of the former Confederacy to create all-white governments. Johnson's leniency, which would later make it possible for Alexander Hamilton Stephens, the vice president of the Confederacy, to enter Congress and later serve as governor of Georgia, enabled former Confederates to create a system that differed little from slavery and ensured white dominance. The all-white legislature in Mississippi, for example, enacted a series of laws called Black Codes that limited the ability of African Americans to own property, serve on juries, move about freely, or even marry. Penalties for violations included unpaid labor, seizure of goods, and the removal of children, who would then be apprenticed to former slave owners. Other states soon enacted similar laws, prompting the Radical Republicans to pass the Civil Rights Act of 1866. The law granted citizenship to all men (other than Native Americans) born in the United States and guaranteed protection under all laws concerning property. Johnson vetoed the bill, but

Congress overrode the veto. Complicating matters in 1868 was the two-month-long impeachment trial of Johnson, who was acquitted in the Senate by a vote that was just one vote shy of the necessary two-thirds majority needed to convict.

In light of these events, the period of "Presidential Reconstruction" ended and "Congressional Reconstruction" (1867–1877) began, and it was early in this period that the Giles/Ratellier engraving was printed. In 1867 and 1868 Congress passed a series of Reconstruction acts that established military rule in the former Confederate states. The right of some high-level Confederate officials to vote was revoked. The bills required the Southern states to extend voting rights to all men and to ratify the Thirteenth and Fourteenth Amendments; the latter amendment stated: "No State shall make or enforce any law which shall abridge the privileges or immunities of citizens of the United States; nor shall any State deprive any person of life, liberty, or property, without due process of law; nor deny to any person within its jurisdiction the equal protection of the laws." But although Black men by law had the right to vote, many were kept from the polls by violence and intimidation. Accordingly, Congress passed the Fifteenth Amendment, which guaranteed that "the right of citizens of the United States to vote shall not be denied or abridged by the United States or by any State on account of race, color, or previous condition of servitude."

White Republicans from the North, derisively called "carpetbaggers" (because their portmanteaus often looked like they were made out of carpet), and white Republicans in the South, called "scalawags," supported the civil rights of Black Southerners so that men who in prior years had been enslaved now became a political majority in some places in the South—and most were Republicans. Between 1863 and 1877, hundreds of thousands of African Americans registered to vote. More than two thousand served in elective office. The first Black U.S. congressman was South Carolina's Joseph H. Rainey, elected in 1869; the first Black U.S. senator was Mississippi's Hiram Revels, who took his seat in 1870. Ironically, South Carolina, the state whose actions sparked the Civil War, had the most representation of Blacks during Reconstruction: in 1868 the state legislature had a Black majority, and throughout the course of Reconstruction, 210 African Americans served in the state house, 28 in the state senate.

For a brief period, it seemed as though, despite setbacks and obstacles, the promise of Reconstruction embodied in the Giles/Ratellier engraving could become a reality. As time passed, however, white resentment grew. Many Southerners believed that the Reconstruction policies imposed on them by the North were overly punitive. Moreover, many believed that Black people were incapable of governing. The backlash against Reconstruction policies led to the emergence of racist paramilitary groups such as the Ku Klux Klan, the Knights of the White Camellia, the White League, and the Red Shirts. These groups intimated Black lawmakers and voters, conducted lynchings, and tried to oust Reconstruction state governments. Reconstruction came to an end after an economic depression and a series of political scandals in the 1870s tarnished the reputation of Republicans and allowed Democrats to regain power. The bitterly contested presidential election of 1876 resulted in a backroom deal that gave the White House to Republican Rutherford B. Hayes over Democrat Samuel Tilden. The tradeoff was an end to Reconstruction.

Reconstruction's end ushered in the Jim Crow era (a term that originated with a stereotyped Black theatrical character in the 1830s). With federal oversight ended, white legislators in the South enacted laws that enforced segregation, criminalized interaction between whites and Blacks, and disenfranchised Black voters through poll taxes, literacy tests, and other obstacles. The hopeful Reconstruction vision of the Giles/Ratellier engraving was ultimately fleeting.

Explanation and Analysis of the Document

The engraving is a complex and multifaceted one that presents an allegory of reconciliation between the North and South during Reconstruction. The image, which was called at the time "Bateman's National Pic-

ture" (referring to Horatio Bateman, the publisher), embodies both patriotic and religious themes. It represents the federal government as an immense structure resembling a pavilion with a broad, flattened dome on which a map of the United States is drawn. Also on top of the dome is an American flag and shield and a federal eagle. Beneath the dome are the members of the Senate, House of Representatives, Supreme Court, and Cabinet. The dome is supported by a number of slender columns, the straight ones representing the state governments, the curved ones representing the people. The bases of the columns represent the former states of the Confederacy; the old ones are called "Foundations of Slavery." These are being replaced with new ones that represent Justice, Liberty, and Education. The structure is undergoing "reconstruction." Under the watchful eye of the army, people are carrying the new columns and putting them into place.

The remainder of the scene includes an abundance of symbols and figures. The sky is filled with numerous faces, including those of American statesmen, public figures, and historical characters, among them Joan of Arc, John Milton, Daniel Webster, and John Calhoun. All of these figures surround an image of Christ, who says, "Do to others as you would have them do to you." Flanking the group are allegorical figures of Liberty on the right and Justice on the left. Beneath the dome, Union generals Benjamin Butler and Ulysses S. Grant are shaking hands with Confederate generals P. T. Beauregard and Robert E. Lee. New York newspaper publisher Horace Greeley is seen embracing Confederate president Jefferson Davis. Below, sleeping in baskets, are two infants, one Black, one white. A streamer reads "All men are born free and equal." The background to all of this teems with people, houses, and buildings, which taken together suggest a rebirth of the United States as a nation of enterprise, peace, and growth.

—Michael J. O'Neal

Questions for Further Study

1. What was the underlying purpose of this image?

2. How could a viewer describe the tone of the image? What attitude might the creator be trying to impart to the viewer?

3. To what extent did this image fail to capture what would turn out to be the reality of Reconstruction?

Further Reading

Books

Foner, Eric. *Reconstruction: America's Unfinished Revolution, 1863–1877.* New York: Harper & Row, 1988; New York: Harper Perennial, 2014.

Foner, Eric. *The Second Founding: How the Civil War and Reconstruction Remade the Constitution.* New York: Norton, 2020.

Franklin, John Hope. *Reconstruction after the Civil War,* 2nd ed. Chicago: University of Chicago Press, 1994.

Guelzo, Allen C. *Reconstruction: A Concise History.* New York: Oxford University Press, 2018.

Perman, Michael, and Amy Murrell Taylor. *Major Problems in the Civil War and Reconstruction: Documents and Essays,* 3rd ed. Boston: Wadsworth Cengage Learning, 2011.

Prince, K. Stephen. *Radical Reconstruction: A Brief History with Documents.* Boston: Bedford/St. Martin's Press, 2015.

White, Richard. *The Republic for Which It Stands: The United States during Reconstruction and the Gilded Age, 1865–1896.* New York: Oxford University Press, 2017.

Websites

"America's Reconstruction: People and Politics after the Civil War." Digital History. https://www.digitalhistory.uh.edu/exhibits/reconstruction/introduction.html.

Blakemore, Erin. "Reconstruction Offered a Glimpse of Equality for Black Americans. Why Did It Fail?" *National Geographic,* February 8, 2021. https://www.nationalgeographic.com/history/article/reconstruction-turbulent-post-civil-war-period-explained.

"U.S. History Primary Source Timeline: Reconstruction and Rights." Library of Congress. https://www.loc.gov/classroom-materials/united-states-history-primary-source-timeline/civil-war-and-reconstruction-1861-1877/reconstruction-and-rights/.

Documentaries

The Civil War: Horatio Bateman's "Reconstruction" Engraving. Brook Thomas, presenter. C-SPAN, May 12, 2017. https://www.c-span.org/video/?428386-1/horatio-batemans-recontruction-engraving.

Reconstruction: American after the Civil War. Henry Louis Gates Jr., narrator. PBS, 2019. https://www.pbs.org/weta/reconstruction/.

Thomas Nast: "This Is A White Man's Government" Cartoon

Author/Creator Thomas Nast	**Image Type** Cartoons
Date 1868	**Significance** Criticizes the Democratic Party's platform prior to the election of 1868 as one of white supremacy

Overview

This editorial cartoon was produced by Thomas Nast in 1868 for *Harper's Weekly*. Promoted as "a journal of civilization," *Harper's Weekly* began publication in January 1857 and continued until May 1916. The journal featured both domestic and foreign news, humor, essays, cartoons, and illustrations. During the Civil War, *Harper's Weekly* was the most widely read publication in the United States. Although originally supporting Stephen Douglas, a Democrat, during the election of 1860, the newspaper shifted its views during the war in support of Abraham Lincoln and the Republican Party.

This cartoon, which was published in *Harper's Weekly* on September 5, 1868, focused on the presidential election of 1868. The Republican candidate, General Ulysses S. Grant, was pitted against the Democratic candidate, Horatio Seymour, the former governor of New York. This election was the first following the Civil War and the first to occur during Reconstruction. The Republican platform centered on support for Congressional Reconstruction of the southern states and African American suffrage. The Democratic Party opposed Congressional Reconstruction, maintaining it was unconstitutional. They argued for the southern states to reorganize themselves and for suffrage to be decided by the individual states.

Thomas Nast was a supporter of the Radical Republicans and of Grant. In this cartoon, Nash sought to demonize the various segments of the Democratic Party and to highlight their use of violence against African Americans. Nash also implies that Democrats were stirring up anti–African American sentiment in the North in their effort to reclaim the presidency. This cartoon highlights the key issues, such as violence against African Americans, suffrage, and racism, that were present during Reconstruction and the presidential election of 1868. Not only are southerners implicated as racist, but so are northern Democrats and Irish Americans, all accused of conspiring to stop the promotion of civil rights and African American suffrage.

About the Artist

Remembered as the father of American political cartoons, Thomas Nast was born in Landau, Germany, in 1840. With his family, Nast immigrated to New York City at the age of six and studied at the National Academy of Design. When he was fifteen, Nast's first drawings were accepted by Frank Leslie's *Illustrated Newspaper*. At this time, he was paid four dollars a

Document Image

"This Is a White Man's Government"
(Library of Congress)

week for his work. Over the next few years, Nast was dispatched to Europe to cover Giuseppe Garibaldi's Italian campaign for American and British newspapers. With the outbreak of the U.S. Civil War in 1860, the fiercely pro-Union Nast found a home with *Harper's Weekly*. Visiting battlefields, Nast sent realistic sketches back to *Harper's Weekly*, where engravers converted them to wood engravings used in publication.

In 1861, Nast married Sarah Edwards. The couple had five children. Sarah Nast contributed to her husband's work by acting as a model for many of his female depictions. Sarah also helped write the captions to her husband's cartoons, something the dyslexic Thomas found difficult.

As a Radical Republican, a subset of the party focused on emancipation and enfranchisement for African Americans, Nast used his cartoons to promote unionism, emancipation, and civil rights. The northern Democratic Party, which sought compromise with the Confederacy, was a constant target. In his 1864 drawing "Compromise with the South," a crippled Union soldier shakes hands with a well-dressed southerner over the grave of Union Heroes of a useless war. Columbia, modeled after Sarah Nast, is depicted weeping at the gravesite. During the election of 1864, the Republican Party reprinted the drawing numerous times in its efforts to reelect Lincoln.

With the collapse of the Confederacy and an end to the Civil War, Nast broadened his artistic endeavors, illustrating 110 books during his career. In 1867, Nast painted thirty-six massive paintings that served as an allegory of U.S. history. These paintings were rolled across a stage accompanied by music and narration. It was in drawings and cartoons that Nast's fame continued to grow. Nast was a devoted supporter of Ulysses Grant, and his cartoons were instrumental in Grant's presidential victories in 1868 and 1872. In 1868, he took on the corrupt New York Democratic machine, Tammany Hall, and was key in the downfall of its leader, William "Boss" Tweed. Having fled to Spain, Tweed was identified and arrested based on one of Nast's cartoon caricatures. In 1879, Nast used a donkey and elephant to represent the Democratic and Republican Parties, which have remained in use to this day. Nast is also credited with the development of the modern depiction of Santa Claus, which appeared in a number of his drawings throughout his career.

By the 1870s, Nast's popularity had begun to wane. The growing purchasing power of women and immigrants led to a journalistic shift to more general entertainment. In 1877, new management at *Harper's Weekly* began to move away from politics to meet the desire for more general topics. Refusing to draw cartoons that he did not believe or support, Nast finally left *Harper's Weekly* in 1886. Desperate for work, in 1902 Nast accepted an appointment as consul general to Ecuador by President Theodore Roosevelt. After serving less than six months, Thomas Nast died of yellow fever on December 7, 1902. He is buried in Woodlawn Cemetery in New York City.

Context

Following the defeat and collapse of the Confederacy, issues such as the status of the southern states and the rights of African Americans took center stage. With the assassination of Abraham Lincoln, Andrew Johnson assumed the presidency. Johnson's lenient Reconstruction policies toward the southern states and racism toward African Americans led to his alienation from the Republican Party. The divide between President Johnson and a Congress controlled by Radical Republicans—those who favored civil rights for African Americans—continued to expand. The Reconstruction Act of 1867, which began Congressional control of Reconstruction, divided the South into five military districts and included universal male suffrage in the establishment of new state government. Johnson's attempt to veto the legislation failed. Southern state governments became dominated by Republicans, and following Johnson's 1868 impeachment, Radical Republicans in congress seized total control of Reconstruction policy.

It was in this context that the election of 1868 and Nast's cartoon occurred. While Grant and the Republican Party campaigned to continue Congressional Reconstruction in the southern states and extend suffrage to all adult men, Seymour and the Democratic Party argued that the states should organize their own post–Civil War governments and had the right to decide who among their citizens could and could not vote. They campaigned that the Reconstruction Acts of 1867, and therefore Congressional Reconstruction, were unconstitutional. At the time, Grant was one of the most popular men in the northern states and easily won the electoral vote, with 214 votes to Seymour's 80. Three states—Virginia, Mississippi, and Texas—had not yet been restored to the Union and did not participate in the election. The popular vote—3,013,650 for Grant and 2,708,744 for Seymour—showed that although the country favored Grant, it was still deeply divided three years after an end to the Civil War.

Explanation and Analysis of the Document

Nast's cartoon attempts to show the viewer the various components and goals of the Democratic Party at the time of the election of 1868. The cartoon is centered on three figures, each representing a segment of the Democratic Party. The three figures are standing on the back of an African American soldier. Above the image is the title, "This Is a White Man's Government," and under the three figures is a caption: "'We regard the Reconstruction Acts (so called) of Congress as usurpations, and unconstitutional, revolutionary, and void.'—Democratic Platform."

The central figure of the cartoon is a depiction of Nathan Bedford Forrest. During the Civil War, Forrest gained infamy in the North for ordering the massacre of more than 200 African American soldiers who had surrendered to Confederate forces at Fort Pillow, Tennessee, in 1864. The medal on Forrest's jacket is meant to show the South honoring his actions at Fort Pillow and represents the South's overall treatment of African American troops during the war. Although Nast's image of Forrest is in civilian clothing, his connection to the Confederacy is displayed on his belt buckle. Raised above his head, Forrest is holding a knife inscribed with "The Lost Cause." The Lost Cause is an interpretation of the Civil War that glorifies the South's struggle against the overwhelming power of the North. It also romanticizes the Antebellum South and slavery and became a basis for the formation of resistance to Reconstruction, in particular the Ku Klux Klan. Forrest had been a founding member of the KKK during Reconstruction and served as Grand Wizard. Nast includes Forrest as a representation of the defeated South trying to maintain its glory and the position of white southerners in the face of emancipation and civil rights. The knife in Forrest's hand represents the violence southern Democrats were willing to employ, while the whip in his back pocket harkens back to the violence used to enforce the slave system.

The figure to the right of Forrest is a caricature of August Belmont, chairman of the Democratic Party in 1868. Belmont's inclusion symbolized the wealthy northern Democrats who supported Horatio Seymour in the election of 1868. Belmont's wealth (Belmont was the founder of the third leg of horse racing's Triple Crown, the Belmont Stakes) is shown in the cartoon by his clothes, his golden watch chain, and his "5th Avenue" button, referring to the wealthy New York City neighborhood. In Belmont's raised left hand is a packet of money labeled "Capital for Votes." This alludes to the Republican accusation that Democrats bought votes.

The left figure is a caricature of an Irish American voter. The apelike figure wearing disheveled clothing, with a liquor bottle in his front pocket and cross on his hat, furthers the stereotypes that the Irish were brutish, heavy drinking, lower-class Catholics. The hat is also labeled "5 points," a reference to the New York neighborhood populated at that time with poor Irish immigrants. A club labeled "a vote" refers to the use of violence to sway voters to support the Democratic Party. Together with the image of Belmont, Nash is insinuating that only through violence or bribery can the northern Democrats garner votes and achieve elector success.

All three figures, hands united, stand on the head and back of a prostrate African American soldier, an American flag lying under him. Having fought to preserve the Union, the soldier is being denied freedom and equality by the combined figures representing the Democratic Party. In the lower right corner of the image, a ballot box representing African American suffrage lies just out of reach.

The background depictions emphasize Nash's accusation that the Democrats use violence to achieve their goals. To the left, one sees the burning of the New York Colored Orphan Asylum by an Irish mob during the drafts riot on July 13, 1863. In front of the burning orphanage, one sees the hanging of an African American from a lamp post. To the right is a depiction of a southern Freeman school also burning.

Taken as a whole, Nash's cartoon is an indictment of the Democratic Party, both northern and southern, in 1868. Racism, bribery, and violence are all implied. The soldier and the flag remind the viewer that African Americans fought for the Union and earned the rights the Democrats were attempting to deny them. The inclusion of the flag also portrays the Democrats as unpatriotic, trampling not only on the rights of African Americans but also on all citizens' rights, represented by the flag. The cartoon can also be a window to Nash's own racism. Although an immigrant himself, Nash's disdain for the Irish is obvious in this image. His anti-Irish and anti-Catholic views were also implied in some of his other illustrations.

—Robert W. Malick

Questions for Further Study

1. Thomas Nast was a staunch Republican throughout the Civil War and Reconstruction. In what ways does this cartoon display his disdain for the Democratic Party?

2. The cartoon was a denunciation of the Democratic Party during the election of 1868. According to Nast, what are the key issues of the election? What is the viewer led to believe will occur if the Democrats win the presidency in 1868?

3. Nast depicts the Democratic Party as being composed of three groups. From the cartoon, what does each group contribute to the party? What does each group hope to gain from their support of the Democrats?

Further Reading

Books

Dewey, Donald. *The Art of Ill Will: The Story of American Political Cartoons*. New York: New York University Press, 2008.

Halloran, Fiona Deans. *Thomas Nast: The Father of Modern Political Cartoons*. Chapel Hill: University of North Carolina Press, 2013.

Hoff, Syd. *Editorial and Political Cartooning: From Earliest Times to the Present*. New York: Stravon Educational Press, 1976.

Navasky, Victor S. *The Art of Controversy: Political Cartoons and Their Enduring Power*. New York: Alfred A. Knopf, 2013.

Articles

Murrell, William, and N. P. Chipman. "Nast, Gladiator of the Political Pencil." *American Scholar* 5, no. 4 (1936): 472–85. http://www.jstor.org/stable/41206437.

Websites

Boissoneault, Lorraine. "A Civil War Cartoonist Created the Modern Image of Santa Claus as Union Propaganda." *Smithsonian*, December 19, 2018. https://www.smithsonianmag.com/history/civil-war-cartoonist-created-modern-image-santa-claus-union-propaganda-180971074/.

Jackson Arn, Artsy. "Why Democrats Are Donkeys and Republicans Are Elephants." CNN, November 3, 2020. https://www.cnn.com/style/article/why-democrats-are-donkeys-republicans-are-elephants-artsy/index.html.

Thomas Nast: "The American River Ganges" Cartoon

Author/Creator Thomas Nast	**Image Type** Cartoons
Date 1871	**Significance** Critiqued the efforts of the Catholic Church and Tammany Hall to undermine the public school system and fund sectarian schools with public money

Overview

"The American River Ganges" was a full-page editorial cartoon drawn by Thomas Nast and published in the September 30, 1871, issue of *Harper's Weekly* and republished in the magazine in 1875. The cartoon was accompanied by an essay written by Eugene Lawrence. Lawrence, a frequent contributor to the magazine, was a nativist who blamed Catholics for what he saw as the demise of the public school system. He argued that "to destroy our free schools, and perhaps our free institutions has been for many years the constant aim of the extreme section of the Romish Church." The essay attacks Jesuits and Irish Catholics, who, Lawrence argues, govern New York because of an unholy alliance between Tammany Hall, the political society run by the politician William "Boss" Tweed, and Irish Catholic immigrants, who looked to Tammany Hall for patronage—and who often received it by pledging to vote for the Democratic political candidates the society supported.

Both the article and Nast's cartoon appeared at a time when nativist impulses, or the view that the interests of native-born Americans had to be protected from an influx of immigrants, were ascendant in the nation. A principal target of nativists was the population of Irish Catholics, who were arriving in the United States in great numbers—as many as 4.5 million between 1820 and 1930. Some segments of American society believed that because they were Catholic, Irish immigrants gave their allegiance to Rome rather than to the culture and institutions of the United States. Nast, while noteworthy as a vigorous opponent of slavery and an equally vigorous supporter of emancipation, shared the anti-Catholic and anti-Irish biases of many Americans, as this cartoon makes clear.

About the Artist

The creator of the cartoon was Thomas Nast, the "Father of the American Cartoon" and arguably the most widely known caricaturist and editorial cartoonist of the nineteenth century. Nast created the Republican Party elephant, popularized the Democratic Party donkey, and created the popular red-suited, bearded image of Santa Claus. He was born in Bavaria in 1840, but he arrived in New York at the age of six. After studying art at the National Academy of Design, he became a draftsman at *Frank Leslie's Illustrated Newspaper* at the age of fifteen. When he was just eighteen, he did his first work for *Harper's Weekly*. He was a staunch

Document Image

"The American River Ganges: The Priests and the Children"
(Library of Congress)

supporter of the Union during the Civil War and used his pen and drawing board to oppose slavery—and to oppose those in the North who only tepidly supported the war and the emancipation of slaves. President Abraham Lincoln called Nast "our best recruiting sergeant," and General Ulysses S. Grant stated that Nast "did as much as any one man to preserve the Union and bring the war to an end." During the postwar Reconstruction period, his cartoons reflected his bitter disappointment with American political developments.

Many of Nast's most famous, and most venomous, cartoons were directed at Tammany Hall, the political machine that essentially ruled New York City through the dirty hands of William M. "Boss" Tweed, and those cartoons likely contributed to the collapse of the machine. In the 1880s, Nast was frequently in disagreement with the editors of *Harper's Weekly*, and his last cartoon appeared in the magazine in 1886. He lost nearly all of his savings and became destitute when his brokerage firm failed. He died in 1902 in Ecuador, having been appointed consul general to that nation by one of his chief admirers, President Theodore Roosevelt.

Context

Nash was a strong supporter of public education and drew a number of cartoons presenting his idealized vision of a school system that all students, regardless of race, religion, or ethnicity, could attend. The result of such a system in his view would be a diverse American society in which religious and racial differences would be diminished. He was unsettled by the efforts of the Catholic Church to create its own schools using public funds supplied through the corrupt influence of Boss Tweed and Tammany Hall. Nast feared that if Tammany Hall succeeded, each ethnic, racial, and religious group would strive to form its own school system at public expense. While the administrators of New York's public schools maintained that that the schools provided a nonsectarian education, many Catholic parents disagreed, pointing to the use of Protestant Bibles in the classroom and believing that the public school system as it existed reflected the values of Protestant small-town America, the mainstay of the Republican Party. Irish Catholics, in particular, believed that having to rely on a secular school system would in time erode their culture and faith.

Debate about the issue dated back to at least 1840, when the governor of New York, William Seward, intimated the possibility of state funds being provided to Catholic schools. In the years that followed, the Catholic Church, under the leadership of Archbishop John Hughes, tried to cultivate political contacts to achieve this end, but with little success. The matter stood in abeyance during the Civil War, but after the war, church leaders and political figures resuscitated the issue and engaged in heated debate over the issue of secular versus religious education.

Enter Boss Tweed (1823–1878). Tweed had served as a New York City alderman and as a U.S. congressman, and at the time the cartoon was drawn, he was a member of the New York senate. Ultimately Tweed and his corrupt cronies gained control of Tammany Hall, the name given to the executive committee of the city's Democratic Party. He used his influence to successfully back candidates for political office, including the mayor of New York City, the governor of the state, and the speaker of the state assembly. He and the "Tweed ring" bilked the city out of millions of dollars, and wielding the power of patronage, he essentially controlled the city's politics until his death. In 1869, he exploited his position in the state senate to slip a provision into a bill specifying that 20 percent of the New York City's excise tax would be used to fund Catholic schools. In response, press outlets such as the *New York Times* and *Harper's Weekly* mounted a crusade against Catholic efforts to drain funds from the public school system, and Nast's cartoons attacking the machine were believed to have tripled the circulation of *Harper's Weekly*.

Nast took issue not with the Catholic Church as a religious institution, nor with Catholics as individuals, but rather with what he saw as the involvement of the church in municipal affairs. He also opposed what he saw as blind allegiance on the part of Catholics to their foreign "monarch"—the pope—which in his view suggested the unwillingness of Irish Catholics to reject European monarchies and assimilate to American society. It was in this context—the nation's large number of Irish Catholic immigrants, the perception that Irish Catholics were unwilling to participate in the great American experiment, the belief that the Catholic Church wanted to fund its own sectarian schools from public coffers, and the corrupt influence of Tammany Hall over the city and its politics—that Nast produced "The American River Ganges."

MILESTONE VISUAL DOCUMENTS IN AMERICAN HISTORY

Explanation and Analysis of the Document

The cartoon is complex, with numerous elements working in concert. The Ganges River is a major waterway that runs through India and Bangladesh. It is the sacred river of Hinduism, giving Nast's American version a religious connotation. The foreground of the image shows Catholic bishops in their pointed, jeweled miters, or ceremonial headgear. They are depicted as crocodiles creeping out of the river on all fours, ready to devour a group of fear-stricken schoolchildren standing on the bank of the river. A Protestant minister, recognizable by his clerical collar, a Bible tucked into his waistcoat, and his parson's hat lying on the ground next to him, is defiantly protecting the children. In the middle of the image, several other bishops in the form of crocodiles are creeping up onto the riverbank, terrorizing another group of non-Catholic schoolchildren. A Chinese child, recognizable by his long braid, is trying to crawl away. The children pressed up against the cliff appear to be Native Americans and African Americans. The depiction of different ethnicities suggests Nast's vision of a U.S. public education system that should be open to all students.

At the top of the cliff, a bearded Boss Tweed and members of Tammany Hall lower a child, presumably a Protestant child, to the grounds below, where slavering crocodiles can feed on it. (In the 1875 republication of the cartoon, the representation of Tweed was eliminated.) To their right is a decayed building with the words "U.S. Public School" on the façade. Above the building, an American flag is flying upside down, a common symbol of distress. An image of Columbia, a goddess-like personification of the United States and a symbol of American liberty, is being led off to a gallows in the distance.

In the background of the cartoon, on the other side of the river, is a building with "Tammany Hall" written over the entrance. (In 1875, the words were replaced with "Political Roman Catholic Church.") The domed building is drawn to look like the Vatican in Rome. Flying over the building are two flags. One is a flag of the Irish harp, the heraldic symbol of Ireland that represented its independence in early Irish mythology. The other is the papal flag, consisting of vertical bands, the crossed keys to heaven of St. Peter, and the papal tiara. The presence of the flags suggest that the Catholic Church and Irish Catholic immigrants are in control of New York City's government. To the right of the building is a structure with the sign "Political Roman Catholic School." Clearly, in Nast's view, Catholic schools were not just religious schools but rather extensions of the political tentacles of Tammany Hall.

Taken together, the details of "The American River Ganges" constitute a bitter satire on the influence of Catholicism, and particularly Irish Catholics, on the public education system and on the influence of Catholicism on municipal government. The details also serve to implicate one of Nast's frequent targets, Tammany Hall, in corrupt processes that threaten the welfare and future of American schoolchildren.

—Michael J. O'Neal

Questions for Further Study

1. What is the principal message of the cartoon?

2. What satirical devices does Nast use in conveying his message?

3. How effective might the cartoon have been in reducing the influence of Tammany Hall and the Catholic Church in New York government?

Further Reading

Books

Dewey, Donald. *The Art of Ill Will: The Story of American Political Cartoons.* New York: New York University Press. 2007.

Fischer, Roger A. *Them Damned Pictures; Explorations in American Political Art.* North Haven, CT: Archon Books, 1996.

Golway, Terry. *Machine Made: Tammany Hall and the Creation of Modern American Politics.* New York: Liveright Publishing, 2014.

Halloran, Fiona Deans. *Thomas Nast: The Father of Modern Political Cartoons.* Chapel Hill: University of North Carolina Press, 2012.

Keller, Morton. *The Art and Politics of Thomas Nast.* London: Oxford University Press, 1968.

Oxx, Katie. *The Nativist Movement in America: Religious Conflict in the 19th Century.* London: Routledge, 2013.

Articles

Boissoneault, Lorraine. "A Civil War Cartoonist Created the Modern Image of Santa Claus as Union Propaganda." *Smithsonian Magazine,* December 19, 2018. https://www.smithsonianmag.com/history/civil-war-cartoonist-created-modern-image-santa-claus-union-propaganda-180971074/.

Justice, Benjamin. "Thomas Nast and the Public School of the 1870s." *History of Education Quarterly* 45, no. 2 (Summer 2005): 171–206.

St. Hill, Thomas Nast. "The Life and Death of Thomas Nast." *American Heritage* 22, no. 6 (October 1971). https://www.americanheritage.com/life-and-death-thomas-nast.

Websites

"Illustrations and Political Cartoons by Thomas Nast." Library of Congress. https://www.loc.gov/pictures/item/2010651579/.

"Thomas Nast: A Life in Cartoons." Massachusetts Historical Society. https://www.masshist.org/features/thomasnast.

Documentaries

A New Look at Tammany Hall. City University of New York, 2009. https://www.youtube.com/watch?v=hGVy702gf84.

Presidents, Politics, and the Pen: The Influential Art of Thomas Nast. Norman Rockwell Museum, 2016. https://www.youtube.com/watch?v=9uYYUW82EfE.

Shannon, Christopher. *Irish Catholics and Tammany Hall.* C-SPAN, October 12, 2021. https://www.c-span.org/video/?515283-1/irish-catholics-tammany-hall.

John Gast: *American Progress* Painting

AUTHOR/CREATOR	IMAGE TYPE
John Gast, for George A. Crofutt	PAINTINGS; FLYERS
DATE	SIGNIFICANCE
1872	An allegorical figure of a woman leading American settlers westward to pursue the nation's manifest destiny

Overview

American Progress, a painting sometimes called *Westward the Course of History*, *Westward Ho!*, or *Manifest Destiny*, is one of the most widely reproduced images from the post–Civil War era having to do with America's westward expansion. It originated as an oil painting by John Gast that was commissioned by publisher George A. Crofutt, who then reproduced and distributed it as a lithograph. The painting is housed in the Autry Museum of Western Heritage in Los Angeles. On the reverse side of the original lithograph was an advertisement for *Crofutt's Western World*, a periodical that was one of Crofutt's popular travel publications promoting travel and tourism in the West; the ad promised a free copy of the image to each new subscriber. The image became emblematic of the concept of "manifest destiny," the belief held by many Americans in the mid- to late nineteenth century that the "destiny" of the United States was to expand its dominion westward across the continent, spreading democracy and progress.

About the Artist

This image originated as an oil painting by John Gast (1842–1896). Gast was born in Berlin, Germany, but his family immigrated to St. Louis, Missouri, where there was a large community of German immigrants. To complete his education, he returned to Berlin and graduated from the Royal Academy of Art. Back in St. Louis, he formed the Gast Lithographic Co., but after three years he sold his interest in the company and went to Paris to study chromolithography, a method for making multicolored prints. When he returned to the United States, he established the *New York Daily Graphic* in 1871. A major feature of the publication was a page devoted to lithographs. He later established the lithographic firm of Gast & Co. He sold his interest in that company to form the Photochrome Company, which relied on several lithographic processes he patented.

Gast was also a painter, and what was arguably his most famous painting, *American Progress*, was commissioned by George Andrews Crofutt (1827–1907), a widely known publisher and printer as well as an ardent promoter of westward expansion. Crofutt was born in Danbury, Connecticut, but he settled first in New York City and then in Philadelphia to work as a journalist and editor. In the Panic of 1857 he went bankrupt, so in 1860, believing he had little to lose, he

Document Image

John Gast's American Progress
(Library of Congress)

joined the gold rush to Pike's Peak in Colorado. He had little success as a prospector, but he became enamored with the beauty and promise of the American West. He returned to journalism after witnessing the completion of the transcontinental railroad with the driving of the Golden Spike at Promontory Summit, Utah, linking the Central Pacific and Union Pacific Railroads in 1869. At that point he became a champion of the westward expansion of the United States, along with tourism in the West. He went on to publish a number of tour guides, among them *The Great Transcontinental Railroad Guide, Crofutt's Overland Tourist, Crofutt's Overland Tours, Crofutt's Grip-Sack Guide,* and the periodical *Crofutt's Western World.* The guides included engravings (and later photographs) of the West's natural wonders and Indigenous peoples. By 1878 he claimed that sales of *Overland Tourist* had exceeded 300,000.

Context

The concept of manifest destiny, as allegorized in *American Progress,* fueled the territorial expansion of the United States throughout much of the nineteenth century. The concept led not just to the acquisition of territory but to the forced removal of Native Americans and others from their land. Further, as the nation rapidly expanded to the west and new states were added to the union, the issue of slavery was intensified, for the persistent question was whether a new state would be a "free state" or permit slavery. This tension, of course, contributed to the outbreak of the Civil War.

The population of the United States in the early decades of the nineteenth century was expanding rapidly because of a high birth rate and immigration. In 1800 the nation's population was about five million. By 1850 it had reached 23 million, and by 1870 it had reached nearly 38.6 million. The Panic of 1819, accompanied by the Banking Crisis of that year, led to a collapse of the U.S. economy. Money was scarce, banks were recalling loans, and Americans were losing everything, motivating them to head west in an effort to recoup their fortunes. The Panic of 1837, caused by risky lending by banks, a housing bubble, and the collapse of cotton prices, among other factors, had a similar effect. Many Americans, their pockets and bank accounts virtually empty and facing an otherwise bleak future, joined the westward movement in search of new opportunities.

The nation's westward march had begun in 1803 with the Louisiana Purchase, which essentially doubled the size of the country by adding some 828,000 square miles that stretched westward from the Mississippi River to the Rocky Mountains and northward from Louisiana to Canada. The Lewis and Clark expedition of 1804 to 1806, sponsored by President Thomas Jefferson, revealed the richness and natural wonders of the West. In 1823 President James Monroe prefigured the concept of manifest destiny when, in his message to Congress, he established the Monroe Doctrine, which cautioned the European powers against interfering with American expansion—and warned that any attempt to do so would be considered an act of war.

Texas became central to the philosophy of manifest destiny. After Mexico won its independence from Spain in 1821, it halted immigration of Americans into Texas, which, along with the present-day American Southwest, was at that time part of Mexico. More Americans than Mexicans, however, had settled in Texas. In 1836 Texas declared its independence from Mexico to form the Republic of Texas. The leaders of the republic successfully urged the United States to annex Texas, which in the course of events became the nation's twenty-eighth state in 1845.

With the annexation of Texas, the inevitability of U.S. expansion all the way to the Pacific Ocean was a concept that began to take hold in the American mindset among people from various regions, ethnicities, races, classes, and political views. In 1839, the widely read editorialist John L. O'Sullivan had written "The Great Nation of Futurity," an editorial published in the journal he founded, *The United States Democratic Review.* He wrote: "The expansive future is our arena, and for our history. We are entering on its untrodden space, with the truths of God in our minds, beneficent objects in our hearts, and with a clear conscience unsullied by the past. We are the nation of human progress, and who will, what can, set limits to our onward march?"

Then, in a July–August 1845 editorial rallying support for the annexation of Texas, he used the phrase "manifest destiny," writing that it was "our manifest destiny to overspread the continent allotted by Providence for the free development of our yearly multiplying millions." The phrase also appeared in an article in the *New York Morning News* that same month. Both the editorial and the article were unsigned, but O'Sullivan was the editor of both publications at the time, so historians are generally firm in the belief that he coined the phrase—especially because it appeared yet again in the *Morning News* in December in support of the acquisition of Oregon. Oregon was added to the country by means of an 1846 treaty with Great Britain and led to the organization of Oregon Territory in 1848. Oregon Territory, which included modern-day Oregon, Idaho, Washington, and most of British Columbia, was regarded as the first success of manifest destiny. Also in 1848, the U.S. War with Mexico concluded with the Treaty of Guadalupe Hidalgo. Under the terms of the treaty, Mexico ceded 525,000 square miles of territory that would encompass modern-day California, Arizona, Colorado, New Mexico, Utah, and Wyoming. This acquisition linked the states and territories of the United States with the Pacific, and thus the nation seemed to have achieved its manifest destiny.

The process, however, was not entirely complete. In 1861 the Western Union Telegraph Company linked its networks, completing a transcontinental telegraph line. This line enabled instantaneous communications between the nation's capital and San Francisco. The completion of the transcontinental railway, which George Crofutt witnessed in 1869, provided a transportation link between East and West so that a trip that had formerly taken weeks by wagon or stagecoach now took just days: in 1876, an express train left New York City and arrived in San Francisco just eighty-three hours later. From the end of the Civil War to the end of the century, nine new states were added to the Union, and three more were added in the early years of the twentieth century. The contiguous United States as it currently exists was complete.

Explanation and Analysis of the Document

American Progress presents an idealized, mythologized image of American expansion and progress. At the center of the image an angelic, allegorical female figure in a flowing, diaphanous white gown is floating above the landscape. The viewer knows that her gaze is fixed westward, for a river, probably the Mississippi River, can be seen in the background. Crofutt described the woman as a "beautiful and charming female." On her head, affixed to her hair, is what he called the "Star of Empire," suggesting the notion that it was America's destiny to extend its empire west to the Pacific Ocean. Crofutt also explained: "In her right hand she carries a book—common school—the emblem of education and the testimonial of our national enlightenment." ("Common school" was the term for "public school" in the nineteenth century.) In her left hand she is holding the wires of the telegraph, symbolizing the linking of East and West in the growth and development of the nation.

On the ground beneath her are people using various forms of transportation, all in a left-to-right sequence that suggests progress. At the head is a group of Native Americans pulling a travois, a framed contrivance used to drag loads. A herd of buffalo is to the Natives' right. In the foreground is a group of prospectors traveling on foot. Behind the prospectors is a pair of farmers plowing a field with a team of oxen; their cabin is in the background. Behind the Native Americans is a Conestoga wagon, presumably transporting settlers. This is followed by a stagecoach and finally by three railroad lines. Taken together, the details of the painting tell a story of technological progress from East to West. They also suggest that the western frontier would be settled by waves of people in sequence, although—notably—the Native Americans are fleeing or being chased by this progress.

—Michael J. O'Neal

Questions for Further Study

1. What was Gast's purpose in creating this painting and Crofutt's purpose in reproducing it for publication as a lithograph?

2. In what ways does the artist idealize the concept of westward expansion and manifest destiny?

3. What is the fundamental message of the image?

Further Reading

Books

Carlisle, Rodney P., and J. Geoffrey Golson, eds. *Manifest Destiny and the Expansion of America*. Santa Barbara, CA: ABC-CLIO, 2007.

Golay, Michael. *The Tide of Empire: America's March to the Pacific*. Hoboken, NJ: Wiley, 2003.

Greenberg, Amy S., ed. *Manifest Destiny and American Territorial Expansion: A Brief History with Documents*, 2nd ed. Boston: Bedford/St. Martin's, 2017.

Johannsen, Robert W. "The Meaning of Manifest Destiny." In *Manifest Destiny and Empire: American Antebellum Expansionism*, edited by Sam W. Haynes and Christopher Morris. College Station: Texas A&M University Press, 2008.

McCullough, David. *The Pioneers: The Heroic Story of the Settlers Who Brought the American Ideal West*. New York: Simon & Schuster, 2020.

Stephanson, Anders. *Manifest Destiny: American Expansionism and the Empire of Right*. New York: Hill and Wang, 1995.

Articles

Pratt, Julius. "The Origin of 'Manifest Destiny.'" *American Historical Review* 32, no. 4 (July 1927): 795–98.

Websites

Fuller, A. James, and Andrew Fisher. "To What Extent Were Manifest Destiny and Westward Expansion Justified?" Bill of Rights Institute. https://billofrightsinstitute.org/activities/to-what-extent-were-manifest-destiny-and-westward-expansion-justified.

"Manifest Destiny and the West." National Gallery of Art. https://www.nga.gov/learn/teachers/lessons-activities/uncovering-america/manifest-destiny-west.html.

"Manifest Destiny: The Philosophy That Created a Nation." *American History: From Revolution to Reconstruction and Beyond*. http://www.let.rug.nl/usa/essays/1801-1900/manifest-destiny/manifest-destiny---the-philosophy-that-created-a-nation.php.

Scott, Donald M. "The Religious Origins of Manifest Destiny." National Humanities Center. http://nationalhumanitiescenter.org/tserve/nineteen/nkeyinfo/mandestiny.htm.

Documentaries

Wood, Sharon. *To Conquer or Redeem: Manifest Destiny*. New York: Films Media Group, 2010.

PHOTOGRAPH OF NICODEMUS, KANSAS

AUTHOR/CREATOR
Unknown

DATE
1877

IMAGE TYPE
PHOTOGRAPHS

SIGNIFICANCE
Shows Washington Street in Nicodemus, Kansas, the earliest Black settlement in the Midwest formed by former slaves who fled oppression in the South during Reconstruction

Overview

This photograph from 1877 shows Washington Street in Nicodemus, Kansas. The town was the earliest and most successful Black settlement formed in the Midwest during the Reconstruction period in the years following the Civil War. Continuing to face discrimination, disenfranchisement, and economic repression, usually because of the abuses of tenant farming, large numbers of newly freed African Americans migrated from the South to form more than two dozen communities such as Nicodemus in the West and Midwest. These settlers came to be called "Exodusters," echoing the Exodus of the Old Testament, when the Israelites fled slavery in biblical Egypt. On April 18, 1877, the Nicodemus Town Company was formed by seven residents, one white and six Black. From 1877 to 1879, separate parties of Black colonists arrived primarily from Tennessee and Kentucky, and these people and their children ultimately constituted the entire population of the town, which totaled nearly 600 by 1879. By 1880 the town had a bank, two hotels, three churches, a newspaper, a drug store, and three general stores, all surrounded by twelve square miles of land that eventually came under cultivation.

The town, however, was short-lived. In 1888 the Union Pacific Railroad bypassed the community, and after most of the town's businesses relocated, Nicodemus withered. A small group of settlers remained, but by 1950 the town's population numbered only sixteen. In the twenty-first century about forty-five descendants of the original colonists still live in Nicodemus, which was designated a National Historic Landmark in 1976 and is operated by the U.S. National Park Service.

About the Artist

It is unknown who took the photograph. The photograph, however, was discovered and preserved by the Historic American Buildings Survey (HABS). Under the auspices of the National Park Service, the HABS was established in 1933 to create a public archive of the nation's architectural heritage. The archive included measured drawings, historical reports, and black and white photographs. The concept of "securing records of structures of historic interest" had been advocated by the American Institute of Architects in 1918, but it was not until the onset of the Great Depression that

Document Image

1877 photograph of Washington Street in Nicodemus, Kansas
(National Park Service)

the proposal took shape in the form of a federal program initiated as part of President Franklin Roosevelt's New Deal. Formation of the HABS, along with the 1935 Historic Sites Act, provided a significant boost to historic preservation throughout the United States. The HABS field-tested a number of the preservation strategies that continue to be used, including surveying, listing, and assembling documentation on historic properties; developing comprehensive information about those properties; and establishing national standards for documenting historic properties.

Context

In 1880, a U.S. Senate committee investigated the causes of Black migration from the South to places like Nicodemus during the 1870s. In its report, the committee stated: "In the spring of 1879, thousands of colored people, unable longer to endure the intolerable hardships, injustice, and suffering inflicted upon them by a class of Democrats in the South, had, in utter despair, fled panic-stricken from their homes and sought protection among strangers in a strange land. Homeless, penniless, and in rags, these poor people were thronging the wharves of Saint Louis, crowding the steamers on the Mississippi River, and in pitiable destitution throwing themselves upon the charity of Kansas. Thousands more were congregating along the banks of the Mississippi River, hailing the passing steamers, and imploring them for a passage to the land of freedom, where the rights of citizens are respected and honest toil rewarded by honest compensation. The newspapers were filled with accounts of their destitution, and the very air was burdened with the cry of distress from a class of American citizens flying from persecutions which they could no longer endure."

The hopes of African Americans in the early days of Reconstruction had been dashed. Many felt that their only hope for a better life as free men and women was to flee the repressive South and settle in towns such as Nicodemus or in the cities of the North. Kansas in particular seemed like a favorable destination. The events of the Bleeding Kansas era, the fame of John Brown (the abolitionist known primarily for leading the raid on Harpers Ferry, Virginia), associations of Kansas with the Underground Railroad, and the prospect of acquiring land by homesteading all made Kansas an attractive destination for African Americans. The 1855 census of Kansas Territory cited just 151 free Blacks and 192 enslaved Blacks in the territory; in 1870, the state was home to more than 17,000 African Americans, and by 1880 the Black population had swollen to more than 43,000.

Much of the increase in the Black population was the work of Benjamin "Pap" Singleton, a formerly enslaved carpenter from Tennessee who, after the Civil War, was motivated by a desire to help other formerly enslaved people improve their lot in life. He encouraged Blacks to move to Kansas, where they could buy land. In 1873 he formed a group that settled and flourished in Cherokee County in southeast Kansas. In 1879, the state's governor, John St. John, formed the Freedman's Relief Association to help the many African Americans who were arriving in the state ill and impoverished. The association would in time establish other colonies for Blacks, one in Wabaunsee, west of Topeka; another in Chautauqua County in southeast Kansas; and yet another in Coffey County, east of Emporia. Black communities were also formed within cities, including Topeka and Kansas City, and in other states.

While Singleton was the impresario behind the Exoduster migration, and while Governor St. John was the Exodusters' initial benefactor (although he later wanted to cut off Black migration to the state out of concern that the Black population would become too large), the driving force behind Nicodemus was a white man, William R. Hill. It was Hill, a land developer from Indiana, who traveled the backwoods of Kentucky and Tennessee and described a "Promised Land" of wide-open territory, game, and the chance to own land through the homesteading process. Hill developed the town site and joined forces with Reverend W. H. Smith, an African American from Kentucky, to form the Nicodemus Town Company, with Smith as president and Hill as treasurer. The town was named Nicodemus in honor of a legendary man who arrived in America on a slave ship but later purchased his freedom. The first settler was the Reverend Simon P. Roundtree, who arrived on June 18, 1877. In July, Zack T. Fletcher and his wife, Jenny Smith (the Reverend Smith's daughter), arrived; Fletcher was named secretary of the Town Company. Later that summer, more than 300 railroad tickets were bought for families in the South to transport them to the nearest railroad station, in Ellis, Kansas. The families who arrived in Ellis walked the thirty-five miles to Nicodemus.

The Town Company publicized the town by means of circulars. They invited "Colored People of the United States" to "Go to Kansas" and settle in the "Great

Solomon Valley." Singleton, who could not read or write, traveled widely, distributing so many circulars that he came to be known as the "Moses of the Colored Exodus." In this way the migrants came to be known as Exodusters.

Life was not easy for the settlers. The original settlers lived in dugouts along the Solomon River. The first winter was harsh. The initial settlers had no tools, seed, or money. Some got by through selling buffalo hides; other worked for the railroad in Ellis. Many survived only because of food, firewood, and other supplies provided by Osage Indians. Many of the settlers, disillusioned by the featureless landscape and harsh weather, returned to the forested hills of Kentucky and Tennessee. Those who stayed were able to begin farming, and in the spring of 1878 more families arrived.

Zack Fletcher became the town's first postmaster and an early entrepreneur. He built a surviving complex that housed the post office, the hotel, a school, and a livery stable. His wife, Jenny, was the town's first postmistress, a schoolteacher, and a charter member of the African Methodist Episcopal Church. In 1878, Edward P. McCabe joined the colony and would later serve two terms as state auditor, making him the first African American to hold a major state office. By 1887, the town had several churches, a literary society, an ice cream parlor, a lawyer, a second newspaper, a baseball team (the Nicodemus Blues), a benefit society, and a band.

Hopes for future growth ran high when the town's residents learned that the Union Pacific Railroad was talking about running a line into Nicodemus. The town raised $16,000 in bonds to attract the railroad. The town and the railroad, however, were unable to agree on financial terms, so the railroad withdrew its plans and instead routed the railroad several miles away, south of the Solomon River, leaving Nicodemus an "island village." The town began its decline when a number of businesses relocated to the other side of the river to be near the railroad camp, which later became the town of Bogue. Those families that remained farmed anywhere from 50 to 1,000 acres each, but the onset of the Great Depression, combined with drought in the early 1930s, forced many of the younger residents to flee.

On the last weekend of every July, the descendants of the original town settlers converge on Nicodemus to celebrate Emancipation Day.

Explanation and Analysis of the Document

The photograph of Nicodemus requires little in the way of explanation. It depicts two buildings in the town. One is the town's first stone church. The other is the Williams General Store. A number of the town's residents are congregated on the street in front of the general store. Four horse-drawn carts or buggies can be seen. Overall, the photograph simultaneously captures the bleakness of the flat terrain, where the settlers would try to scratch out a living, and the sense of hopefulness as the settlers gather to preserve the memory of their newly created, self-governing community, far from the oppressions of the South. This photo is part of an array of photos that includes images of many of the early settlers, including Charles Williams and his family, various other individuals and buildings, and the Nicodemus Blues baseball team.

—Michael J. O'Neal

Questions for Further Study

1. In what ways does this photograph convey what life might have been like for the settlers of Nicodemus?

2. What thoughts might have been going through the minds of the people in the photo as it was being taken?

3. What is the importance of preserving the heritage of a community like Nicodemus through photographs such as this?

Further Reading

Books

Athearn, Robert G. *In Search of Canaan: Black Migration to Kansas, 1879-80.* Lawrence: Regents Press of Kansas, 1978.

Crockett, Norman L. *The Black Towns.* Lawrence: University Press of Kansas, 2021.

Hinger, Charlotte. *Nicodemus: Post-Reconstruction Politics and Racial Justice in Western Kansas.* Norman: University of Oklahoma Press, 2016.

Painter, Nell Irvin. *Exodusters: Black Migration to Kansas after Reconstruction.* New York: Norton, 1992.

Promised Land on the Solomon: Black Settlement at Nicodemus, Kansas. Washington, DC: National Park Service, U.S. Department of the Interior, 1986. http://npshistory.com/publications/nico/promised-land-solomon.pdf.

Slocum, Karla. *Black Towns, Black Futures: The Enduring Allure of a Black Place in the American West.* Chapel Hill: University of North Carolina Press, 2019.

Articles

Davis, Damani. "Exodus to Kansas: The 1880 Senate Investigation of the Beginnings of the African American Migration from the South." *Prologue Magazine* 40, no. 2 (summer 2008). https://www.archives.gov/publications/prologue/2008/summer/exodus.html.

Websites

"The African-American Mosaic: Nicodemus, Kansas." Library of Congress. https://www.loc.gov/exhibits/african/afam010.html.

"Nicodemus, Graham County." *Kansapedia: Kansas Historical Society.* April 2015. https://www.kshs.org/kansapedia/nicodemus-graham-county/12157.

Nicodemus Historical Society & Museum. https://www.nicodemushistoricalsociety.org/nicodemus-kansas-settlers.

Weiser-Alexander, Kathy. "Nicodemus—A Black Pioneer Town." *Legends of America.* https://www.legendsofamerica.com/ks-nicodemus/.

Joseph Keppler: "The Modern Colossus Of (Rail) Roads" Cartoon

Author/Creator Joseph Ferdinand Keppler	**Image Type** Cartoons
Date 1879	**Significance** Lampooned the monopoly power of the railroads and the business magnates who owned them

Overview

The history of the United States in the years between the end of the Civil War in 1865 and the dawn of the twentieth century can, from one perspective, be told through the history of the railroad industry. Before the early 1870s, about 45,000 miles of track had been laid. By 1900, 170,000 miles of track had been added. It was the Gilded Age, when business tycoons like William Henry Vanderbilt amassed immense fortunes, not just in the railroad industry but also in steel, oil, banking, timber, textiles, liquor, and other industries. The names of many of these tycoons, often characterized as "robber barons," remain familiar, for many of their descendants remain active in industry and politics, and many of the names—John D. Rockefeller, Henry Ford, Andrew Carnegie, Leland Stanford, Andrew W. Mellon, J. B. Duke, Cornelius Vanderbilt—can be found above the entryways of the universities, museums, foundations, and other enterprises they endowed. In some cases, their priceless art collections preserved the works of the Old Masters for posterity and found homes in museums. These men, however, often expanded their business empires through shady and sometimes coercive tactics—union busting, fraud, intimidation, bribery, backroom deals with politicians—all while ignoring accepted business practices and often ignoring the law.

One of these tycoons, the featured character in the cartoon, was William Henry Vanderbilt, the son of Cornelius Vanderbilt, "The Commodore," who had amassed a fortune first in steam shipping and then in the railroad industry. On his death in 1877, the elder Vanderbilt left an estate of $105 million (well over $2 billion in 2022 dollars) to his son. Until his death in 1885, William more than doubled the fortune he inherited and became possibly the richest person in the United States. Among his competitors, depicted in the cartoon, was Jay Gould, also a railroad magnate, an unpopular figure known for unscrupulous tactics. Gould had acquired control of the Union Pacific Railroad during the Panic of 1873, when the price of the company's stock was depressed. Gould made William M. "Boss" Tweed, the boss of Tammany Hall, the political machine that essentially ran New York, a director of the Erie Railroad, in this way gaining favorable treatment for his rail enterprises. Gould also issued fraudulent stock, bribed legislators, started price wars, manipulated the gold market, and even duped the U.S. Treasury, setting off a stock market panic in 1869. Cyrus West Field, also depicted in the cartoon, was a financier and one of the entrepreneurs who created the Atlantic Telegraph Company, which laid a telegraph cable across the Atlantic in 1858. From 1877 to 1880

Document Image

"The Modern Colossus of (Rail) Roads"
(Library of Congress)

he was president of the New York Elevated Railroad Company, but unlike many other Gilded Age tycoons, he made some bad investments and lived out the remainder of his life in modest circumstances. He died in 1892.

About the Artist

Joseph Ferdinand Keppler, the cartoonist who created this illustration, was born in Vienna, Austria, in 1838. Early on he showed promise as an artist (and actor) and enrolled in an art academy in Vienna in 1856. His father immigrated to Missouri, primarily because of the failure of the Revolution of 1848. Keppler followed his father in 1867 and settled in St. Louis, where there was a large population of German immigrants. In 1869, he began publishing a humor weekly, *Die Vehme, Illustriertes Wochenblatt für Scherz und Ernst* ("The Vehme, Illustrated Weekly for Joking and Seriousness"), the first American humor periodical with lithographic cartoons. The publication lasted for only a year, but in 1871 he launched *Puck, Illustrierte Wochenschrift* ("Puck, Illustrated Weekly"). That publication, too, was short-lived, but it brought him to the attention of Frank Leslie, who offered him a job as an illustrator for his *Frank Leslie's Illustrated Newspaper*, where he specialized in cartoons drawing attention to political corruption. In 1876 he left the newspaper and, with Adolph Schwarzmann, founded *Puck, Humoristisches Wochenblatt*. The English edition of the periodical, begun in 1877, survived until 1918. Generally, Keppler's cartoons, like "The Modern Colossus of (Rail) Roads," were large (this one covered two pages), often with depictions of numerous figures. He gained particular fame in 1880 with a cartoon skewering presidential candidate (and eventual winner) James Garfield for his involvement in the Crédit Mobilier scandal, a scandal that entangled the Union Pacific Railroad. Keppler died at his home in New York in 1894.

Context

Throughout the final three decades of the nineteenth century, as the nation's railroad system expanded exponentially, the industry was often in the news. Its expansion contributed to the growth of labor unions—which in turn led to labor strife and major strikes. In 1877, for example, the Baltimore and Ohio Railroad Company announced that for the second time in eight months that it was cutting the pay of its workers in Martinsburg, West Virginia. The workers, fed up, announced that they would prevent trains from leaving the roundhouse. The National Guard and federal troops were called in, but the strike spread to eight other railroads, leading to violence. At its peak, the strike, known as the Great Upheaval, involved 100,000 railroad workers.

Additionally, railroad tycoons were guilty of shenanigans with regard to the rates they charged. The chief shady practice involved rebates, which were special reduced rates that the carriers charged preferred customers. The purpose in granting the rebates was to discriminate in favor of a particular shipper by offering a secret rate below the rate charged by the carrier's competitors, putting competitive pressure on them. This practice continued into the next century. In 1908, for example, the U.S. Supreme Court, in *New York Central & Hudson River Railroad Company v. United States*, upheld the verdict of a lower court in finding the New York Central, one of Vanderbilt's companies, guilty of paying rebates to the American Sugar Refining Company and others in New York for the shipment of sugar. The Standard Oil Company, under the generalship of John D. Rockefeller, was able to procure from Vanderbilt rebates worth millions of dollars in shipping its crude oil from wells in Pennsylvania to refineries in Cleveland, in this way squeezing out competing refineries and contributing to the violence that erupted during the rail strike of 1877.

As the railroads become critical to the success of American enterprise in the late nineteenth century, they needed the output of other large industries, including iron, steel, copper, glass, machine tools, and oil. The need to finance these enterprises caused the investment markets to reorganize to handle their immense capital requirements. This capital flow enabled them to scale their businesses in ways that could not have been conceived a generation earlier. The railroads, however, were worried about production shortfalls in any of the commodities they needed. To stabilize their business, they formed "pools" that combined all the associated industries under centralized management. These combinations, which amounted to vertical monopolies, gave the railroads extraordinary power over the nation's economy, for they gave them the ability to drive out competitors, force down their costs for labor and raw materials, artificially raise the prices they charged customers, and wangle special treatment from state and national governments. With immense war chests at their disposal, they were able to finance political campaigns to bring into office men who would back their schemes and turn a blind eye to their malfeasances. Because they controlled the prices, they had all the power: Customers had to pay whatever rates the railroad companies set.

A lengthy article in *The Atlantic*, published in 1881, outlined the abuses. The article stated in summary: "In less than the ordinary span of a life-time, our railroads have brought upon us the worst labor disturbance, the greatest of monopolies, and the most formidable combination of money and brains that ever overshadowed a state. The time has come to face the fact that the forces of capital and industry have outgrown the forces of our government. The corporation and the trades-union have forgotten that they are the creatures of the state. Our strong men are engaged in a headlong fight for fortune, power, precedence, success. Americans as they are, they ride over the people like Juggernaut to gain their ends."

Ultimately, the government responded. On February 4, 1887, the U.S. Senate and House of Representatives passed the Interstate Commerce Act. The act applied the Commerce Clause of the U.S. Constitution, which granted Congress the power "to Regulate Commerce with foreign Nations, and among the several States," to regulate railroad rates. The law required the railroads to charge rates that were "reasonable and just." It outlawed rebates to high-volume customers. It made charging higher rates for shorter hauls illegal. To adjudicate cases on the matter, the act created the Interstate Commerce Commission.

Other federal legislation followed. The 1903 Elkins Act prohibited railroad companies from extending rebates to customers that shipped large quantities of goods. This law was reinforced in 1906 with passage of the Hepburn Act, which gave the Interstate Commerce Commission the power to set maximum railroad rates. The Railway Rate Act of 1910 extended the power of the Interstate Commerce Commission to regulate shipping rates.

Explanation and Analysis of the Document

The editorial cartoon, covering two pages in the December 10, 1879, issue of *Puck*, is dominated by an image of William Henry Vanderbilt, president of the New York Central Railroad and several other rail companies. He was regarded as the most powerful business tycoon in the railroad industry at the time. His legs are spread astride three intersecting sets of railroad tracks. He is described as a Colossus, referring to any object or person that is of enormous size or importance; the original colossi were statues created in ancient Greece and Rome, and "Colossus of Roads" is a play on one of the Seven Wonders of the World, the Colossus of Rhodes, an immense statue of the sun god Helios on the ancient Greek island of Rhodes.

Superimposed over Vanderbilt's right leg is an image of Cyrus West Field, the controller of the New York Elevated Railroad Company. To his right is an elevated railway station. Superimposed on Vanderbilt's left leg is an image of Jay Gould, another major tycoon who controlled the Union Pacific Railroad. Vanderbilt is holding what appear to be leashes attached to the engines of Field and West, suggesting that he has enough clout to control them. A sign posted in the foreground reads: "All freight seeking the seaboard must pass here and pay any tolls we demand." Over Field's rail station is a flag that reads: "L Road. Many nickels stolen are millions gained." The implications of the sign and flag are that the railroad magnates are using their monopoly power to gain fortunes at the expense of the passenger public and of companies wishing to ship their products by rail.

—Michael J. O'Neal

Questions for Further Study

1. What is the chief purpose of this cartoon?

2. How effective might the cartoon have been in drawing the public's attention to abuses by the railroad industry?

3. To what extent might this cartoon, and others like it, have contributed to efforts on the part of public officials to regulate the rail industry?

Further Reading

Books

Cooper, Anderson, and Katherine Howe. *Vanderbilt: The Rise and Fall of an American Dynasty*. New York: HarperCollins, 2021.

Frey, Robert L., ed. *Railroads in the Nineteenth Century*. New York: Facts on File, 1988.

Hiltzik, Michael. *Iron Empires: Robber Barons, Railroads, and the Making of Modern America*. Boston: Mariner Books, 2021.

Kelly, Jack. *The Edge of Anarchy: The Railroad Barons, the Gilded Age, and the Greatest Labor Uprising in America*. New York: St. Martin's Press, 2019.

Vanderbilt, William H. *The Last Will and Testament of the Late William H. Vanderbilt*. New York: Taggart & Miller, 1886. Available at Internet Archives. https://archive.org/details/lastwilltestamen00vand/page/14/mode/2up.

Websites

"Development of the Railroad Monopoly." Stanford University. https://cs.stanford.edu/people/eroberts/cs201/projects/corporate-monopolies/development_rrmon.html.

"Interstate Commerce Act (1887)." National Archives. https://www.archives.gov/milestone-documents/interstate-commerce-act.

Lloyd, H. D. "The Story of a Great Monopoly." *Atlantic*, March 1881. https://www.theatlantic.com/magazine/archive/1881/03/the-story-of-a-great-monopoly/306019/.

Documentaries

Jeserich, Mitch. *The Robber Barons: A History of the Railroads* (interview with author Michael Hiltzik), June 8, 2021. https://www.youtube.com/watch?v=IoHx8JZ0Xu4.

Haymarket Mass Meeting Flyer

Author/Creator
Adolph Fischer, August Spies

Date
1886

Image Type
Flyers

Significance
Example of the "mass communication" method of promoting nineteenth-century community meetings, in this case one associated with the tragic Haymarket Square Bombing

Overview

This document is an example of an American broadside. Broadsides were used during the eighteenth and nineteenth centuries for mass communication. Printed on a single sheet of paper, broadsides were posted in public places and handed out to people to advertise merchandise for sale, notify people about public events, such as entertainment productions or speeches, or advocate religious or political positions. In a nation where the population was growing rapidly but technology was limited, these posters or flyers were the primary form of reaching large numbers of people, particularly in urban areas.

This particular flyer is an announcement to draw people to Haymarket Square, the site of an important event in United States labor history. The late 1800s was a period of significant labor unrest in America as rapid industrialization resulted in long work hours and dangerous working conditions for many industries. As workers unionized, they found ways to fight back against these conditions—most often using the work stoppage, or strike. There were many strikes in the United States in this era, and many of them involved violence. The Great Railroad Strike of 1877 brought the country's transportation system to a halt and resulted in bloody clashes between troops and strikers in many major cities across the United States. The McCormick Reaper Plant in Chicago was a flash point for union action, and strikes often attracted anarchists and other radicals. The event advertised by this document was a public protest against police action at the McCormick Reaper Plant the previous day, where the Chicago police killed two workers and injured many more. At the Haymarket Square protest on May 4, 1886, an unknown person threw a homemade bomb at the police who were on guard. The resulting panic and violence at Haymarket marked a milestone moment in American labor history, where unions and the labor movement became associated with anarchism and bombs in the mind of the public. This document is thus an important piece that allows us to reflect on how a particular event in history can represent larger historical issues such as industrialization, power imbalances in gender and class, and attitudes about immigrants and immigration. Visual documents such as the Haymarket broadside reveal not just specifics about one event in history, but also social and cultural attitudes of the time.

Document Image

The "Attention Workingmen!" Flyer
(Library of Congress)

About the Artist

This document was written by local anarchists in Chicago known as the Executive Committee. The primary author was Adolph Fischer. Fischer was born in Germany in 1858 and immigrated to the United States in 1873. In 1883 he moved his family to Chicago, where he worked as a typesetter for the German-language newspaper *Arbeiter-Zeitung*. Fischer became a member of the International Working People's Association and a radical splinter group, Lehr-und-Wehr Verein.

The leader of the Chicago anarchist movement was August Spies, and he played an important role in the creation of this document. Spies was born in Germany in 1855 and immigrated to Chicago after his father died suddenly in 1871. Spies had relatives in the burgeoning and successful German community that settled in Illinois in the late 1800s, so he became part of the German working class in Chicago, working as an upholsterer. Attracted to socialist politics, he joined the Socialist Labour Party in 1877 and rose to a leadership position. As part of Chicago's more radical socialist wing, Spies helped form the International Working People's Association in 1883 as an alternative to the Socialist Labour Party. He became the editor of the pro-labor newspaper *Arbeiter-Zeitung* in 1884.

Spies was one of several speakers at labor events on May 3, 1886. After workers were killed and injured at the riot at the McCormick Reaper Plant, Fischer attended a meeting during which he and others formulated a plan to respond. The attendees decided to hold a mass meeting at Haymarket Square the next evening, and Fischer was asked to create a flyer to publicize the event. The original flyer contained the words "Workingmen Arm Yourselves and Appear in Full Force!" Spies, who was scheduled to be one of the "good speakers" at the Haymarket meeting, feared that that such inflammatory language would turn away potential attendees. He refused to speak at the rally unless this sentence was removed from the document. Most of the original flyers were destroyed, and some 20,000 copies of the new broadside were distributed.

Following the violence at the Haymarket meeting, both Fischer and Spies were arrested along with six others accused of participating in the bombing and violence. Although Fischer and Spies attended the meeting—Spies as the primary speaker of the evening—both men left before the bombing and violence began. Fischer and Spies were convicted and sentenced to death by hanging. Both men were hanged on November 11, 1887.

Context

During the late 1800s, the United States rapidly expanded its manufacturing capacity. Whereas earlier manufacturing, such as textile production, was driven by steam technology, this Industrial Revolution included heavy manufacturing, including steel production and equipment. Most of the new factory jobs were filled with immigrants who came in large numbers to the United States to seek economic opportunity and escape from poverty, political violence, and religious persecution.

As these workers grew in number, they began to organize to fight back against what in many cases were dangerous and grueling work conditions. In industrial centers such as Chicago, workers typically worked six days a week, often for more than ten hours a day. Workers formed unions to have some bargaining power with management for better wages and conditions. Founded in 1869, the Knights of Labor grew from 70,000 members in 1884 to over 700,000 by 1886, primarily because of the union's advocacy for an eight-hour workday, a position supported by most workers regardless of gender, ethnicity, or skill level. However, as socialists and others embracing more radical leftist politics joined the labor movement, Samuel Gompers organized the Federation of Organized Trades and Labor Unions (FOTLU, later known at the American Federation of Labor) in 1881 with the goal of divorcing labor interests from politics. In October 1884, the FOTLU called for federal legislation mandating an eight-hour workday and set a deadline for May 1, 1886. If the federal government failed to pass such legislation, workers would call a general strike, in which all workers regardless of industry would refuse to report to their jobs. Although the FOTLU and the Knights of Labor were at odds with each other, the members of the Knights of Labor overwhelmingly agreed to support the May Day strike.

Labor activists in Chicago were particularly organized and motivated. Illinois's rapid transformation from agriculture to industry spawned a working class that did not shy away from demands for reform. The state formed the nation's first coal miners' union in 1861, and by 1867, Illinois' legislature passed an eight-hour workday law. Because the law was not enforced,

Chicago workers were particularly irritated when subjected to ten-hour days and grueling work conditions. By the time the May Day strike deadline approached, labor activists in Chicago had years of experience with organizing strikes and other actions; in 1884, the Illinois State Federation of Labor expressed solidarity with the FOTLU, calling for May Day 1886 to be the day to finally win the eight-hour-day goal.

As the May Day deadline came and no federal legislation was passed, strikes erupted throughout industrial centers, including Chicago. Some 80,000 workers marched up Michigan Avenue on May 1, 1886. The labor actions attracted supporters who were not necessarily peaceful. Radical anarchists and others who had previously promoted violence joined in, prompting law enforcement to be concerned for public safety. The peaceful protests ended in violence at a particularly hot flash point: the McCormick Reaper Plant. Striking workers had been replaced by non-union workers, and, on Monday, May 3, union workers began to physically attack their non-union replacements. The Chicago police, aided by the private Pinkerton Security Agency of hired law enforcement, were on duty, anticipating trouble. As violence broke out, the police and Pinkerton agents moved in, killing two workers and injuring many more. Angered by the police's actions, Chicago leaders called for a meeting at Haymarket Square, a busy commercial center in the city, to protest not just labor conditions but also police brutality.

Inclement weather prevented a massive turnout for the May 4, 1886, Haymarket event, and it started much later than the time indicated on the document. Perhaps two thousand people attended, and by the end of the evening, the crowd had dwindled to some 200. Expecting a much larger crowd and trouble, the Chicago police had sent a contingent of 176 officers to the scene. In one of the most unexplainable incidents in American history, an unknown person launched a home-made bomb into the police squad, setting off a frenzy of panicked response. Police shot indiscriminately, killing six of their own; one died from the bomb blast. Four workers also died.

The Haymarket incident marked a turning point for the American labor movement. The violence associated with the bombing of police officers turned public sentiment away from supporting labor causes, such as the eight-hour day. The diverse nature of Chicago's labor activists, including immigrants, women, socialists, unskilled laborers, and anarchists, as well as native-born Americans, skilled workers, and more established immigrants, fueled an increasing fear of disorder. Anti-labor laws and sentiment increased after this event; union newspapers were shut down and leaders rounded up. The trial of the eight men supposedly responsible for the Haymarket bombing is the source of much historical discussion, but it is clear that it was politically driven; the man accused of throwing the bomb had witnesses proving he was a mile away from the scene at the time. The Haymarket meeting shows us how immigration, industrialization, power imbalances, and social action converged in one particular event—represented by one important document.

Explanation and Analysis of the Document

One of the first aspects of this document that likely strikes a modern reader is the gendered language used to describe the target audience. The headline screams in bold type "Attention Workingmen!" The reality of history is that many women worked in industrial factory jobs. They also played an important role in labor activism during the nineteenth century, particularly in Chicago. The Knights of Labor voted to admit women as members in 1881. Its emphasis on equal pay and the eight-hour day, regardless of gender, ethnicity, or skill level, helped the organization grow its ranks and influence. The Knights of Labor used charismatic women to draw in new members. One notable speaker was Mary Harris Jones, known as Mother Jones. Jones was a Chicago seamstress who became a self-proclaimed "hell-raiser" intent on fighting wealth inequality in the Gilded Age of the late 1800s.

One of the most prominent activists in the Chicago labor movement was Lucy Parsons. Parsons was born in Texas to enslaved parents and married a Confederate soldier. Their advocacy for the rights of the formerly enslaved and for mixed-race marriage resulted in violent threats against them in Texas, and they relocated to Chicago. Lucy became an advocate for women of color in Chicago labor unions, and she and her husband, Albert, founded the anarchist newspaper *The Alarm*, with Albert as editor and Lucy as contributing writer. Lucy and Albert supported the events at the McCormick Reaper Plant and Haymarket Square. Ultimately, Albert Parsons was hung alongside Fischer and Spies for conspiracy. Lucy continued her work as a labor activist. Although the document called on

"Workingmen" to appear, working women were an important force in the nineteenth-century labor movement.

Another interesting feature of this document is the use of a language other than English. Many contemporary critics of twenty-first-century immigrants claim that earlier immigrants from the nineteenth century were much more amenable to learning English and blending into American culture. It is true that immigrants from the 1800s, particularly the latter half of the century, were mocked if they did not speak English correctly, which pressured immigrants to learn the new language rather than retain their old culture. However, not every immigrant to the United States simply learned English and gave up any remnant of their home culture. The very existence of the *Arbeiter-Zeitung*, Spies's pro-labor newspaper, proves that there was a considerable population of workers in Chicago for whom German remained their language of choice. Germans immigrated in droves to Chicago in the mid-to late 1800s. From 1850 to 1890, Chicago's population doubled almost every year, and the single reason was German immigration. By 1884, they accounted for over 24 percent of the city's population. Unlike Germans who immigrated in the early part of the nineteenth century, these Germans were less educated, less rural, and more rooted in craftsman trades and radical politics. They brought with them their traditions of the *Arbeiter-Vereine*, or workers' associations, that allowed working-class men to gather socially. What started as social activities became more political in the late 1800s. In Chicago and elsewhere, these meetings became places for recruiting activists, not just perpetuating German culture through food, dance, and song. The document's use of the German language shows the persistence of retained culture in early immigrant groups despite the often-used narrative of early assimilation. In fact, early immigrants, even Western Europeans, clung to their culture, traditions, and language.

—Karen Linkletter

Questions for Further Study

1. As the urban population in America grew in the 1800s, so did the need for mass communication. Why would this flyer have been an effective way to reach a large number of working-class people in Chicago?

2. The document states that "good speakers" would appear at the Haymarket meeting. Why would the authors have chosen to add that specific text to the flyer? How do organizers today use "star" speakers to draw people to mass meetings and protests?

3. What does this document tell us about the nature and function of public urban spaces in the nineteenth century?

Further Reading

Books

Hirsch, Eric L. *Urban Revolt: Ethnic Politics in the Nineteenth-Century Chicago Labor Movement.* Berkeley: University of California Press, 1990.

Websites

Adelman, William J. "The Haymarket Affair." Illinois Labor History Society. http://www.illinoislaborhistory.org/the-haymarket-affair.

"The Popularity of Broadsides." Printed Ephemera: Three Centuries of Broadsides and Other Printed Ephemera, Library of Congress. https://www.loc.gov/collections/broadsides-and-other-printed-ephemera/articles-and-essays/introduction-to-printed-ephemera-collection/the-popularity-of-broadsides/.

Sclater, Karla Kelling. "The Labor and Radical Press, 1820 to the Present: An Overview and Bibliography." Labor Press Project, Pacific Northwest Labor and Radical Newspapers, University of Washington, 2001. https://depts.washington.edu/labhist/laborpress/Kelling.shtml.

Documentaries

Haymarket: The Bomb, the Anarchists, the Labor Struggle. Adrian Prawica, director. Filmadria, 2021.

Photograph Of Carlisle Indian School Students

Author/Creator
Unknown

Date
1887

Image Type
Photographs

Significance
A photo of several Chiracahua Apache children in western dress taken shortly after their arrival at the Carlisle Indian School in 1887

Overview

This photograph shows a group of Native American students taken four months after their arrival at the United States Indian Industrial School in Carlisle, Pennsylvania, generally called the Carlisle School or Carlisle Indian School. The Carlisle School, founded in 1879 and housed in an unused military barracks, the Carlisle Barracks, was one of twenty-six federally funded boarding schools for Native American youth operated under the auspices of the U.S. Bureau of Indian Affairs. They operated alongside numerous private institutions for Native youth run by religious organizations in the late nineteenth century and into the twentieth. Until the school closed in 1918, a total of 10,000 students from 140 tribes had attended. The tribes with the largest number of students were the Lakota, Ojibwe, Cherokee, Apache, Cheyenne, Alaska Native, Seneca, and Oneida.

The school was founded by Captain (later General) Richard Henry Pratt, who believed that the only way Native Americans could survive was through assimilation to European American culture and institutions. He is perhaps most famous for his statement "Kill the Indian, save the man." When students arrived at the school, the boys' hair was cut, and all the children were given new names. They were not allowed to speak their native tongues or to engage in traditional religious or recreational practices. They were not allowed to return to their homes for visits. Pratt's life was shaped by the military, leading him to adopt a military regimen for the boys at the school and teach them trades, while girls were schooled in domestic skills. Discipline was harsh and could include solitary confinement and corporal punishment. Buried on the grounds of the school are the remains of 146 students.

Pratt, who served as superintendent of the school, was by no means a monster. Taking into account the views of the era in which he lived, his attitudes related to Native Americans were relatively benevolent, born of a genuine desire to improve their lot. He was affiliated with a philanthropic organization called Friends of the Indian, and at a convention of the organization held at Lake Mohonk in New York State in 1902, he stated: "The Indian's property and our greed for it stands in the way of the Indian's progress." Pratt is responsible for the first recorded instance of the use of the word "racism" when he went on to state: "Segregating any race of class of people apart from the rest of the people kills the progress of the segregated people or makes their growth very slow. Association of races and classes is necessary in order to destroy racism and

Document Image

A photo of Chiracahua Apache children at the Carlisle School
(Granger)

classism. Almost all the humanitarian and Government contrivances for the Indian within my knowledge are segregating in their influences and practically accomplish only segregation."

One of the ways the school tried to "Americanize" the students was with such activities as a lacrosse team, a track team, and a marching band. The school was particularly noted for its intercollegiate football team, a rather successful one at that. From 1893 to 1917 the Carlisle football team—not surprisingly called the Carlisle Indians—compiled a record of 167 to 88, with 13 ties. Among the wins was a rout of Army in a battle of the "Warriors" versus the "Long Knives," the Army team whose members included a linebacker and future president named Dwight D. Eisenhower. Many of the Carlisle victories were over established Ivy League teams and other football powers. The Carlisle team, coached by Pop Warner, was responsible for a number of football innovations, including the forward pass, the spiral, and the hidden-ball trick. Among the best and most famous Carlisle players was Jim Thorpe, who had been born Wa-tho-huck, or "Bright Path." Thorpe later won two gold medals at the 1812 Olympic Games in Stockholm, Sweden (in the pentathlon and decathlon), played for six seasons with the New York Giants baseball team, and played professional football for the Canton Bulldogs in Ohio. He even played basketball with a barnstorming team in the 1920s. He was so popular in the world of sports that he was named the first commissioner of the new National Football League in 1920.

About the Artist

It is unknown who took the photo. The provenance of the photo is the Cumberland County Historical Society, founded in 1874. The society is located in Carlisle, Pennsylvania, the location of the Carlisle Indian School. The city is also home to Dickinson College, which maintains archives of materials documenting the history of the Carlisle Indian School and is the source of this photo.

Context

Not long after the formation of the United States, the government tried to address what was called the "Indian problem." The "problem" was a problem because of the large numbers of immigrants who were pushing the boundaries of the United States to the west, encroaching on the eastern borders of the land occupied by Native tribes. Conflicts between white settlers and the Indians emerged. They were competing for resources, and the cultural, economic, and religious systems under which they operated were widely different. Many white Americans believed that the two societies would never be able to coexist, and many believed that the Indians were "savages," less than fully human, who had to be exterminated. One solution was proposed by William Medill, a former U.S. congressman who served as Commissioner of Indian Affairs from 1845 to 1850. He proposed setting aside reservations (or "colonies") that would be occupied only by Indians, much along the lines of the reservations the Indians had created for themselves in the East. The notion was that the U.S. government would remove Native Americans to regions west of the Mississippi River, allowing white Americans to settle in the Southeast. Indeed, the Indian Removal Act of 1830, signed into law by President Andrew Jackson, had already provided for the removal of Indians to territory west of the Mississippi.

In the latter half of the century, many Native tribes resisted relocation to reservations, giving rise to Indian Wars that culminated with the massacre at Wounded Knee in 1890. Essentially, the Native tribes had gone down to defeat, and many returned to the reservations. Each tribe was allotted a claim to new lands and the right of self-governance. The reservations system, however, created its own difficulties. The tribes tried to maintain their traditions, including the cohesive tribal unit with hereditary leadership; managing the land as owners was new to them. The administration of the reservation system led to malfeasance, as supplies and money were siphoned off by corrupt U.S. agents.

By the 1880s, when the Carlisle School was founded, the consensus among non–Native Americans was that the only solution to the "Indian problem" was assimilation of Indians to the American way of life. Only in this way could the Indians survive. It was widely believed that they needed to abandon the concept of tribal landholding and reservations. Ultimately, it was believed, they had to cast aside their tribal identities and join "mainstream" society.

It was in this context that U.S. senator Henry Dawes introduced the Dawes Allotment Act, also called the Dawes Severalty Act, in 1887. The act was signed into law by President Grover Cleveland. The purpose, according to Dawes, was to "rid the nation of tribalism through the virtues of private property, allotting land parcels to Indian heads of family." Put differently, the purpose of the Dawes Act was to convert the Indians into settled property owners and subsistence farmers in large part by breaking up the tribes as social units. The act also had the effect of ensuring that parts of reservation land remained under the ownership of Indians while opening the remainder of the land to white settlement.

The Dawes Act and later acts that extended its provisions were intended to protect the property rights of Native Americans. In too many cases, however, the outcome was not what was expected. Much of the land allotted to the Indians was desert or near desert, unsuitable for farming. Indians, accustomed to a tribal way of life, did not know the methods needed for self-sufficient farming, and they had no money to buy the necessary tools, seeds, and supplies. Many simply did not want to become farmers. When individual tribal members refused the requirements of the government, their land was sold to white settlers, resulting in the loss of nearly a million acres of tribal land. Many individuals lost their land to swindlers. The issue of inheritance became a problem, too. When there were multiple heirs, the piece of land was divided and perhaps later divided again, creating small landholdings that were simply too small to make a profit. In many cases, children who had been sent to the boarding schools, including the Carlisle School, were unable to farm allotments they had inherited.

This was the broad context, carried out in the halls of Congress at a national level. The belief was the that "Indian problem" could be solved by Americanizing Indians by turning them into settled, self-sufficient, Christian farmers—and that one step in that direction was to Americanize Native youth in schools like the Carlisle Indian School. The schools would contribute to the end of tribalism, and graduates of the school would go out into the world not as Indians but as American citizens. In March 2022, the pope met with tribal leaders in Canada to apologize for the mistreatment of indigenous students at similar schools conducted by missionaries in Canada.

Explanation and Analysis of the Document

The photograph is simple. It shows eight boys and three girls who were students at the Carlisle School. The picture was taken about four months after their arrival. All of the students seem to be in their early adolescence. The boys are dressed in military-style uniforms buttoned up to the neck. The two boys in front are holding military-style hats. All have had their hair cut. The three girls in the photo are dressed in floor-length dresses commonly worn by girls and women at the time. The girls' hair was not cut, but their hair in this photo is pulled back. None of the students are smiling, although the lack of smiles was commonplace in nineteenth-century photos. A viewer looking at the photo without any context might not even perceive that the students are Native Americans, for the process of assimilating them to European American culture had already begun. For many viewers, the photo is a horrid reminder of the nineteenth-century (and later) efforts to stamp out the traditional cultures of Native Americans.

—Michael J. O'Neal

Questions for Further Study

1. Other than simply children, what does this photo depict?

2. What impact might a photo such as this have had on non-Native viewers at the time?

3. How might the descendant of a Carlisle student react to looking at this or similar photos today?

Further Reading

Books

Adams, David W. *Education for Extinction: American Indians and the Boarding School Experience, 1875–1928*. Lawrence: University Press of Kansas, 1995.

Black, Jason Edward. *American Indians and the Rhetoric of Removal and Allotment*. Jackson: University Press of Mississippi, 2015.

Fear-Segal Jacqueline, and Susan D. Rose, eds. *Carlisle Indian Industrial School*. Lincoln: University of Nebraska Press, 2016.

Hoxie, Frederick E. *A Final Promise: The Campaign to Assimilate the Indians, 1880–1920*. Lincoln: University of Nebraska Press, 2001.

Prucha, Francis Paul, ed. *Documents of United States Indian Policy*, 3rd ed. Lincoln: University of Nebraska Press, 2000.

Websites

"The Carlisle Indian Industrial School: Assimilation with Education after the Indian Wars." National Park Service. https://www.nps.gov/articles/the-carlisle-indian-industrial-school-assimilation-with-education-after-the-indian-wars-teaching-with-historic-places.htm.

Carlisle Indian School Digital Resource Center, Dickinson College. https://carlisleindian.dickinson.edu/.

Carlisle Indian School Project. https://carlisleindianschoolproject.com/.

"Dawes Act (1887)." National Archives. https://www.archives.gov/milestone-documents/dawes-act.

Kliewer, Addison, Miranda Mahmud, and Brooklyn Wayland. "'Kill the Indian, Save the Man': Remembering the Stories of Indian Boarding Schools." University of Oklahoma College of Journalism and Mass Communications. https://www.ou.edu/gaylord/exiled-to-indian-country/content/remembering-the-stories-of-indian-boarding-schools.

Yu, Jane. "Kill the Indian, Save the Man." Pennsylvania State University. Spring 2009. http://pabook2.libraries.psu.edu/palitmap/CarlisleIndianSchool.html.

Documentaries

O'Gara, Geoffrey. *Home from School: The Children of Carlisle*. PBS, 2021. https://www.pbs.org/independentlens/documentaries/home-from-school-the-children-of-carlisle/.

Rose, Susan D., and Manuel Saralegui. *The Lost Ones: The Long Journey Home: A Documentary Film*. Dickinson College. Community Studies Center, 2009.

Jacob Riis: "Bayard Street Tenement" Photograph

Author/Creator
Jacob Riis

Date
c. 1889

Image Type
Photographs

Significance
A prime example of muckraking photojournalism, in this case highlighting the living conditions of the urban working class in New York City tenements

Overview

As photography technology and techniques evolved in the latter decades of the nineteenth century, photographs became an increasingly important way to disseminate information, reflecting the advertising dictum coined later that "a picture is worth a thousand words." While technology had yet to evolve to allow quality mass reproduction of photographic images in printed material, photos were increasingly used as the basis for the drawings and engravings that were used in print media. They were also rapidly becoming an effective and central element in presentations and exhibitions.

The population of urban areas of the United States swelled in the late 1800s, both from immigration and from internal migration from rural areas. The new arrivals were lured by the prospect of jobs in America's booming industrial economy. Typically, however, they had few skills associated with manufacturing or urban living. Their numbers created a surplus of minimally skilled labor, resulting in chronically low wages and household income. There was little urban planning for residential areas, nor was there much in the way of regulation of building standards or occupancy limits. Consequently, conditions in the areas inhabited by the growing urban working class, commonly known as tenements, were cramped, dangerous, unhealthy, and downright deplorable.

These conditions soon caught the attention of the progressive movement, which added improving the living conditions of the urban working class to its agenda. Movement activists used a variety of techniques and media to spread awareness of the circumstances of working-class life to gain support for their attempts to improve it. The photo "Lodgers in a Crowded Bayard Street Tenement," taken by Jacob Riis around 1889, is an example of the photography used by progressives in their efforts. Riis, a journalist by trade, recognized the impact of photography and devoted much of his energy to producing visual documentation of the life and physical environment of the tenement districts. His work was exhibited, used in lantern slide-show presentations, many of which he gave himself, and ultimately published in books. He is credited as a major force in helping the progressives achieve many of their reforms in urban life and as a pioneer of gritty, realistic urban photography who inspired generations of successors.

Document Image

"Lodgers in a Crowded Bayard Street Tenement"
(Museum of the City of New York)

About the Artist

Jacob Riis was born in Denmark in 1849. Like many of those he photographed, he immigrated to the United States, arriving near the beginning of the post–Civil War immigration wave in 1870. His early years in the country were spent living the hardscrabble life of an immigrant in New York City's tenement neighborhoods. As the son of a teacher and newspaper columnist, Riis had advantages most immigrants did not. He was literate (in both Danish and English) and had experience with several aspects of newspaper publication. While he preferred carpentry to journalism, job opportunities were better for him in journalism. By the mid-1870s he was a successful journalist with a stable career. He began to turn his efforts to improving the lot of those he had lived among when he first arrived in the United States.

Riis's writings were already having an impact by the mid-1880s; however, he felt he could be even more effective with photos. Annoyed by the frustrations of working with professionals, Riis learned the basics of photography and began collaborating with other amateur photographers. His passion for the mission of improving life in the tenements gave him the courage to try new techniques. Perhaps most importantly, he is credited with being one of the early adopters and innovators of flash photography, a necessity to capture images in the dimly lit tenements. His innovations did not always go well, causing him to catch his clothes on fire, spark at least two building fires, one of which was in his home, almost blind himself, and frighten dozens of his subjects. Nevertheless, he took over a hundred strikingly powerful images that stoked the conscience of his contemporaries and preserved pictures of the daily life of the working class in late-nineteenth-century New York. Many say his work invented the field of photojournalism. As his speaking career progressed, his increasingly crowded schedule of lantern slide presentations eventually forced him to again leave the actual picture taking to others.

His work made him not only a sought-after speaker but earned him publishing contracts and friendships with powerful people. He wrote countless articles and more than a dozen books, including the famous *How the Other Half Lives* in 1890, followed up by *Children of the Poor* in 1892, both credited with providing the impetus for much of the tenement reforms of the Progressive Era in New York. He published an autobiography, *The Making of an American*, in 1901. A

friend of Theodore Roosevelt, with whom he worked as police reporter and social reformer when Roosevelt was the New York City police commissioner, Riis wrote what in later times would be called a campaign biography for Roosevelt, *Theodore Roosevelt: The Citizen*. While his photos provided the basis for images in these works, printing technology did not allow them to be reproduced effectively for publication, and it was only generations after his death in 1914 that reissued versions of his works, and later several websites, brought them widely to the general public.

Context

A burgeoning manufacturing economy in the Northeast and Great Lakes states attracted millions of migrants to the urban areas of those regions in the decades after the Civil War. With no centralized planning for population growth and the overriding ethic of laissez-faire capitalism deterring government regulation of living conditions, housing for these masses of people was put up in a haphazard, unsanitary, and dangerous manner. People were cramped together in unimaginably crowded conditions beset with a myriad of problems, from inconveniences like a lack of running water to major health hazards such as virtually no sanitation or ventilation. Such conditions bred not only disease but enormous amounts of interpersonal and domestic violence. Chronically low wages and little job security combined with frequent economic downturns created a desperately poor population that often turned to theft and robbery for survival. Criminal gangs preyed on this desperation and peddled all manner of vices and pleasures driven underground by the prudish values of the middle class. These gangs amassed great wealth and established bases of power in this maelstrom of filth, misery, and despair. Yet, thousands rushed to join the chaos every day, making certain neighborhoods of New York and other urban areas some of the most densely populated places on Earth.

Having lived in these tenement areas intermittently in his first couple of years in the United States, sometimes even being homeless at times in those mean streets, Riis had firsthand knowledge of the conditions facing the urban poor and how to navigate the tenement neighborhoods and interact with their residents. His literacy and writing skill allowed him to escape the tenements, but he never truly left them behind. He continually chose jobs in journalism that sent him back to the dark corners of poverty-stricken New York City, often as a police reporter. With a messianic fervor, he sought to prick the conscience of America's middle and upper classes toward reforms to make the tenements more livable. First with newspaper and magazine articles, then later with books and lantern slide shows, which he started presenting in 1888, Riis showed America in lurid detail what life was like in the tenements.

Riis's contemporaries saw him as an essential driver of tenement reform. Shortly before assuming the presidency, his friend Theodore Roosevelt called him "the most useful citizen of New York" in an article in *McClure's*. One important and long-lasting example of Riis's work directly leading to action was the construction of the New Croton Reservoir. He published a massive five-column investigation of the hazards of the city's water supply titled "Some Things We Drink" in August 1891 in the *Evening Sun*, a weekly New York newspaper. Along with Riis's shocking prose, the article included six pictures. Construction began on the New Croton Reservoir and on the existing water delivery system, which was overdue for updates, the next year. The reservoir is still an important part of New York City's water system.

Perhaps most important, although not necessarily as immediate in results, Riis's writings are credited with the state legislature's Tenement House Commission Report of 1884. The report made twenty or so recommendations. One of the recommendations, breaking up the infamous Mulberry Bend, generally acknowledged as the most dangerous and unsanitary section of the tenement district, came forth in the Small Parks Act, which led to the creation of Mulberry Bend Park, now known as Columbus Park. The others would have to wait until Riis's photos and presentations had created more public awareness and sympathy for reform. Most of the remaining recommendations were put in place by the Tenement House Act of 1901. This act not only mandated improved ventilation, water, and sanitation for tenements but established a systematic process of inspection to ensure compliance.

Explanation and Analysis of the Document

The photograph "Lodgers in a Crowded Bayard Street Tenement," dated 1889, is a gelatin silver print, a fairly new chemical process at the time. It is housed with the rest of Riis's photos in the Museum of the City of New York. The picture itself is designed to show the crowded conditions of tenement house living, in particular the overcrowding in rooms rented out by the night, often located in the basements and less usable spaces of tenement buildings. A drawing of the image appeared on page sixty-nine of the original edition of *How the Other Half Lives*. It first appeared as a halftone photo on page 273 in Riis's autobiography, *The Making of an American*. By the 1970s it was appearing as a high-quality photograph in reissues of his works.

As Riis describes the scene, "A room not thirteen feet either way slept twelve men and women, two or three in bunks set in a sort of alcove, the rest on the floor. A kerosene lamp burned dimly in the fearful atmosphere." The photo only shows those on the bunks, who number at least six, all of whom seem to be male. The location is on Bayard Street in the infamous Mulberry Bend. The image was taken as Riis followed police inspectors on patrol seeking to make sure the minimal regulations on short-term lodging that existed were being followed.

Those critical of Riis accused him of intruding on people's lives and staging his photos, some suggesting in this one that he woke his subjects up and had them look at the camera. Given the police and photographic assistants with him, as well as the landlord, who gave them access to the room, this was clearly not an unannounced snapshot of a night's lodging in a quasi-legal rooming house. Nevertheless, the degree to which one can say the photo does not reflect the reality of a night-to-night lodging space in the tenements is questionable. Whether the boarders that night would have been sleeping, groggy, or awake and staring at a camera, there still would have been twelve people in less than 170 square feet. The general state of disorder and the dirty appearance of the room and bedding were not a concoction of Riis, although perhaps the flash made the light contrast in the room harsher, which highlighted it.

This was one of several of Riis's images that exposed the decrepit physical conditions and human misery of the Mulberry Bend. The Tenement House Commission Report of 1884 had called for destruction of the Bend by extending Pell Street to Leonard Street, which would require demolition of some of the most dilapidated and densely packed tenements of the Bend. "Lodgers in a Crowded Bayard Street Tenement" was taken a half block or so north of the proposed Pell

Street expansion designed to bust the Bend. The block formed by Bayard Street to the west, Park Street to the east, Mulberry Street to the south, and Baxter Street to the north had twenty-eight tenement houses with 5,650 people living in them. Tenements typically had five stories, with four apartments per floor. All that averages out to a little over 200 people per building: forty people per floor, and ten people per apartment.

Ultimately, the solution of replacing the unhealthy, crime-ridden Mulberry Bend neighborhood with a roadway was rejected. Using the Small Park Act of 1887, New York instead eventually built the Mulberry Bend Park in the area, a fix Riis had advocated. Construction of the park was started in 1895, no doubt spurred on by Riis's photos, including this one, that were shown and discussed in a growing number of presentations. Riis's contributions were acknowledged at the park's dedication in 1897. His estrangement from Tammany Hall had cost him a VIP invitation to the event, but Sanitation Commissioner George Waring noticed Riis in the crowd and asked for three cheers for the man, which the crowded enthusiastically gave. Since that impromptu verbal acclamation, Riis has been honored in many ways, with monuments, parks, museums, and schools named for him in New York and beyond.

—G. David Price

Questions for Further Study

1. What problems resulting from the physical space of the tenements existed for those living in them?

2. Looking closely at the photo, how does the image reflect those problems? What emotions does it stir in those viewing it?

3. What does the photo and Jacob Riis's career suggest about the role of journalism in pushing for change? Are journalists merely reporting facts and recording events? What can they do beyond chronicling facts and events? Should journalists go beyond reporting facts and events?

4. Once the most dilapidated tenements of Mulberry Bend had been destroyed and part of the area turned into a park, where might the people who used to live there have gone instead? How did the Tenement House Act of 1901 address the issue of lodging for the working class?

Further Reading

Books

Riis, Jacob. *How the Other Half Lives*. New York: Dover, 1971.

Yochelson, B., and D. J. Czitrom. *Rediscovering Jacob Riis: Exposure Journalism and Photography in Turn-of-the-Century New York*. Chicago: University of Chicago Press, 2014.

Articles

deNoyelles, Adrienne. "'Letting in the Light': Jacob Riis's Crusade for Breathing Spaces on the Lower East Side." *Journal of Urban History* 46, no. 4 (July 2020): 775–93.

Flint, Kate. "'More Rapid Than the Lightning's Flash': Photography, Suddenness, and the Afterlife of Romantic Illumination." *European Romantic Review* 24, no. 3 (2013): 369–83.

Welch, Shawn. "A Working Faith: Social Gospel Theology, Pragmatism, and Jacob Riis's Consecration of the Camera." *Journal of American Culture* 44, no. 3 (September 2021): 210–22.

Yotova, Denitsa. "Presenting 'The Other Half': Jacob Riis's Reform Photography and Magic Lantern Spectacles as the Beginning of Documentary Film." *Visual Communication Quarterly* 26, no. 2 (April 2019): 91–105.

Websites

"Jacob Riis." International Center for Photography. https://www.icp.org/browse/archive/constituents/jacob-riis.

LOUIS DALRYMPLE: "SCHOOL BEGINS" CARTOON

AUTHOR/CREATOR Louis Dalrymple	IMAGE TYPE CARTOONS
DATE 1899	SIGNIFICANCE A cartoon offering commentary on American expansionist ambitions in the late nineteenth century

Overview

This cartoon appeared in the January 25, 1899, issue of *Puck*, a leading American humor magazine. It was published in support of American expansionism, which seemed to be cresting in the late 1890s. The United States had already annexed Texas, acquired California and the American Southwest as a result of war with Mexico, and purchased Alaska from Russia. Cuba, the Philippines, Puerto Rico, and Hawaii had come under U.S. hegemony in the 1890s as the nation was continuing to achieve its "Manifest Destiny" by expanding into the Pacific and the Caribbean. These expansionist aims were a source of considerable controversy in the last years of the nineteenth century and the early years of the twentieth. To some Americans, the nation was appropriately flexing its muscles and evolving from a small, fledgling nation into one ready to take its rightful place among the world's powers, defend its interests abroad, and spread Anglo-American culture, institutions, and civilization, including Christianity. To others, "imperialism" had the ring of bullying and the exploitation of other nations, particularly those whose people were brown-skinned, for ends that were less than honorable. Pro-imperialists tended to mock anti-imperialists in the press as meddlesome "old women" and "aunties."

About the Artist

The cartoon was drawn by Louis Dalrymple. Dalrymple was born in 1866 in Cambridge, Illinois. He studied at the Pennsylvania Academy of Fine Arts and the Art Students League of New York. In 1885 he became the chief cartoonist of the *New York Daily Graphic*, but his cartoons also appeared in the humor magazines *Puck* and *Judge*. He died in 1905.

The outlet for this cartoon by Dalrymple was *Puck*, the humor magazine founded in 1871 by Austrian Joseph Keppler and his partners as a German-language publication. It was named after the airy, sprightly character in William Shakespeare's comedy *A Midsummer Night's Dream*, best remembered for his line "Lord, what fools these mortals be." The magazine's first English-language issue was published in 1877, and it soon became a major competitor of *Frank Leslie's Illustrated Newspaper* and *Harper's Weekly*, Keppler's former employer. *Puck* was unique among U.S. magazines in the late nineteenth century. Rather than relying on wood engravings, it was illustrated with lithographs, and each issue featured three cartoons rather than the usual one. In the early years the cartoons were black and

Document Image

"School Begins"
(Library of Congress)

white, but later, tints were added, and later still, the cartoons were printed in full color. Historians believe that the *Puck* cartoons supporting Democrat Grover Cleveland in his run for the presidency in 1884 likely contributed to his election victory. *Puck*, along with its main competitor, *Judge*, published numerous cartoons in these years providing commentary on the issue of imperialism.

Context

The cartoon presents what amounts to a narrative history of American expansion and the achievement of its "Manifest Destiny" in the nineteenth century. Among the early "class" of students that were schooled by Uncle Sam in civilization was Texas, which declared its independence from Mexico in 1836 to become the Republic of Texas. Texas leaders, however, called for annexation by the United States, and their desire came to fruition in 1845 with the admission of Texas as the nation's twenty-eighth state. Mexico was not happy with this development, believing that the United States was in effect dismembering Mexico, and in 1846, warfare between the two nations was the result. After the American victory in the Battle of Buena Vista and the successful march on Mexico City by U.S. troops in 1847, the war ended with the 1848 Treaty of Guadalupe Hidalgo. A key feature of the treaty was the Mexican cession of much of its northern territory to the United States. That territory would become, among others, the U.S. states of California, New Mexico, and Arizona—"students" that in 1899 had already been schooled by Uncle Sam. Meanwhile, the United States had acquired Alaska from Russia in 1867. At the time, the purchase was mocked as "Seward's folly," in reference to Secretary of State William H. Seward, who closed the transaction, but at two cents an acre, Alaska, with its wealth of resources, turned out to be a bargain.

A key series of events in the 1890s bearing on U.S. expansion was the Spanish American War of 1898. The war was significant because it was the concluding chapter of Spain's empire in the Western Hemisphere. It also established the role of the United States as a power in the Pacific. The war began in 1898 after three years of efforts by armed Cuban revolutionaries to throw off the yoke of Spanish rule. Americans paid close attention to the conflict because of the possibility of instability in the region just off American shores and because they were outraged by stories of brutal

tactics on the part of the Spanish. Further, ever since the Monroe Doctrine of 1823, the United States had been trying to purge the Western Hemisphere of European colonialism and the threat it posed to American interests. Tension was building. It grew after the U.S. battleship *Maine* exploded and sank in Havana Harbor on February 15, 1898. On April 11, President William McKinley asked Congress for a resolution that would ensure the stability of an independent Cuba. On April 20, Congress responded with a resolution acknowledging Cuban independence and demanding that Spain relinquish control of the island. The resolution also authorized the use of American arms to guarantee Cuba's independence. After Spain rejected American demands and declared war on April 22, Congress passed a war resolution on April 25.

What took place was what U.S. Ambassador John Hay called a "splendid little war." Press barons such as William Randolph Hearst, publisher of the *New York Journal* and the *San Francisco Examiner*, were enthusiastic supporters of the war, coverage of which boosted circulation. On May 1, Commodore George Dewey defeated the Spanish naval force defending the Philippines at Manila Bay. In June, U.S. troops landed at Guantanamo Bay and Santiago. In the most celebrated battle of the war, future president Teddy Roosevelt led his "Rough Riders" in the Battle of San Juan Hill in July.

A cease-fire was signed on August 12, and the war ended when the United States and Spain signed the Treaty of Paris on December 10, 1898. The treaty guaranteed the independence of Cuba and forced Spain to cede Guam, Puerto Rico, and the Philippines (new "students" in the cartoon) to the United States. By a margin of just one vote over the required two-thirds margin needed, the U.S. Senate ratified the treaty on February 6, 1899. Opposing ratification was Senator Benjamin Tillman, who stated: "The commercial instinct which seeks to furnish a market and places for the growth of commerce or the investment of capital for the money making of the few is pressing this country madly to the final and ultimate annexation of these people regardless of their own wishes." Tillman's words were indicative of the views of those Americans who opposed American imperialist aims. Among them were members of the American Anti-Imperialist League, founded on June 15, 1898, in opposition to annexation of the Philippines as a violation of the republican concept of "consent of the governed."

The war became a pretext for the annexation of Hawaii. In 1893, white planters and businessmen had staged a coup against Queen Liliuokalani and installed a new government. President Grover Cleveland rejected their requests that the United States annex Hawaii, but the McKinley administration, and much of the American public, supported annexation, partly for economic reasons and partly because Hawaii would provide a base of operations that would enable the United States to protect its interests in Asia. On August 12, 1898, Hawaii was annexed to the United States by a joint resolution of Congress. In 1993, President Bill Clinton signed a joint resolution passed by Congress apologizing for the events of the 1890s.

These were the events that brought the issue of American imperialism to the fore in the late 1890s. *Puck*, however, was not the only publication that expressed views on the matter. In February 1899, during the Senate debate over ratification of the Treaty of Paris, "The White Man's Burden: The United States and the Philippine Islands," a jingoistic poem by English author Rudyard Kipling, was published in *McClure's* magazine. The poem urged the United States to "send forth the best ye breed . . . To serve your captives' need . . . Take up the White Man's burden." In 1899, *Judge* published an editorial cartoon titled "The White Man's Burden." It depicted a sweating Uncle Sam carrying a hamper filled with colonial subjects. He is following the British John Bull, who is carrying the people of the British Empire and China. Their goal in the cartoon is "Education" and "Liberty."

Explanation and Analysis of the Document

Dominating the cartoon "School Begins" is a stern-faced caricature of Uncle Sam with a teacher's pointer in his hand. He is leaning over a teacher's desk, glaring at the students in front of him. His new "students" include Cuba, Porto Rico (that is, Puerto Rico), Hawaii, and the Philippines, who all appear to be terrified by their "teacher." On the teacher's desk is a book titled *U.S. First Lessons in Self-Government.* Behind these new students, who had been added to the "class" in the 1890s, are established students, labeled California, Texas, New Mexico, Arizona, and Alaska. Uncle Sam is saying to his "new class in civilization": "Now, children, you've got to learn these lessons whether you want to or not! But just take a look at the class ahead of you and remember that, in a little while, you will feel as glad to be here as they are!" In the background is a Native American boy sitting by himself reading an upside-down book labeled "ABC," suggesting that he has failed to achieve the benefits of civilization because of his inability to read. A Chinese boy is standing just outside the door of the schoolhouse, suggesting the exclusion of the Chinese from American society. A Black boy is washing a window, suggesting that African Americans are denied educational opportunities and are relegated to the performance of menial tasks. Above and to the left of the door is a caption that reads: "The Confederate States refused their consent to be governed; but the union was preserved without their consent." The blackboard facing the teacher reads:

"The consent of the governed is a good thing in theory, but very rare in fact. / England has governed her colonies whether they consented or not. By not waiting for their consent she has greatly advanced the world's civilization. / The U.S. must govern its new territories with or without their consent until they can govern themselves."

These words suggest that the concept of "consent of the governed" was inapplicable to the world's peoples of color, who were regarded as backward and uncivilized and needing to be "schooled" in civilization.

—Michael J. O'Neal

Questions for Further Study

1. What is the primary message of the cartoon?

2. What position did the creator of the cartoon, and by extension *Puck* magazine, take with regard to American expansion?

3. How effective might the cartoon have been in shaping readers' views about American expansion?

Further Reading

Books

Beisner, Robert L. *Twelve against Empire: The Anti-Imperialists, 1898–1900.* New York: McGraw Hill, 1968.

Healy, David. *US Expansionism: The Imperialist Urge in the 1890s.* Madison: University of Wisconsin Press, 2011.

Immerman, Richard H. *Empire for Liberty: A History of American Imperialism from Benjamin Franklin to Paul Wolfowitz.* Princeton, NJ: Princeton University Press, 2010.

Immerwahr, Daniel. *How to Hide an Empire: A History of the Greater United States.* New York: Farrar, Straus and Giroux, 2019.

Sexton, Jay, and Ian Tyrell. *Empire's Twin: U.S. Anti-imperialism from the Founding Era to the Age of Terrorism.* Ithaca, NY: Cornell University Press, 2014.

Stephanson, Anders. *Manifest Destiny: American Expansion and the Empire of Right.* New York: Hill and Wang, 1995.

Winks, Robin W. "The American Struggle with 'Imperialism': How Words Frighten." In *The American Identity: Fusion and Fragmentation*, edited by Rob Kroes, 143–77. Amsterdam: Universiteit van Amsterdam, 1980.

Articles

Kramer, Paul A. "Power and Connection: Imperial Histories of the United States in the World." *American Historical Review* 116, no. 5 (December 2011): 1348–91.

Loy, Edward H. "Editorial Opinion and American Imperialism: Two Northwest Newspapers." *Oregon Historical Quarterly* 72, no. 3 (September 1971): 209–24.

Zevin, Robert. "An Interpretation of American Imperialism." *Journal of Economic History* 32, no. 1 (March 1972): 316–60.

Websites

"Address Adopted by the Anti-Imperialist League." Anti-Imperialist League, February 10, 1899. Internet Archive. https://archive.org/details/AddressOfTheAnti-imperialistLeague/mode/1up.

"American Imperialism." GlobalSecurity.org. https://www.globalsecurity.org/military/world/usa/history/08-09.htm.

Davies, Dave, with Daniel Immerwahr. "The History of American Imperialism, from Bloody Conquest to Bird Poop" (interview). *Fresh Air*, February 18, 2019. NPR. https://www.npr.org/2019/02/18/694700303/the-history-of-american-imperialism-from-bloody-conquest-to-bird-poop.

"1898: Birth of an Overseas Empire." History, Art & Archives, U.S. House of Representatives. https://history.house.gov/Exhibitions-and-Publications/APA/Historical-Essays/Exclusion-and-Empire/1898/.

Tillman, Benjamin. "Address to the U.S. Senate." Library of Congress, February 7, 1899. http://nationalhumanitiescenter.org/pds/gilded/empire/text7/tillman.pdf.

Documentaries

Miller, Daniel A., and Daniel B. Polin. *Crucible of Empire: The Spanish-American War.* Great Projects Film Company and South Carolina ETV for PBS, 1999.

Photograph Of Freed Slaves At A County Almshouse

Author/Creator Unknown	**Image Type** Photographs
Date 1899	**Significance** A photo capturing the bleak lives of impoverished former slaves living at a county almshouse

Overview

A U.S. Census report compiled in the early 1900s indicated that there were more than 2,700 almshouses in the United States as of 1903, just a few years after this photo was taken. Most of these almshouses would have been operated by counties, although a relatively few were operated by cities or states. The total number of "paupers," as they were called, living in these almshouses was more than 81,700, according to the report. Among these, the number of "colored paupers" was more than 6,900 in 1903. That number grew to more than 7,400 in 1905.

The first almshouse in the United States was founded in Boston in 1622. In the nineteenth century, the number of "poorhouses," an alternative term for almshouses, grew rapidly. Many of these early almshouses were small, holding perhaps ten or a dozen people under the care of a superintendent and a matron, who was typically the superintendent's wife. Some cities and states, however, had large concrete-block almshouses that held thousands of people and that almost resembled prisons. (Indeed, the occupants were called "inmates.") A notorious example was the Tewksbury Almshouse in Massachusetts, near the industrial city of Lowell; Anne Sullivan, the "miracle worker" teacher of blind and deaf Helen Keller, was a resident of Tewksbury in the 1870s. Others included the Bellevue Almshouse in New York City, which later became Bellevue Hospital, and the Cook County Almshouse in Chicago, which later became Cook County Hospital. In the early to mid-nineteenth century, the people who occupied almshouses on a permanent basis tended to include the mentally and physically disabled, children, the "feeble minded," and "fallen women" (that is, women who worked in the sex trade). Throughout much of the century, the federal government stayed out of the social services business after President Franklin Pierce vetoed the Bill for the Benefit of the Indigent Insane in 1854.

Almshouses were often situated on the grounds of what was called a "poor farm." Able-bodied residents of the almshouse were expected to perform work. Most of these farms provided at least a portion of the foodstuffs needed to support the residents, including grain, produce, and livestock. Otherwise, residents were expected to perform housekeeping chores and in some cases provide care for other residents. Accommodations were minimal. Conditions were sometimes abusive.

By late in the century, the almshouse was a feared institution, primarily because it was regarded as a place to go to die. A viewer of this photo is perhaps left won-

Document Image

Freed slaves at a county almshouse
(Bettmann / Getty)

dering whether the people depicted in the photo believed that they were simply being warehoused and waiting to die.

About the Artist

Nothing is known about the photographer or the circumstances under which the photo was taken, including its location.

Context

This photo was taken in the context of the precarious condition of African Americans in the late nineteenth century. Before the Civil War, virtually all African Americans were excluded from public welfare services. Enslaved African Americans were the responsibility of their owners, and free Blacks were left to fend for themselves. In 1863, President Abraham Lincoln issued the Emancipation Proclamation, which declared that enslaved people in the states that were in rebellion "are, and henceforward shall be free." Contrary to popular belief, the Emancipation Proclamation did not have the effect of "freeing the slaves," for of course the Confederacy paid no attention to Lincoln. It was not until the years after the Civil War, with the ratification of the Thirteenth, Fourteenth, and Fifteenth Amendments to the U.S. Constitution—collectively the "Reconstruction Amendments"—that genuine freedom became a hope. The Thirteenth Amendment, ratified in 1865, abolished slavery and "involuntary servitude." The Fourteenth, ratified in 1868, created the legal concepts of due process and equal protection under the law for all citizens, including African Americans. The Fifteenth, ratified in 1870, prohibited discrimination in voting rights on the basis of "race, color, or previous condition of servitude." The purpose of the amendments was to guarantee the freedom of those formerly enslaved. Meanwhile, with the end of the Civil War, Black people, particularly southern Blacks, celebrated what seemed to be the end of the brutalities of slavery—the beatings and whippings, the backbreaking labor, the breakup of families, the sexual assaults, and the denial of such rights as marriage, education, property ownership, and more.

The problem, of course, was that formerly enslaved people in most cases lacked the tools—literacy, education, money, land—that would enable them to take advantage of their newly acquired freedom. One freed-

man wrote, "We colored people did not know how to be free." To aid in the transition to freedom, Congress, in 1865, created the Bureau of Refugees, Freedmen, and Abandoned Lands, commonly called the Freedmen's Bureau. The bureau performed most of its work from 1865 to about 1870. Although one of its primary purposes was to deal with matters pertaining to land that had been seized or abandoned during the war, it also provided relief to former slaves. It issued rations and clothing, operated hospitals and refugee camps, and supervised labor contracts between planters and freedmen. It managed apprenticeship disputes for formerly enslaved people trying to enter trades (although many of these "apprenticeship" agreements essentially re-enslaved workers under their former owners), facilitated the legalization of marriages that had been entered into during slavery, provided transportation for freedmen who were trying to find lost relatives in other parts of the country, and helped Black soldiers get back pay and pensions. The Freedmen's Bureau helped benevolent societies in the creation of schools and supervised some 3,000 schools in the South. In some schoolhouses during this era, grandparents sat side by side with their grandchildren, learning to read.

The promise of Reconstruction (1866–1877) meant that Blacks could and exercise the rights of citizenship, including holding public office: some 700 Black people were elected to public office, including two U.S. senators and sixteen congressional representatives, and another 1,300 held government jobs during Reconstruction. The promise of freedom, however, quickly eroded. The states of the former Confederacy regarded Reconstruction as a humiliating occupation by "carpetbaggers" from the North. Governments in the South enacted Black Codes, or laws that circumscribed the civil rights of Blacks by making it illegal for them to serve on juries, to testify against white defendants, or to serve in the militias. Poll taxes and literacy tests impeded the right of Blacks to vote. The codes required sharecroppers (who paid rent on land owned by white landowners with a share of their crop) and tenant farmers to sign contracts with white landowners, and if they refused, they could be arrested. Large numbers of Black people, particularly in the South, lived in crushing poverty.

Southern whites, instead of helping, tried to continue to exclude Blacks from access to social services. The so-called Redeemers, the southern wing of the Democratic Party, tried to reaffirm white supremacy and regain their political power by, among other steps, enforcing segregation in facilities for the poor. Opposing them were the "Radical Republicans," a group of legislators in Congress who were committed to the emancipation of slaves and the enfranchisement and equal treatment of Blacks. They spearheaded reforms, many of them at the urging of prominent activists such as Dorothea Dix, that allowed Blacks to be admitted to insane asylums, institutions for the blind and deaf, orphanages, hospitals, and almshouses.

Reconstruction came to an end with the Compromise of 1877, in which Democrats agreed to acknowledge Rutherford B. Hayes as the winner of the disputed presidential election of 1876 in exchange for the withdrawal of federal troops from the South—troops that had been sent there to enforce the Reconstruction amendments. The withdrawal led to the resurgence of the Ku Klux Klan and renewed oppression of African Americans. The result was that significant numbers of African Americans, particularly the elderly, were left destitute and forced into almshouses as the only means of survival. It was the last resort for many.

Explanation and Analysis of the Document

Little is known about the photograph. The photograph is dated 1899, but it is unknown who took it or where it was taken. It could have been taken in virtually any county in the United States. The image shows four elderly African Americans in the foreground, three women and one man. An additional person can be seen far in the background. The people in the foreground appear to be doing chores. The woman in the center appears to be performing a task such as shelling peas into a basin at her feet. The woman on the right appears to be sewing. It is unclear what the man in the bowler hat, seated to the left, is doing. The fourth person, a woman, is standing behind the other three. All appear to be under a covered area projecting from a brick building, the almshouse. In front of the seated figures are a metal tub, a wooden crate, and a half barrel. The image presents a stark picture of the poverty and tedium of the life of former slaves who failed to realize the initial hope of emancipation and who are living out the remainder of their lives under the care of the local government in an almshouse.

—Michael J. O'Neal

Questions for Further Study

1. What might be the primary message of this photograph?

2. What might have been going through the minds of the people depicted in the photograph as they were going about their chores?

3. To what extent did the almshouses and the condition of African Americans in the decades after the Civil War represent another type of enslavement?

Further Reading

Books

Blackmon, Douglas A. *Slavery by Another Name: The Re-Enslavement of Black Americans from the Civil War to World War II.* New York: Anchor Books, 2009.

Kretz, Dale. Administering Freedom: The State of Emancipation after the Freedmen's Bureau. Chapel Hill: University of North Carolina Press, 2022.

Smethhurst, James. *The African American Roots of Modernism: From Reconstruction to the Harlem Renaissance.* Chapel Hill: University of North Carolina Press, 2011.

Wagner, David. *Ordinary People: In and Out of Poverty in the Gilded Age.* London: Routledge, 2016.

Wagner, David. *The Poorhouse: America's Forgotten Institution.* Lanham, MD: Rowman-Littlefield, 2005.

Articles

Carlton-Laney, Iris. "Old Folks' Homes for Blacks during the Progressive Era." *Journal of Sociology and Social Welfare* 16, no. 3 (September 1989): 43–60. https://scholarworks.wmich.edu/cgi/viewcontent.cgi?article=1907&context=jssw.

Rabinowitz, Howard N. "From Exclusion to Segregation: Health and Welfare Services for Southern Blacks, 1865–1890." *Social Service Review* 48, no. 3 (September 1974): 327–54.

Websites

Blakemore, Erin. "Poorhouses Were Designed to Punish People for Their Poverty." *History.com.* August 29, 2018. https://www.history.com/news/in-the-19th-century-the-last-place-you-wanted-to-go-was-the-poorhouse.

Ford, Kathy Roberts, and Bryan Bowman. "Exploiting Black Labor after the Abolition of Slavery." *The Conversation*, February 6, 2017. https://theconversation.com/exploiting-black-labor-after-the-abolition-of-slavery-72482.

"The Freedmen's Bureau." National Archives. https://www.archives.gov/research/african-americans/freedmens-bureau.

Wagner, David. "Poor Relief and the Almshouse." Virginia Commonwealth University Social Welfare History Project. https://socialwelfare.library.vcu.edu/issues/poor-relief-almshouse/.

BUFFALO BILL'S WILD WEST FLYER

AUTHOR/CREATOR	IMAGE TYPE
Courier Lithographic Co.	FLYERS
DATE	SIGNIFICANCE
c. 1899	A poster advertising *Buffalo Bill's Wild West*, a show that created and fostered perceptions of the Old West in the late nineteenth century and beyond

Overview

William F. "Buffalo Bill" Cody (1846–1917) began his rise to fame at the age of twenty-three when he met a pulp novelist, Ned Buntline, who based his novels loosely on Cody's adventures as a scout, Pony Express rider, Civil War soldier, and bison hunter in the West. Those novels, and many others like them, gave rise to a national mania for the rough, rollicking, boisterous western frontier. In 1872 Buntline produced a theatrical show, *The Scouts of the Prairie*, with Cody himself as the star. Then in 1883, Cody opened his own show, called *Buffalo Bill's Wild West*, a type of living history that formed the foundation of the world's image of the Old West.

Cody was a consummate promoter. As his show moved into a community, his "roadies" plastered advertising posters like this one on virtually every vertical surface they could find. The posters were effective in generating interest and attracting a large, enthusiastic audience willing to pay to see the spectacle. The *Wild West* show was an extravagant outdoor performance, with a cast of hundreds, including fast-shooting, hard-riding cowboys and Indians, Cossacks, and *vaqueros* and featuring real-life stars like markswoman Annie Oakley and Chief Sitting Bull. The show recreated the capture of the Deadwood stagecoach in South Dakota, a Pony Express ride, a lynching, Custer's Last Stand, and other historical events. It is estimated that between 300 and 400 surviving versions of the *Wild West* posters are extant. When a poster comes up for auction, it can attract bids in the tens of thousands of dollars.

About the Artist

It is not known who, specifically, created this poster. The major producer of *Buffalo Bill's Wild West* posters, however, was the Courier Lithographic Co., founded in 1860 in (appropriately) Buffalo, New York. The company was organized by the publishers of the *Buffalo Courier* newspaper and would grow into the largest poster production company in the United States, and possibly in the world. In later years, the company moved into book printing, commercial and railroad printing, bookbinding, wood engraving, lithography, and catalogs. Among the firm's customers were not only Cody but also the Ringling Brothers circus and P.T. Barnum. The company, with a production facility of 130,000 square feet, three hundred employees, and sixty-three printing presses, was a fixture in Buffalo, in part because of its efforts to promote fire safety, so in

Document Image

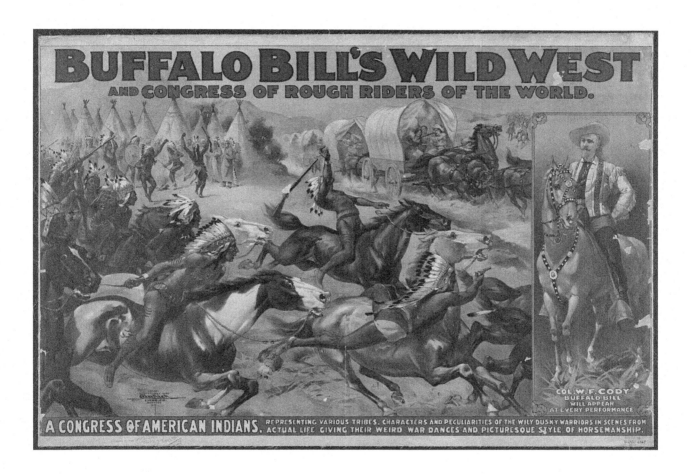

Poster advertising Buffalo Bill's Wild West
(Library of Congress)

a remarkable stroke of irony, the company went out of business in 1908 when a fire destroyed its offices, many of its presses, and a $180,000 worth of circus posters.

Context

For most Americans, and for many people around the world, the image of the Wild West of the post–Civil War era is indelible. Children of a certain generation were thrilled at the Saturday-morning adventures of *The Lone Ranger* and the title character's sidekick, Tonto. In the 1958–59 television season, seven of the top ten rated shows were westerns, including *Gunsmoke* and *Have Gun—Will Travel*. Hollywood churned out westerns by the score, and even today, movies with lantern-jawed, six-gun-toting, hard-drinking, cigar-chomping western characters are produced by major studios, although contemporary westerns tend to resist the romanticizing of earlier western fare in favor of a more gritty, realistic feel.

The romantic perception of the Wild West was in large part a product of the work of Buffalo Bill Cody and his twice daily, rain-or-shine *Wild West* show, which, from 1893 to 1913, performed in a thousand cities in ten countries and attracted fifty million patrons. (The show was originally titled *Buffalo Bill and Doc Carver's Wild West, Rocky Mountain and Prairie Exhibition*, but the partnership between Cody and sharpshooter William "Doc" Carver ended after six months; Carver was "Doc" because he had trained as a dentist.) The show was a spectacle, a blend of historic reenactment, pageantry, patriotism, sport, dare-devilry, and education. It was an amalgamation of fact and fiction that was wildly popular and cemented the place of Buffalo Bill Cody in the popular imagination as an American icon.

Cody was nothing if not a promoter—the P.T. Barnum of the Wild West. A key component of his marketing strategy was colorful, action-filled posters, which not only fired the imagination of large and appreciative audiences but had an impact on the western art of such figures as Frederic Remington, Louis Maurer, Charles Schreyvogel, Gertrude Käsebier, Irving R. Bacon, and James Abbott McNeill Whistler. All of these artists created a body of work that gave rise to and sustained the idolization of the Wild West. *Buffalo Bill's Wild West* was often touted as "America's National Entertainment." The posters fostered the popularity of the show, bolstered the celebrity of Cody, and elevated the reputation of its performers, including Annie Oakley and Chief Sitting Bull.

Buffalo Bill's Wild West had been the main attraction at the American Exhibition in London, England, in 1887. The scale of the enterprise that had to be carted across the Atlantic was nothing short of astonishing. The company boarded the *State of Nebraska* steamship carrying several dozen saloon passengers, more than three dozen steerage passengers, nearly a hundred Native American passengers, nearly two hundred horses, eighteen buffalo, ten elk, five Texas steers, four donkeys, and two deer. An advance party plastered posters all over London, leading one London newspaper to report: "I may walk it, or bus it, or hansom it: still I am faced by the features of Buffalo Bill. Every hoarding is plastered, from East-end to West, with his hat, coat, and countenance, lovelocks and vest." More than a million people saw one of the show's more than three hundred performances in England. Queen Victoria called for a command performance in connection with her Golden Jubilee. During that performance, the Prince of Wales and the kings of Denmark, Greece, Belgium, and Saxony climbed aboard the Deadwood Stage, which was driven around the arena by Buffalo Bill himself as the stagecoach was "attacked" by Indians. After leaving London, the show toured the British Isles, then moved on to the Continent, performing in Germany, France, Spain, and Italy. In 1893, three million people saw the show during its run adjacent to the World's Columbian Exposition in Chicago.

Most historians would argue that the image Cody created was of a West that never really existed, or at least of a West that by the 1890s was rapidly changing. Indeed, when the first performance of the show took place in Omaha, Nebraska, on May 19, 1883, the West it depicted was largely gone. Native American tribes had been relocated to reservations and were no longer attacking white settlers. The immense herds of buffalo that had roamed the Plains had been largely killed. (Cody himself quipped that one could see more buffalo in his show than in the wild.) The prevalence of cowboys had waned as countless miles of barbed wire enclosed the cattle that had previously grazed on open ranges. Two major transcontinental railroads cut across the prairies such that immigrants who previously had traveled to the West in covered wagons now road the rails. The gunslingers who presumably terrorized small towns throughout the West had been tamed by police forces and a law-abiding citizenry.

Despite these transformations, the allure of a romanticized West still held, and Cody's nostalgic re-creation of the West increased that allure. Indeed, in 1888 an article in *Field and Stream* stated: "The performance is thoroughly realistic and is enough to stir the blood in the veins of any old timer whose memory can go back twenty years ago when all the scenes were common in the wild, wild West, now, alas, wild no longer."

Explanation and Analysis of the Document

This colorful lithograph depicts numerous elements. To the right is an iconic image of William F. Cody in his signature hat and colorful costume sitting astride his horse. The foreground is dominated by Native Americans, all on horseback and wearing traditional war bonnets, most carrying rifles or pistols. The Natives and their horses are depicted as attacking a wagon train carrying white settlers in the background. Also in the background is a group of Natives who appear to be doing a war dance around a fire in front of several tepees. The caption at the top reads "Buffalo Bill's Wild West and Congress of Rough Riders of the World."

"Rough Riders" is a phrase generally associated with Theodore Roosevelt and his corps of Rough Riders during the Spanish American War, but the expression had been coined by Cody in an effort to promote the "manly" image of the nation's frontiersmen. The caption at the bottom of the poster reads, "A Congress of American Indians." In smaller print are the words "Representing various tribes, characters, and peculiarities of the wily dusky warriors in scenes from actual life giving their weird war dances and picturesque style of horsemanship." The word "Congress" in both captions reflects Cody's efforts to include performers from various cultures and nations, including Indians, *vaqueros* from Spanish-speaking parts of North America, and Cossacks, who were eastern European Slavs known for their prowess as horsemen. For many people at the time, both in North America and Europe, an image such as this captured the essence of the American frontier and the Old West. That image was one of peaceful settlers in covered wagons seeking a better life as farmers in the West but facing the threat of attack by American Indians, who were often regarded as warlike and savage.

—Michael J. O'Neal

Questions for Further Study

1. What image of Native Americans does the poster portray?

2. How effective would a poster like this have been in attracting the public to Cody's shows?

3. To what extent does a poster such as this contribute to perceptions of the American Old West?

Further Reading

Books

Blackstone, Sarah J. *Buckskins, Bullets, and Business: A History of Buffalo Bill's Wild West*. New York: Greenwood Press, 1986.

Carter, Robert A. *Buffalo Bill Cody: The Man behind the Legend*. New York: John Wiley & Sons, 2000.

Delaney, Michelle. *Art and Advertising in Buffalo Bill's Wild West*. Norman: University of Oklahoma Press, 2019.

Friesen, Steve. *Buffalo Bill: Scout, Showman, Visionary*. Golden, CO: Fulcrum Publishing, 2010.

Hall, Roger A. *Performing the Frontier, 1870–1906*. New York: Cambridge University Press, 2001.

Kasson, Joy S. *Buffalo Bill's Wild West: Celebrity, Memory, and Popular History*. New York: Hill and Wang, 2001.

Moses, L. G. *Wild West Shows and the Images of American Indians, 1883–1933*. Albuquerque: University of New Mexico Press, 1999.

Rebhorn, Matthew. *Pioneer Performances: Staging the Frontier*. New York: Oxford University Press, 2012.

Reddin, Paul. *Wild West Shows*. Urbana: University of Illinois Press, 1999.

Rennert, Jack. *100 Posters of Buffalo Bill's Wild West*. New York: Darien House, 1976.

Rydell, Robert W., and Rob Kroes. *Buffalo Bill in Bologna: The Americanization of the World, 1869–1922*. Chicago: University of Chicago Press, 2005.

Articles

Gowarts, Mary. "'Playing Cowboy': America's Fascination with the 'Wild West.'" *Barre Montpelier Times Argus*, August 4, 2018. https://www.timesargus.com/playing-cowboy-americas-fascination-with-the-wild-west/article_67c016c1-3c37-5fa0-9625-904d95e33209.html.

Hall, Alice J. "Buffalo Bill and the Enduring West." *National Geographic* (July 1981): 76–103.

Polacsek, John. "The Marketing of Buffalo Bill's Wild West Shows." *Bandwagon* (March/April 1990): 24–29.

Websites

"The Artistic Legacy of Buffalo Bill Cody." Buffalo Bill Center of the West. http://codystudies.org/bonner/.

"Buffalo Bill's Wild West Show." *American Experience*, PBS. https://www.pbs.org/wgbh/americanexperience/features/oakley-show/.

Jones, Michaela. "Buffalo Bill's Wild West: A Performance for Everyone." Buffalo Bill Center of the West, August 15, 2016. https://centerofthewest.org/2016/08/15/buffalo-bills-wild-west-performance-everyone/.

Documentaries

Buffalo Bill's Wild West Show: 1898, 1902, 1910. Buffalo Bill and Pawnee Bill Film Company/Blackhawk Films, 1898, 1902, and 1910; Oklahoma Historical Society, 2015. https://www.youtube.com/watch?v=3Bl4_2HhzdI.

"Buffalo Bill." *American Experience*, PBS, February 8, 2006. https://www.pbs.org/wgbh/americanexperience/films/cody/.

William McKinley Campaign Poster

Author/Creator
Unknown

Date
1900

Image Type
Flyers

Significance
Touted the accomplishments of incumbent President William McKinley and compared the country in 1896 to its condition four years later

Overview

This poster from 1900 touted the accomplishments of President William McKinley. That year McKinley, a Republican, was running for reelection along with his running mate, New York governor Theodore Roosevelt. McKinley had been elected president in 1896, a time when the United States had a range of economic problems and faced a series of foreign policy challenges. The economy improved significantly during McKinley's first term. In addition, the United States had fought a war with Spain to end Spanish colonialism in Cuba. However, not all Americans had enjoyed the rising prosperity of the first McKinley term, and many critics of the president asserted that Cuba had simply traded Spanish domination for American control.

The Republican campaign poster was designed to do four things. First, it sought to remind voters that McKinley had fulfilled his campaign promises. Second, the flyer asserted that Americans were better off financially after the president's first term in office than they had been under his Democratic predecessor, Grover Cleveland. Beginning in 1893, the United States underwent a period of deep economic decline known as the "Panic of 1893," but by 1900, the economy had recovered. One factor in the economy's downturn had been the collapse of several large banks, which caused average Americans to lose their savings. McKinley's economic policies helped stabilize the banking system and reduce weaknesses in the banking sector. Third, the poster argued that the U.S. occupation of Cuba was not done to colonize the island but to liberate it from the tyranny of Spain for "humanity's sake." Finally, the campaign advertisement highlighted the inclusion of Theodore Roosevelt as McKinley's running mate. Roosevelt was immensely popular at the time. He had become a war hero during the brief Spanish-American War (1898) and was widely known as a reformer.

McKinley was easily reelected in 1900, but he was shot in an assassination attempt and died on September 14, 1901, less than six months after being inaugurated for his second term.

About the Artist

The artist who created this advertisement is unknown. The flyer was very similar to others printed to support various political parties at the time. In some cases, these political advertisements were commissioned by the political parties themselves. In other cases, private

Document Image

"The Administration's Promises Have Been Kept"
(DeGolyer Library, Southern Methodist University)

companies or individuals would pay to have them created and distributed.

Context

As a result of the Panic of 1893, the U.S. economy fell into a depression, a period of deep economic decline and stagnation. The Panic was the result of a number of factors, including the collapse of some financial markets overseas and overspeculation in some industries in the United States, including the railroads. In the United States, more than 15,000 companies went out of business, including more 500 banks, and the unemployment rate rose from about 3.5 percent in 1892 to more than 18 percent in 1894. The economy became so bad that the United States government had to borrow about $65 million in gold from private sources, including millionaire J. P. Morgan. By 1896 the economy had begun to recover, only to go into a depression again. This economic downturn was likewise dubbed a panic—the Panic of 1896. The 1896 depression was marked by the collapse of a number of large banks, which in turn caused many depositors to lose some or all of their savings.

McKinley was the Republican presidential candidate in 1896. He had previously served in the U.S. House of Representatives (1885–1891) and was governor of Ohio from 1892 to 1896. McKinley was elected president in 1896 with 51 percent of the vote, defeating his Democratic challenger, William Jennings Bryan, who had received 46.7 percent. During McKinley's first term in office, the U.S. economy improved significantly. Unemployment rates, for instance, fell from 14.5 percent in 1896 to 5 percent in 1900. Businesses prospered as the president and his party implemented tariffs, or taxes, on imported goods and products. The tariffs made U.S.-made products cheaper but raised the costs of the items for consumers.

The United States annexed Hawaii in 1898. It also fought the Spanish-American War from April to August of that year, ostensibly to liberate Cuba from Spanish rule. However, as a result of the war, the United States gained the territories of Puerto Rico and Guam, and it secured the Philippines in exchange for a $20 million payment. The war was generally popular among Americans as the result of "yellow journalism"—a style of reporting that exaggerated or misrepresented events to influence public opinion or generate sales. Nonetheless, some groups opposed the conflict, criticizing the war as imperialistic and denouncing the acquisition of any new territory outside of the continental United States. McKinley himself had tried to avoid going to war.

As McKinley began his reelection campaign in 1900, he faced the ardent anti-imperialist Bryan, who was again the Democratic presidential candidate. McKinley adopted a low-key "front-porch" campaign strategy whereby he remained in Washington or in his home state of Ohio. He sought to appear presidential and busy with the business of government. To counter Bryan, who was renowned as a great orator, McKinley chose Roosevelt as his vice-presidential candidate.

Roosevelt's heroism in the Spanish-American War helped him win election as governor of New York in 1898, where he established a reputation as a reformist and proponent of good government. During the campaign, Roosevelt was dispatched to travel the country, give speeches, and advocate for McKinley.

In the 1900 election, McKinley won an even larger majority, defeating Bryan with 51.6 percent of the vote to his opponent's 45.4 percent. He was inaugurated for his second term on March 4, 1901. On September 5, the president was shot twice in the stomach by Leon Czolgosz, an anarchist. McKinley's wounds became infected, and he died on September 14. Roosevelt became president and was reelected in 1904.

Explanation and Analysis of the Document

The campaign advertisement was designed to highlight the accomplishments of McKinley and reinforce the idea that he had kept his campaign promises. The title "The Administration's Promises Have Been Kept" appears across the top. On the left side of the flyer are three images from 1896, before McKinley took office. In the top left, under the label "Gone Democratic," an image portrays the country as economically stagnant, with no one working and businesses shut down. There are abandoned factories with "closed" signs and merchant ships rotting at anchor. Next, in the middle left, is an image of desperate people in front of a closed bank. The implication is that they are unable to access their savings or investments. The title of this section, "A run on the Bank," is a reference to the Panic of 1896 and the numerous banks that closed. The top and middle areas are related in that the failure of the banks under-

354   Milestone Visual Documents in American History

mined the economy and contributed to the closure of many businesses. In the bottom left is a picture labeled "Spanish Rule in Cuba" showing a group of Cubans in chains in a prison. The image is meant to symbolize the tyranny of Spanish colonialism.

This part of the flyer serves as a warning to voters. If they did not want a return to the economic problems caused by the Panics of 1893 and 1896, Americans should vote Republican. This theme implicitly emphasizes the role of McKinley in improving the economy even though the president's policies were only partially responsible for the economic recovery.

In the center of the poster are two American flags, under a wreath with a patriotic cap in the middle and a blazing sun in the background. President McKinley is in the middle left of the campaign flyer, with Roosevelt in the middle right. These images are clearly designed to appeal to the patriotism of voters. The pictures of the two politicians serve another purpose. McKinley symbolizes experience and wisdom, while Roosevelt epitomizes youth and vigor. McKinley also represented the more traditional and conservative wing of the Republican Party, while Roosevelt was the champion of its reformist wing.

The flyer features McKinley's July 12, 1900, quote: "The American flag has not been planted in foreign soil to acquire more territory but for humanity's sake." The statement is an attempt to counter accusations of imperialism or colonialism by McKinley's administration. Despite his rhetoric, however, the United States did plant its flag, first in Hawaii and later in Guam, the Philippines, and Puerto Rico, to secure more territory. The flyer does not mention the administration's role in gaining these areas or the fact that there was an ongoing, bloody rebellion in the Philippines. (The rebellion would last until 1902 and cause thousands of casualties on both sides of the conflict.)

The right side of the campaign advertisement is designed to showcase the accomplishments of McKinley in his first term. All of the images on the right contrast sharply with those on the left. Under the heading "1900," the picture at the top right conveys prosperity and wealth with a farmer tilling his fields, a railway, a canal, and working factories. In the center right, Americans are carrying bags of money into a bank. This image is titled "A run to the Bank." Finally, the bottom right presents an idealized view of "American Rule in Cuba," showing children in school, busy farmers, and factories in the distance. While Cuba had not been formally annexed to the United States, U.S. forces remained in the country. The United States would continue to intervene in Cuba for the next sixty years.

Although the campaign flyer is not entirely accurate, especially about U.S. imperialism, it effectively highlights the economic improvements that the country experienced during McKinley's first term in office. The message presented in the campaign advertisement was effective and reflected public sentiment about McKinley. He remained highly popular until his death.

—Tom Lansford

Questions for Further Study

1. What was the main purpose of the campaign advertisement? Did it succeed in its goals? Please explain.

2. How does the flyer portray economic conditions in the United States under McKinley's Democratic predecessor?

3. Why is Theodore Roosevelt featured in the advertisement? What was his role during the campaign? Why was he chosen as McKinley's running mate?

4. What are the most significant accomplishments of the first McKinley administration, according to the flyer? What are some inaccuracies in the flyer?

Further Reading

Books

Merry, Robert W. *President McKinley: Architect of the American Century.* New York: Simon & Schuster, 2018.

Pafford, John M. *William McKinley versus William Jennings Bryan: The Great Political Rivalry of the Turn of the 20th Century.* Jefferson, NC: McFarland, 2020.

Roberts, Robert North, Scott John Hammond, and Valerie A. Sulfaro. *Presidential Campaigns, Slogans, Issues and Platforms: The Complete Encyclopedia.* 2nd ed. 3 Vols. Westport, CT: Greenwood, 2012.

Steinle, John F. *Colorado and the Silver Crash: The Panic of 1893.* Charleston, SC: History Press, 2021.

Vestner, Eliot. *Ragtime in the White House: War, Race, and the Presidency in the Time of William McKinley.* Westport, CT: City Point Press, 2020.

Websites

"Presidential Election of 1900: A Resource Guide." Library of Congress. https://www.loc.gov/rr/program/bib/elections/election1900.html.

"DREAMLAND AT NIGHT" PHOTOGRAPH OF CONEY ISLAND

AUTHOR/CREATOR
Detroit Publishing Co.

DATE
1905

IMAGE TYPE
PHOTOGRAPHS

SIGNIFICANCE
An iconic image of one of three large amusement parks on New York City's Coney Island during its heyday, showing the novelty of so many electric lights in one place and the ability to escape to a permanent fantasy entertainment location

Overview

This 1905 photograph shows the resort neighborhood of Coney Island, New York. Coney Island began as a place for New Yorkers to escape the heat during the late nineteenth century. With the advent of the subway system at the turn of the century, large amusement parks attracted even more visitors than the area's famous beach. While other cities installed their own amusement parks at the end of their respective streetcar lines, none of these were as famous or as influential as the parks on Coney Island.

Dreamland was the last of the three major amusement parks designed to attract visitors to Coney Island, opening in 1904. Built by William H. Reynolds for $3.5 million, the park exhibited both highbrow and lowbrow aspects of American culture. The 375-foot Beacon Tower, pictured here, was more sophisticated than most amusement park attractions because it invoked the White City from the World's Columbian Exposition, the 1893 world's fair in Chicago, in its placement next to a lagoon and in the many electric lights that illuminated it at night.

About the Artist

The photographer is unknown.

Context

Coney Island first attracted New Yorkers who wanted to beat the heat during the mid-nineteenth century. However, as in other resort areas, the only people who could take the time to bathe in the ocean were the comparatively wealthy. Four steam railroad lines connecting the resort area to the city during the 1870s began the process of democratizing this kind of leisure. While nature was the initial attraction, man-made attractions gradually took precedence as the entertainment industry gradually expanded there. The first roller coaster in the United States, built on Coney Island in 1884, helped attract tens of thousands of leisure seekers during the summer months.

Coney Island's most important period was the era of three large amusement parks, each one influenced in some way by the famous World's Columbian Exposition of 1893. George C. Tilyou's Steeplechase Park opened in 1897 and copied the universally beloved Ferris wheel from the earlier event, albeit at a smaller

Document Image

Night view of Dreamland at Coney Island, New York
(Library of Congress)

scale. The Pavilion of Fun at Steeplechase mimicked the midway of the World's Columbian Exposition while breaking new ground in creating excuses for visitors of different genders to get closer to one another. One example was the Barrel of Fun, which tossed people on top of one another as they were forced to walk through it. Coney Island's Luna Park invoked the name of the most popular ride at the 1901 Buffalo Pan-American Exposition, "A Trip to the Moon." When Luna Park opened in 1903, it contained new thrills besides simulated space flight, like a ride called 20,000 Leagues under the Sea and a display of 250,000 electric lights.

Dreamland tried to provide a more highbrow version of the titillating fun found elsewhere on the island. It included a Biblical Creation exhibit, a ballroom, and a Japanese pavilion. Even its famous Infant Incubators were designed to educate park visitors about the wonders of modern science while they gawked at the preemies on display there. This may explain why the park went bankrupt in 1910. It was largely destroyed by fire the very next year, shortly before it would have opened for the summer season. In the spirit of Coney Island, the park's manager opened shows that didn't depend on physical structures—like the freak show—at the site of the ruined park, which attracted visitors for years afterward.

The long-term significance of Coney Island is visible in today's amusement parks, movies, and even video games. Before entertainment could be mass-produced, leisure had to be made accessible to all. While nineteenth-century theater, for example, offered short-term enjoyment for those who could afford tickets, amusement parks were places working-class city dwellers could spend the day or maybe even the weekend. They became vacations for people who couldn't afford train tickets out of town. Because amusement parks depended upon mass visitation, the rides and buildings created there reflected the mass culture of the Progressive Era. The closest thing we have to Coney Island today is the Las Vegas Strip, in that it too depends upon spectacle, even though the kind of spectacle necessary for Las Vegas to attract mass visitation requires more than just bathing opportunities and strange rides.

Explanation and Analysis of the Document

The Columbian Exposition of 1893, a world's fair held in Chicago, had two main areas: the Midway and the White City. The Midway was the place where visitors saw the beginnings of American carnival culture, like the Ferris wheel. The White City showcased the achievements of science and industry and inspired the creation of Beacon Tower in Coney Island's Dreamland, shown in this photograph. The 375-foot Beacon Tower, the tallest structure on Coney Island, did not physically resemble the administration building in the White City from the Columbian Exposition, but the decision to build a permanent structure in a historic style demonstrates that Dreamland took its inspiration from both parts of the Columbian Exposition rather than just the Midway. The statuary, the castle-like shapes of the buildings on either side of the artificial pool, and even the one visible sign reading "The Canals of Venice" invoke the more highbrow part of the Columbian Exposition.

Electric light was itself a symbol of modernity in 1905. Electric utilities began in New York City in the early 1880s, but electricity hadn't affected the average American that much by 1905. Most Americans saw their first modern electric lights in Chicago in 1893, and there were electrified signs in Times Square, for example, by the dawn of the twentieth century. Coney Island's ostentatious display, therefore, would have impressed its visitors. In fact, the lights of Coney Island's Dreamland were supposedly visible thirty miles out to sea. Thrills like the site of the Beacon Tower lit up at night only make sense in the context of their time. The fact that the novelty of this much electric light proved very temporary only demonstrates the influence of Coney Island on the rest of American culture.

What this picture doesn't show are the more titillating aspects of the park, like the Hell Gate Boat Ride or the Infant Incubator, which allowed visitors to gawk at premature babies at the same time they marveled at the new technology that could keep them alive. Even the Canals of Venice, the entrance of which is visible in the picture, had low-culture implications despite invoking one of Europe's most sophisticated cities. The tunnels containing these rides were dark, so men and women on a single boat could snuggle up to one another completely unobserved, at least for a few moments.

Something virtually unseen in this picture is people. Coney Island was notoriously crowded on summer nights, and a viewer looking closely can see those crowds on the left and right sides of the picture, behind the strings of lights. The focus of the picture, however, is deliberately upon the tower and the lights because the photographer's intention is to highlight the man-made spectacle—the main reason to pay one's admission fee to enter the park.

In the empty space in front of the tower sits an artificial lake surrounded by a performing ring, where horses or acrobats could perform. Behind the tower there was a place for a sixty-foot-long, cigar-shaped airship with a 35-foot-long gondola for passengers hanging from it. It was borrowed from the Buffalo Exposition, where it had been one of the most popular attractions. This photograph was taken from the top of a ride called "Chute the Chutes," which allowed visitors to slide down a ramp in a small boat out into the ocean. That ride, like so much else in any American amusement park, was borrowed from earlier amusement parks. Indeed, Samuel Gumpertz, the manager at Dreamland, was famous for acquiring rides and sites from elsewhere and then opening them in his park. While the technology has gotten better over time, the basic desire to thrill visitors one way or another remains intact.

—Jonathan Rees

Questions for Further Study

1. Why would an amusement park want to create a promotional photograph that featured a building?

2. Why did the photographer choose to leave the foreground of the picture empty?

3. What was the advantage of keeping all the buildings white?

4. What aspects of the buildings pictured here remind you of modern amusement parks?

Further Reading

Books

Baker, Kevin. *Dreamland.* New York: HarperCollins, 1999.

McCullough, Edo. *Good Old Coney Island: A Sentimental Journey into the Past.* New York: Charles Scribner, 1957.

Parascandola, Louis J., and John Parascandola, eds. *A Coney Island Reader: Through the Dizzy Gates of Illusion.* New York: Columbia University Press, 2015.

Peiss, Kathy. *Cheap Amusements: Working Women and Leisure in Turn-of-the-Century New York.* Philadelphia: Temple University Press, 1986.

Edgar Thomson Steel Works Photograph

AUTHOR/CREATOR Detroit Publishing Co.	IMAGE TYPE PHOTOGRAPHS
DATE 1908	SIGNIFICANCE A historical photo of a Pennsylvania steel mill that was part of the empire of industrialist Andrew Carnegie.

Overview

This photograph depicts the Edgar Thomson Steel Works, which was constructed in 1874. The land where the plant stood was purchased for just over $219,000 in 1873 by Carnegie, McCandless & Company. The land, which later became known as the town of Braddock, is located along the Monongahela River, about ten miles north of Pittsburgh. The plant was named after John Edgar Thomson, an early financial backer of the firm and the president of the Pennsylvania Railroad, which became a major purchaser of the mill's iron rails. Production on the mill began in 1875, and within a year it created more than thirty-two tons of steel rail. In the 1880s, the mill became part of Carnegie Brothers and Company, which was created by the consolidation of several steel operations that Andrew Carnegie owned. In 1901 the plant became part of what would become U.S. Steel, which continues to own and operate the plant—one of the few surviving steel mills in the Monongahela Valley. The plant's significance was as the first integrated Bessemer steel works built in the area around Pittsburgh by Andrew Carnegie. The plant launched a transformation of the industrial base of the valley from a center of smaller iron works to an integrated steel manufacturing center.

About the Artist

The Detroit Publishing Co. was the copyright holder of this photograph. The company was founded as the Detroit Photographic Company by William A. Livingstone, a publisher, and Edwin H. Husher, a photographer, in the late nineteenth century. The company was later renamed the Detroit Photochrom Company and then, starting in 1905, the Detroit Publishing Company. The company's stock in trade was a color printing process called Photochrom, which had been developed by Hans Jakob Schmid of the Swiss firm Orell Fussli & Company. The process allowed the company to mass produce color postcards, but it suffered from declining sales during World War I. In 1924 the company declared bankruptcy, and in 1932 it was liquidated. This photo of Edgar Thomson Works is currently part of the Library of Congress's American Memory collection, which consists of nearly a million historical prints and photographs documenting the nation's past.

Context

In the decades after the Civil War, the United States underwent a profound transformation. As smokestacks rose over the landscape, as the shrill sound of factory whistles kept time in mill towns, and as the

Document Image

The Edgar Thomson Steel Works in Braddock, Pennsylvania
(Library of Congress)

railroad system was linking all parts of the country, the U.S. economy grew at a rapid pace, supplanting the United Kingdom as the world's leading economy. Behind this growth was the expansion of the iron industry, fueled in turn by the growth of the coal mined from midwestern coalfields. Large steel mills, such as the Edgar Thomson Steel Works, grew up in the vicinity of these coalfields. For a century and a half, the Thomson Works turned out steel around the clock, contributing to the industrialization of the nation.

The mill was one of the first Bessemer mills in the country. Industrialist Andrew Carnegie, a Scotsman by birth who had already made a fortune in the railroad industry as an investor, was traveling in Europe in the summer of 1872 when he learned of the Bessemer process, an inexpensive method of converting molten pig iron, a crude, brittle iron with high carbon content, into steel by injecting it with air that removes impurities. When he returned to Pittsburgh, he set about building a Bessemer mill. Construction on the mill began in 1874, and because Carnegie wanted to gain favor with Edgar Thomson, the president of the Pennsylvania Railroad and potentially a major customer, he named the mill after him. Carnegie hired Alexander Holley, an expert in the Bessemer process, as the mill's engineer, and Holley set about making improvements in the process.

The mill had distinct geographical advantages. It was located near the coalfields in Connellsville, which produced what was regarded as the finest metallurgical coke in the world. Further, it was located near lines of the Pennsylvania Railroad and the Baltimore and Ohio Railroad. And it was located near the junction of the Monongahela, Ohio, and Allegheny rivers. These latter two advantages made the transportation of raw materials and completed rails easier. On August 22, 1875, the mill's Bessemer converter produced its first "heat" (batch) of liquid steel. The Pennsylvania Railroad would use the steel in the production of 2,000 rails.

Also adding to the efficiency of the mill was the work of its general manager, William R. Jones, who improved the process of transporting molten iron from the furnaces to the Bessemer converters. In large part because of the innovations of the Thomson Works, total Bessemer rail production in the United States rose from 6,451 tons in 1868 to nearly 1.19 million tons in 1881. The Thomson Works, for its part, altered the steel industry and contributed to the nation's rapid indus-

trial growth. Its steel was stronger and more resistant to wear, making it an ideal choice for railroads. The Edgar Thomson Works was only the first step, for in the years that followed, Carnegie acquired a network of mills, coke plants, and blast furnaces. Together, these operations became the Carnegie Steel Company.

Carnegie transformed not only the steel industry but also the town of Braddock. At the time the mill was built, Braddock was a farming community. It was known as the place where General Edward Braddock was killed in 1755 during the French and Indian Wars. It was also the site of a protest rally by farmers and militiamen during the Whiskey Rebellion in 1794. After the mill was constructed, the area around Braddock began to flourish. Because of the need for stores, restaurants, and bars, entrepreneurs and merchants surged into Braddock, changing the nature of life in the community. Immigrants from around the world, mainly from Eastern Europe and Italy, along with African Americans, worked in the mill. These unskilled workers lived in tenements near the mill. Skilled workers, mostly of northern European ancestry, lived farther away on the hills surrounding the town.

The workday of a steelworker was by no means an easy one. The work was backbreaking and dangerous. Workers were dealing with molten metal. They were inhaling toxic fumes. They were operating heavy machinery. Few safeguards were in place. The workday initially was twelve hours, so fatigue was a factor. To blow off steam, many workers turned to drinking and gambling during their off-duty hours. Jones, however, was more far-sighted. He convinced Carnegie that an eight-hour workday would make the workers not only more content but also more efficient and productive. Carnegie agreed, and in the early years of the firm he supported the labor union and agreed to its wage scales. By the end of the 1880s, however, conditions in the steel industry had changed. Carnegie was facing intense competition from other mills. Believing he had to cut costs, he reinstated the twelve-hour workday, slashed wages, and hired Pinkerton detectives to break strikes and, in 1888, force the union out of the Thomson Works. As a form of compensation to the community, Carnegie financed the Braddock Carnegie Library, one of more than 2,500 libraries he financed worldwide in the belief that education would enable people to achieve the kind of success he did.

The plant was the site of a major labor dispute in 1892. Henry Clay Frick, one of the "robber barons" of the Gilded Age, was one of Carnegie's partners. The contract with the labor union was set to run out. Carnegie was traveling to his native Scotland, so he turned operations over to Frick, who, as an opening gambit in negotiations with the union, tried to cut the workers' wages at the nearby mill in Homestead, a company that was part of the Carnegie operations. When the workers at Homestead went out on strike, the workers at Edgar Thomson joined them in solidarity. Frisk fired all the workers at the Homestead plant and replaced them with nonunion workers. He called in Pinkerton detectives to break the strike. A riot broke out, resulting in a number of injuries, beatings, and deaths. The rioting got so bad that the governor of Pennsylvania ordered up two brigades of the National Guard to end it.

In 1901, the Carnegie Steel Company, including the Thomson mill, was sold to a group of investors, among them J. P. Morgan, for $480 million (more than $16 billion in 2021 dollars) and became the foundation of U.S. Steel. At this point, Carnegie retired to devote himself to philanthropic activities. In the years that followed, U.S. Steel moved the mill into the modern age. The company created a safety program, made improvements in the Braddock sanitation system, supported industrial training in area high schools, and provided classes to help immigrant workers adapt to life in the United States. The Edgar Thomson plant hired a welfare worker to reduce turnover among African American workers. Meanwhile, the town operated according to the rhythms of the mill. Restaurants stayed open all night to accommodate workers coming off second and third shifts. Shower facilities were provided for men to wash up after coming off their shifts.

Walls around town were regularly scrubbed to remove the soot produced by the mill. Teenagers drove up the surrounding hills to watch the "fireworks display" produced by the glare of the blast furnaces.

In 1995, ASM International, a society that recognizes works of structural engineering, designated the mill a historic landmark, joining such structures as the Statue of Liberty and the Eiffel Tower.

Explanation and Analysis of the Document

This black and white photo captures the essence of a major industrial operation in the early twentieth century. The photo is an aerial view, likely taken from one of the hills surrounding the Monongahela Valley, where Braddock is situated. The image demonstrates that a steel mill is actually a complex of numerous buildings where materials are offloaded and stored, and iron is melted in batches then taken to the Bessemer converters. The complex would also include administrative offices, maintenance sheds, temperature exchanges, equipment for moving materials, garages for vehicles, and other buildings needed to support the mill operations. A number of smokestacks, virtually a symbol of the industrialization of America, rise above the buildings and belch smoke into the air. In the background is the Braddock Bridge over the Monongahela River. In the foreground are the rail lines that would have carried in coke and carried out the steel rails.

—Michael J. O'Neal

Questions for Further Study

1. In what ways would the construction of a major industrial plant like this one change a community?

2. How concerned about environmental issues would the owners and operators of the Thomson Works likely have been?

3. What does the photo tell modern viewers about the early industrialization of the United States?

Further Reading

Books

Burns, Daniel J. *Homestead and the Steel Valley*. Charleston, SC: Arcadia Publishing, 2007.

MacGregor, J. R. *Andrew Carnegie: Insight and Analysis into the Life of a True Entrepreneur, Industrialist, and Philanthropist*. Sheridan, WY: CAC Publishing, 2019.

Misa, Thomas J. *A Nation of Steel: The Making of Modern America, 1865–1925*. Baltimore, MD: Johns Hopkins University Press, 1995.

Perelman, Dale Richard. *Steel: The Story of Pittsburgh's Iron and Steel Industry, 1852–1902*. Charleston, SC: History Press, 2016.

Warren, Kenneth. *Big Steel: The First Century of the United States Steel Corporation 1901–2001*. Pittsburgh, PA: University of Pittsburgh Press, 2001.

Articles

Boselovic, Len. "Carnegie Plant That Made Pittsburgh the Steel City Marks 125th Anniversary." *Pittsburgh Post-Gazette*, August 22, 2000.

Websites

"The Edgar Thomson Steel Works and Blast Furnaces." Norman B. Leventhal Map and Education Center, Boston Public Library. https://collections.leventhalmap.org/search/commonwealth:ht250c523.

McKeever, Amy. "In the Shadow of the Steel Mill." *Topic*, August 1, 2018. https://www.topic.com/in-the-shadow-of-the-steel-mill.

Meese, Hugh P. "Edgar Thomson Steel Works." The Hopkin Thomas Project. http://www.thehopkinthomasproject.com/TheHopkinThomasProject/TimeLine/GenealogyPortraits/CaptWRJonesBios/EdgarThompsonSteelworks.htm.

Potter, Chris. "I Grew Up Near U.S. Steel's Edgar Thomson Plant. Who Was Edgar Thomson?" (journalist's response to reader query). *Pittsburgh City Paper*, May 19, 2005. https://www.pghcitypaper.com/pittsburgh/i-grew-up-near-us-steels-edgar-thomson-plant-who-was-edgar-thomson/Content?oid=1337573.

Documentaries

Empires of Industry—Andrew Carnegie and the Age of Steel. A&E Home Video, The History Channel, 2005.

Louis Wickes Hines: Photograph Of Boys Working In Arcade Bowling Alley

Author/Creator Louis Wickes Hine	**Image Type** Photographs
Date 1909	**Significance** One of numerous photos and records documenting the prevalence of child labor in the early twentieth century

Overview

A patron at a modern bowling alley, where a mechanical device called a pinsetter or pinspotter sets the pins back into their original positions, returns bowling balls to the front of the alley, and clears fallen pins, might need to be reminded that these devices perform tasks that in a former era were performed manually by "pinboys." Gottfried Schmidt was awarded a patent for the first mechanical pinsetter in 1940; he sold the patent to American Machine and Foundry (AMF) in 1941, and AMF "pinspotters" were first marketed in 1952. Until then, boys were hired to sit on a ledge behind the pins. After a bowler had bowled the first of two balls, the boy would jump down, reset the pins (if the bowler bowled a strike), sweep those that had been knocked down off the lane, and return the ball to the bowler by pushing it down the return track. Sometimes bowlers attempted to bribe pinboys to fake a perfect game for them by knocking down standing pins with something like a coat hanger.

The work of pinsetting was done by boys such as those who appear in this photograph. Typically, boys were chosen to do this work for a number of reasons. They were smaller than young men, so they could fit into the area behind the pins. As children, they were unlikely to complain about working conditions. Many were disadvantaged children from the streets who were glad to earn any money they could. Many boys who worked as pinsetters, however, came away from an evening's work with broken ribs, bruised shins, and smashed fingers. These children—and child laborers in other settings—typically did not attend school, perpetuating a cycle of poverty. During the Progressive Era of the early twentieth century, reformers and labor committees focused their attention on child labor and mounted efforts to restrict it through legislation, primarily at the state level. They used photographs such as this to document the abuses of child labor.

About the Artist

The photograph was taken by Louis Wickes Hine, who was born in Wisconsin in 1874. Early in his career, Hine, educated as a sociologist, photographed immigrants who had arrived at New York's Ellis Island and the tenements and sweatshops where many of these immigrants lived. In 1909 he published two collections, *Child Labor in the Carolinas* and *Day Laborers Before Their Time*, both documenting child labor, which was usually performed by children as young as

Document Image

Louis Wickes Hine's 1909 photograph of "pinboys"
(National Archives)

eight years old. These children worked under dangerous conditions and typically worked six days a week for as little as forty-five cents a day. In 1911 Hine was hired by the National Child Labor Committee (NCLC) to examine the issue of child labor. He traveled throughout the eastern United States, taking some 7,000 photos of exploited children that the NCLC assembled in 1912. His photos played a major role in drawing the attention of the public to the child labor problem. Ultimately, they had the effect of giving rise to federal legislation on conditions for children in the workplace. Hine died in 1940.

The National Child Labor Committee was formed under the auspices of the Children's Bureau of the Department of Commerce and Labor. The mandate of the Children's Bureau, created on April 9, 1912, was as follows: "The said Bureau shall investigate and report to said Department upon all matters pertaining to the welfare of children and child life among all classes of our people, and shall especially investigate the questions of infant mortality, the birth rate, orphanage, juvenile courts, desertion, dangerous occupations, accidents and diseases of children, employment, legislation affecting children in the several States and Territories."

Context

Child labor was a practice through virtually the entirety of human history. In the United States, the Puritan work ethic of the early colonies valued work as a means of combating idleness and temptation, and the agrarian and handicraft society of the colonial and pre–Civil War years typically required children to work on the family farm or otherwise help parents in supporting the family. Boys often began apprenticeships when then were as young as ten, and many children were sent to work on farms as indentured servants. Enslaved children, of course, were required to work from their earliest days.

Child labor was particularly prevalent during the Industrial Revolution following the Civil War and into the early years of the twentieth century. Many children worked long hours for little pay in dangerous, dirty, unsafe factories, mills, and mines. Children were selected for many jobs because their small stature enabled them to squeeze into places where adults could not go. Many child laborers were the children of immigrants and came from impoverished classes. In the 1880s, im-

migrants in large numbers were arriving from southern and eastern Europe. These people were not "Americanized" and spoke little or no English, so it was easy for business owners and robber barons to exploit them and their children. During this era, trains often carried children from faraway orphanages to become laborers in cities and industrial centers in the east.

By the early years of the twentieth century, working-class children worked in a variety of settings. Many worked in mines breaking up coal. "Breaker boys" in the mines sat precariously on benches above a conveyor belt and used a coal breaker to remove impurities from coal before it was shipped. Others worked on farms. One study concluded that a fourth of the boys under the age of sixteen who worked on farms were actually under the age of ten. In the textile industry of the South and New England, children worked in the textile mills. By 1904, 50,000 workers in the cotton mills of the South were under the age of sixteen, 20,000 under the age of twelve. On the coasts, children worked in activities supporting seafood production, often by shucking oysters or cleaning shrimp. In industrialized areas, children could be found in steel mills and manufacturing plants. In the cities, children called "newsies" often survived by selling newspapers. They frequently resorted to unethical tactics to attract buyers, such as shouting out lurid but false headlines or claiming to a sympathetic buyer that they could not go home until their one remaining newspaper was sold—then taking out another newspaper from a hidden stash to sell to another buyer in the same way.

This photo of pinboys was taken in the midst of the Progressive movement, which extended roughly from 1880 to 1920. During this period, reformers worked to combat the negative effects of industrialization. They sought stiffer regulation for private industry and more protections for workers and consumers, and they exposed corruption among business leaders and elected officials. In general, Progressive reformers sought a better society and to that end backed Progressive candidates for office. Among the concerns of Progressive reformers was the condition of labor in general and the prevalence of child labor in particular. In 1904 the National Child Labor Committee was formed, and in concert with state child labor committees, efforts were launched to eliminate the use of child labor. These organizations hired experts to compile reports and used photographers to document the conditions under which children worked. They also began intense lobbying efforts, relying on leaflets, pamphlets, and mailings to bring the issue to the attention of the public.

Until about 1915, the committees sought reform through state legislatures, and as a result of their efforts, numerous state laws restricting child labor were passed. Resistance to similar legislation was widespread in the southern states because of a longstanding belief that children were needed to work the fields, earn income in mills, and support the family. Because of this resistance, reformers concluded that federal legislation was needed. The Keating-Owens Act of 1916 addressed the issue of child labor by prohibiting the interstate sale of goods produced in factories that employed children, but the U.S. Supreme Court declared the law unconstitutional in 1918. Congress tried again in 1919 by taking an indirect approach: the Revenue Act of 1919, also called the Child Labor Tax Law, imposed a 10 percent tax on the profits of companies that employed children in industries such as mining and manufacturing, but that law failed to end the practice. In 1924, both the U.S. House of Representatives and the U.S. Senate approved a constitutional amendment that would have banned child labor, but the amendment met with opposition from farm and church groups that feared growing federal authority over children. It was ratified in only a handful of states and after ten years was regarded as dead. Finally, the Fair Labor Standards Act of 1938 banned all child labor on the part of businesses that engaged in interstate commerce.

Explanation and Analysis of the Document

The photo shows four lanes of a bowling alley. In the photo are several pinboys or pinsetters, who have been hired to reset the bowling pins after the bowler has taken his or her turn. The boys all appear to be roughly ten or twelve years old. In front of them are bowling pins. In comparison to many photos from this era, many of them heartbreaking images of children working at looms in the textile industry or covered with soot and dirt from working in mines or factories, this one might suggest that the boys work under relatively benign conditions. They are indoors, and they appear to be clean and dressed relatively well. Nevertheless, pinboys at the time were exploited. The pay was low, typically ten cents per game. Generally, they had to work until at least midnight, if not longer. The work was dangerous, frequently resulting in broken bones or other injuries. Often pinboys were unable to attend school and used the money they earned for unsavory purposes.

—Michael J. O'Neal

Questions for Further Study

1. What message, if any, does this photograph convey?

2. How would photos such as this one by Hine—and he took many of them—have influenced the public and legislators?

3. What might have been the attitudes of these boys toward their work as pinboys?

Further Reading

Books

Burgan, Michael. *Breaker Boys: How a Photograph Helped End Child Labor.* Mankato, MN: Compass Point Books, 2011.

Fliter, John A. *Child Labor in America: The Epic Legal Struggle to Protect Children.* Lawrence: University Press of Kansas, 2018.

Freedman, Russell. *Kids at Work: Lewis Hine and the Crusade against Child Labor.* New York: Clarion Books, 1998.

Macieski, Robert. *Picturing Class: Lewis W. Hine Photographs Child Labor in New England.* Amherst: University of Massachusetts Press, 2015.

Websites

"Child Labor in U.S. History." University of Iowa Labor Center. https://laborcenter.uiowa.edu/special-projects/child-labor-public-education-project/about-child-labor/child-labor-us-history.

Hansan, J. "The American Era of Child Labor." *Social Welfare History Project*, 2011. https://socialwelfare.library.vcu.edu/programs/child-welfarechild-labor/child-labor/.

Liao, Kristy. "Child Labor in the United States." *The Borgen Project.* https://borgenproject.org/child-labor-united-states/.

Schuman, Michael. "History of Child Labor in the United States." *Monthly Labor Review*, U.S. Bureau of Labor Statistics, January 2017. "Part 1: Little Children Working," https://www.bls.gov/opub/mlr/2017/article/history-of-child-labor-in-the-united-states-part-1.htm; "Part 2: The Reform Movement," https://www.bls.gov/opub/mlr/2017/article/history-of-child-labor-in-the-united-states-part-2-the-reform-movement.htm.

Taylor, Alan. "Child Labor in America 100 Years Ago." *Atlantic*, July 1, 2015. https://www.theatlantic.com/photo/2015/07/child-labor-in-america-100-years-ago/397478/.

Documentaries

"Cotton Mill Girl: Behind Lewis Hine's Photograph & Child Labor Series." *Time.* https://www.youtube.com/watch?v=pOIvdhmMaOE.

Photograph Of Congested Chicago Intersection

Author/Creator Unknown	**Image Type** Photographs
Date 1909	**Significance** Shows the almost unimaginable congestion and chaos of Chicago's streets before the advent of more rational city planning

Overview

By 1909, the year this photo was taken, Chicago had grown into a major U.S. city, second only to New York City. The growth had been rapid, and in the eyes of many Chicagoans and the city's planners, the growth had gotten out of control, leading to congestion and overcrowding. This widely reproduced photograph from the Chicago History Museum has become emblematic of the city's chaos and congestion at the time. It was taken in conjunction with the 1909 publication of *The Plan of Chicago*, popularly called the Burnham Plan after one of its authors, Daniel H. Burnham. The document's production was backed by city leaders and the Commercial Club, a social welfare organization created in 1877 to improve the city's social and economic climate. Using images such as this one, Burnham and the Commercial Club made numerous recommendations for putting the planning and organization of the city on a more rational footing and prevent the kind of bottlenecks that impeded Chicagoans as they tried to go about their business, particularly in the city's central business district.

About the Artist

It is not known who took the photograph, which is part of a collection curated by the Chicago Historical Society. The society is a privately endowed institution that collects, interprets, and presents the history of Chicago and of Illinois through exhibitions, programs, research collections, and publications. In 2006, the Chicago Historical Society, founded in 1856, announced that it was changing its name to the Chicago History Museum. The museum houses more than 22 million items in a number of collections: Archives and Manuscripts, including sound recordings; a library; Costumes and Textiles; Decorative and Industrial Arts; Paintings and Sculpture; and Prints and Photographs. The Prints and Photographs division contains more than 6.5 million images and more than 4 million feet of moving images. These images document the history of the city from the early nineteenth century to the present. Included are photos, prints, broadside images, engravings, etchings, lithographs, stereocards, negatives, postcards, greeting cards, films, and of course photographs.

Document Image

A 1909 photograph of the intersection of Dearborn and Randolph streets in Chicago
(Chicago History Museum)

Context

Urbanization and industrialization were prominent features of nineteenth-century life, particularly in the United States and western Europe. Between 1800 and 1900, the percentage of Americans who lived in urban areas rose from 3 percent to nearly 40 percent, although an "urban area," according to the U.S. Census Bureau, was defined as a city with 2,500 or more residents. During this period, New York City grew from 60,500 people to 3.44 million. By 1900, thirty-eight American cities had more than 100,000 residents.

The story of growth was enacted dramatically in Chicago. In 1914, poet Carl Sandburg, in his famous poem "Chicago," called Chicago "City of Big Shoulders" and concluded the poem with the words: "Laughing the stormy, husky, brawling laughter of Youth, half-naked, sweating, proud to be Hog Butcher, Tool Maker, Stacker of Wheat, Player with Railroads and Freight Handler to the Nation." One might imagine Sandburg as having been inspired by this photograph, or one very much like it, in his characterization of the city, but he was by no means the only observer who thought of Chicago as boisterous, unrefined, and rough around the edges as it moved into the modern age.

In 1889, Chicago occupied less than 37 square miles, but in 1889–90, local residents voted to annex a number of adjacent communities, increasing the size of the city fivefold to more than 179 square miles, and by 1900, the city occupied an area of about 190 square miles. By 1909 the city encompassed more than 2,800 miles of streets, only about half of them paved, and 1,400 miles of alleys, less than a tenth of them paved. Going under or over the Chicago River were three tunnels and ninety-one bridges owned by either the city or railroad companies. Among the city's 38,000 streetlights, 8,500 were powered by electricity, the remainder by gas. Water consumption from Lake Michigan amounted to nearly half a billion gallons a day, 223 gallons for each resident. In early 1900, the city opened the Sanitary Canal, which reversed the flow of the Chicago River to reduce pollution of the lake water.

Streetcars were a common feature of Chicago life. They ran along the city's major roads, generally a half mile apart. They also ran along diagonal routes, and commercial centers sprang up at points where the streetcar lines converged. Beginning in 1890, the streetcars were being electrified, and by 1909 the process of electrification was almost complete. Despite the prevalence of streetcars, people still used cabs or carriages for transport. A one-mile ride in a vehicle drawn by a single horse cost fifty cents. In 1910, the number of registered automobiles in the city was just under 13,000.

Beginning in 1890, rapid transit lines were erected. Four companies—the Chicago and South Side Rapid Transit Company, the Lake Street Elevated Railway, the Metropolitan West Side Elevated Railroad, and the Northwestern Elevated Railroad—provided service to the city. In 1897 the Union Elevated Railroad (the "El") constructed the rectangular Loop, which linked the various lines around the central downtown district. By 1911 the rapid transit lines had merged.

In terms of transportation into and out of downtown, the amount of traffic was staggering. One historian counted 1,300 trains each day, carrying collectively 175,000 passengers. By 1920 that number had swelled to 270,000. Railroad tracks crisscrossed the city, leading to traffic delays and deadly accidents. In his 1894 book *If Christ Came to Chicago,* investigative journalist William Stead wrote: "If the stranger's first impression of Chicago is that of the barbarous gridironed streets, his second is that of the multitude of mutilated people whom he meets on crutches. . . . The railroads which cross the city at the level in every direction, although limited by statute and ordinance as to speed, constantly mow down unoffending citizens at the crossings, and those legless, armless men and women whom you meet on the streets are merely the mangled remnant of the massacre that is constantly going on year in and year out."

In his 1997 book *An Early Encounter with Tomorrow,* historian Arnold Lewis wrote: "Regardless of how we identify the causes—progress, economic expansion, or the 'go-ahead' mentality—[rail traffic] speeded up Chicago's daily life, which, in turn, increased the likelihood of accidents and deaths on the job and in the streets. In this respect Chicago was again the Western world's most dramatic clarifier of unintended consequences of progress."

Population growth added to the congestion. In 1830, the population of Chicago was a mere 100 souls. According to census figures, its population in 1870 was nearly 300,000 and in 1900 was 1,698,575. By 1909, the population had passed the 2 million mark, and the 1910 census reported a population of 2,185,183. During the decade, the population of Cook County increased

31 percent. By this point, Chicago was the fourth largest city in the world, trailing only London, New York, and Paris. Incidentally, in 1910, more than 35 percent of the city's population was foreign born, and nearly 42 percent had at least one parent who had arrived from another country. This rate was twice that of the country as a whole. Just 2 percent of the population was African American.

It was in this context of spiraling and uncontrolled growth that the Commercial Club, led by architect and city planner Daniel H. Burnham, issued *The Plan of Chicago* in 1909. The central thesis of the document was that the city had to institute major changes if it had any hope of being livable in the future. The authors concluded that despite the presence of some well-established cultural institutions, and despite the achievements of the World's Columbian Exposition of 1893 (also called the Chicago World's Fair), Chicago was rough-edged and unruly. The authors noted that much of the cityscape was unappealing and dirty. The air was polluted by smoke, and poor sanitation created health hazards. Freight and passengers moved through the downtown at a glacial pace. Many streets were not paved. Railroad tracks separated the commercial center from the lakefront. The working classes lived in squalid conditions, and class conflict and labor violence were habitual. The authors of the report made numerous suggestions to improve planning for the city's future.

The Plan of Chicago was not the only document that exposed the troublesome underside of the city during this era. Upton Sinclair's *The Jungle*, published in 1906, exposed the horrid conditions faced by immigrants in Chicago's meat-packing industry. In 1910, reformer Jane Addams published *Twenty Years at Hull-House*, documenting her work among the poor and among immigrants on Chicago's West Side. These and other authors had the same goal: envisioning a city that was more humane and more orderly and that reconciled the public good with economic interests.

The problem of congestion and overcrowding was by no means unique to Chicago. The nation's major metropolitan areas from Boston to San Francisco confronted similar problems as frustrated citizens contended with horses, cars, trams, streetcars, and buses at a time when city streets were used to transport goods, conduct business, and serve as playgrounds, parade routes, venues for political meetings and rallies, and marketplaces.

Explanation and Analysis of the Document

The photo graphically documents the congestion of downtown Chicago at the intersection of two of its major thoroughfares, Dearborn Street and Randolph Street. The image shows electric trolleys contending with horse-drawn vehicles of various types and with motorized vehicles. Some of the vehicles are carrying cargo; most prominent is the vehicle in the center, which appears to be transporting cylindrical items that could be barrels or kegs. Hundreds of pedestrians are trying to make their way through the streets, which extend like a canyon between tall buildings. Vehicular and foot traffic appears to be at a complete standstill. Cables crisscross above the street. The air is filled with smoke. The photo offers a startling image of almost unimaginable urban congestion in the early years of the twentieth century. It conveys in graphic detail the chaos and disorder of a city that grew at a rate that was perhaps too fast for city authorities to control and place on a sound and rational foundation.

—Michael J. O'Neal

Questions for Further Study

1. What would likely be a viewer's immediate response to this photo?

2. To what extent might photos such as this have contributed to more sensible planning in Chicago and other cities?

3. What might have the pedestrians in the photo have been thinking as they tried to negotiate the congestion and overcrowding they encountered as they tried to go about their business?

Further Reading

Books

Burnham, Daniel H., and Edward H. Bennett. *The Plan of Chicago*. Chicago: The Commercial Club, 1909. Available at Chicago Architecture Center website. https://www.architecture.org/learn/resources/architecture-dictionary/entry/1909-plan-of-chicago/.

Chicago Tribune. *Chicago Flashback: The People and Events That Shaped a City's History*. Evanston, IL: Agate Midway, 2017.

Chudacoff, Howard P., Judith Smith, and Peter Baldwin. *The Evolution of American Urban Society*, 8th ed. London: Routledge, 2014.

Cronon, William. *Nature's Metropolis: Chicago and the Great West*. New York: Norton, 1992.

Maguire, Kathleen. *Chicago Then and Now*. London: Pavilion Books, 2015.

Reardon, Patrick T. *The Loop: The "L" Tracks That Shaped and Saved Chicago*. Carbondale: Southern Illinois University Press, 2020.

Smith, Carl. *The Plan of Chicago: Daniel Burnham and the Remaking of the American City*. Chicago: University of Chicago Press, 2006.

Spinney, Robert G. *City of Big Shoulders: A History of Chicago*. DeKalb: Northern Illinois University Press, 2020.

Websites

Boustan, Leah Platt, Devin Bunten, and Owen Hearey. "Urbanization in the United States, 1800–2000." Working Paper 19041, National Bureau of Economic Research, Cambridge, Mass., 2013. https://scholar.princeton.edu/sites/default/files/lboustan/files/research21_urban_handbook.pdf.

Rees, Jonathan. "Industrialization and Urbanization in the United States, 1880–1929." *Oxford Research Encyclopedias: American History*, 2016. https://oxfordre.com/americanhistory/view/10.1093/acrefore/9780199329175.001.0001/acrefore-9780199329175-e-327.

"Urbanized America." Smithsonian American Art Museum. https://americanexperience.si.edu/historical-eras/modern-united-states/pair-eviction-tanagra/.

Documentaries

Chicago: City of the Century, three-part series written, produced, and directed by Andrew Hoyt. *American Experience*, PBS, 2003.

Photograph Of Garment Workers Strike

Author/Creator
George Grantham Bain/Bain News Service

Date
1910

Image Type
Photographs

Significance
A depiction of strikers from the International Ladies Garment Workers Union on the picket line during the "Uprising of the 20,000," a garment workers strike in New York City

Overview

This photograph shows garment workers on strike in New York City. In September 1909, the workers at the Triangle Shirtwaist Factory, one of some 600 such shops and factories in New York City, went on strike. (A shirtwaist is a tailored woman's blouse worn with a skirt.) The workers at two other shops joined them. Then on November 22, 1909, thousands of workers in the "needles trade" filled the Great Hall at Cooper Union on East Seventh Street in Manhattan. Among them were Samuel Gompers, head of the American Federation of Labor, and Clara Lemlich, a Jewish immigrant who worked in the garment trade. That day, Lemlich called for a general strike, launching the New York Shirtwaist Strike of 1909, often referred to as the "Uprising of the 20,000." Backing the garment workers was the Women's Trade Union League, formed in 1903 as the first national organization formed for the purpose of organizing women workers. The strikers, like those depicted in the photograph, demanded shorter hours, better treatment by managers, the end of night work, and a decent wage. Most of the women who went out on strike were, like Lemlich, Yiddish-speaking Jewish immigrants, although a significant number were Italian; many were in their teens or early twenties. The strike lasted until February 1910. Modest reforms, however, were unable to prevent the Triangle Shirtwaist Fire of 1911, when 146 employees of the factory, including 123 women, lost their lives. Nevertheless, because of the strike, the garment industry in the ensuing years became one of the nation's best-organized trades.

About the Artist

The photograph was published by the Bain News Service and was likely taken by George Grantham Bain, a New York photographer. Bain was born in Chicago, Illinois, in 1865, but he grew up in St. Louis, Missouri. He studied chemistry at St. Louis University, where he learned the fundamentals of photography. After completing a law degree from St. Louis University in 1883, he became a reporter for the *St. Louis Globe-Democrat*. A year later he took a position with the *St. Louis Post-Dispatch*, which assigned him as a bureau correspondent in Washington, D.C. He later worked for United Press before founding Bain News Service in 1898. In the years that followed, he became a driving force in the linkage of photos with text in newspapers and magazines. He was considered the "father of for-

Document Image

The Garment Workers Strike
(Library of Congress)

eign photographic news," for his company gathered photographs from around the world and distributed them to newspapers for publication. The photos he took himself were principally of people and events in New York City, and by 1905 he had amassed a million photographs. Sadly, the building that housed Bain News Service was destroyed by fire in 1908, taking with it all of the photos he had accumulated, but he started over and created another collection before his death in New York City in 1944. Today, most of his surviving photos are curated by the Library of Congress, which holds about 40,000 of his glass plate negatives and 50,000 photographic prints. His subjects included celebrities, sporting events, politics, immigration, aviation, World War I, and the Mexican Revolution.

Context

Until the late nineteenth century, the production of women's clothing was largely done in the home. Clothing made outside the home, usually for the well-to-do, was typically made by male tailors. The emergence of the shirtwaist, or tailored blouse, marked a change, as hundreds of small shops and factories for the production of less expensive, more convenient women's clothing opened in the garment district of New York City. These operations collectively employed about 30,000 workers, mostly immigrant women and their male managers, and produced some $50 million in merchandise each year. A typical factory employed from fifty to three hundred workers.

The jobs for many of these women were poorly paid. At the bottom rung were unskilled "learners," who earned as little as three to four dollars a week, often working sixty-five hours a week or even seventy-five hours during busy seasons. Semiskilled "operators," who comprised the majority of workers, earned more, from seven to twelve dollars a week, but they too worked long hours under harsh conditions. The top rung consisted of pattern makers, sample makers, and cutters. These workers, mostly men, could earn up to twenty-three dollars a week and were more likely to unionized, particularly in a climate when gender bias among conservative labor leaders, including those of the American Federation of Labor, impeded the efforts of women to organize. Nevertheless, at the turn of the century, women began to push back, as they did in a 1902 boycott of kosher meat butchers (which actually led to rioting outside the shops) and the 1907–08 rent strike, which was organized and led by sixteen-year-

old Pauline Newman and was the largest rent strike in the city's history.

The general strike arose from smaller strikes against three companies, including the Triangle Shirtwaist Company, the largest of the three, during the industry's busy season in the fall of 1909. The strikers' demands included not only fairer wages and shorter hours but also greater workplace safety and an end to indignities, such as sexual harassment, threats, and the like. At the Triangle factory, to cite one example, the women were locked in because metal doors were bolted shut to prevent them from taking unauthorized breaks. The women were required to ask for permission to use the bathroom.

The strikers met with resistance. The companies hired ruffians and even prostitutes to harass the strikers. In many cases they were aided by the police, who arrested strikers on false charges of assault. The courts were of no help. Arrested strikers appeared before hostile judges who scolded them, fined them, and in some cases sentenced them to workhouses.

The International Ladies Garment Workers Union (ILGWU), which had been formed in 1900, stepped in. To monitor the picket lines, the union solicited the help of the Women's Trade Union League (WTUL), which had been formed in 1903 by upper-class suffragists with the goal of promoting the interests of working-class women. The public remained indifferent until the widely publicized arrest of one of the strikers. Backing the strikers were several other organizations: *Forverts*, a Yiddish-language newspaper whose name means "Forward"; the United Hebrew Trades, an association of Jewish labor unions formed in New York City in the 1880s; the Arbeter Ring, or Workers Circle, an organization founded in 1900 to promote the welfare of the Jewish community; and the Socialist Party, including its weekly publication *The Call*.

By November 1909, the strike fund was largely depleted. Many strikers, to avoid arrest and injury, returned to work. Triangle and the Leiserson Company were able to carry on by subcontracting work to smaller shops. It was at this point that the executive committee of the local chapter of the ILGWU proposed a general strike to curtail production entirely in the industry. This decision led to the meeting at the Cooper Union on November 22, 1909. The speakers at the meeting supported the workers, but their approach to the issues remained hesitant. After two hours of debate that seemed to be going nowhere, Clara Lemlich, a Leiserson worker who had been badly beaten by thugs, rose and demanded the floor. She gave what was by all accounts an impassioned speech, stating: "I am a working girl, one of those who are on strike against intolerable conditions. I am tired of listening to speakers who talk in general terms. What we are here to decide is whether we shall or shall not strike. I offer a resolution that a general strike be declared—now." She added: "I have listened to all the speakers. I would not have further patience for talk, as I am one of those who feels and suffers from the things pictured. I move that we go on a general strike!"

Lemlich stirred the audience, who cheered her en masse. The chairman of the meeting, Benjamin Feigenbaum, summoned her to the platform and had her raise her right hand and repeat a famous Jewish oath: "May my right hand wither from my arm if I betray the cause I now pledge." The following day, 20,000 garment workers, including many of the male craftsmen, went on strike. The garment industry in New York City was largely brought to a standstill, although some workers at small shops returned to their jobs. Many of the women who walked out were no strangers to labor agitation. Many had belonged to labor unions in Europe or were members of the Bund, also called the Jewish Labour Bund, a secular labor party founded in Russia and active in eastern Europe.

The strikers continued to meet with stiff, sometimes brutal, opposition. Arrests and harassment continued: during one month, 723 strikers were arrested, and nineteen of these were sentenced to the workhouse. Bail was a prohibitively high $2,500 a day. Court fines amounted to $5,000. The strike overall cost $100,000 (about $3.12 million in 2021 dollars). Lemich was arrested seventeen times and suffered six broken ribs. A ten-year-old girl was arrested and sentenced to the workhouse on a charge of assaulting a "scab" (a replacement worker). In response to the harassment, the WTUL organized rallies at the Hippodrome Theatre, Carnegie Hall, and City Hall. Most of the spadework of the strike was carried out by learners and operators, who distributed leaflets, raised money, distributed strike benefits, and boosted morale, often under bitterly cold conditions. The strike dragged on for eleven weeks, until the point was reached that the workers could not go on in the face of intransigence from the Associated Waist and Dress Manufacturers. The strike was called off on February 15, 1910.

The workers, however, achieved a number of gains. Among the 353 firms affiliated with the Associated Waist and Dress Manufacturers, 339 signed contracts that created a fifty-two-hour week, paid holidays, and negotiation of wages. By the strike's end, 85 percent of the workers had joined the local chapter of the ILGWU, whose membership swelled from just a hundred workers to 10,000.

Working conditions, however, remained poor. On March 25, 1911, a fire broke out at the Triangle factory, which occupied the eighth, ninth, and tenth floors of the Asch Building in New York City. The fire spread rapidly. A fire hose was rotten, and the water valves were rusted shut. A freight elevator was barred. Narrow stairways allowed passage of only one person at a time, and doors to the stairs were locked. Panicked women, some of them on fire, jumped from the windows, in some cases embracing one other as they fell, and their bodies scattered on the street impeded the work of firefighters. Public pressure forced the New York state legislature to appoint a factory investigating commission, whose findings led to industrial reforms, including thirty-six new laws in the state labor code and rigorous fire-protection laws.

Explanation and Analysis of the Document

The photograph depicts four of the strikers. Each is wearing a sash that reads "Picket Ladies Tailors Striker." The four women are posing in a row in front of a building. A look of grim determination is on their faces, although the woman on the right appears to be smiling. All are wearing coats, and two hold muffs to keep their hands warm, indicating that they are walking in the picket line in cold weather. The photo reminds viewers of the courage and resolve of women workers—and indeed all workers—in fighting for human dignity and a decent life for themselves and their families, often under the most difficult conditions. It is particularly significant that the workers are women at a time when women generally were fighting for their rights, including the right to vote, against the conservative belief that the proper place of women was in the home.

—Michael J. O'Neal

Questions for Further Study

1. What would be the purpose of a photo such as this?

2. Would photos of strikers such as this one have influenced the public's perceptions of unions and of striking workers?

3. Although the strike was abruptly called off, did it have any positive effects?

Further Reading

Books

Babson, Steve. *The Unfinished Struggle: Turning Points in American Labor, 1877–Present*. Lanham, MD: Rowman & Littlefield, 1999.

Dye, Nancy Schrom. *As Equals and as Sisters: Feminism, the Labor Movement, and the Women's Trade Union League of New York*. Columbia: University of Missouri Press, 1980.

Edge, Laura B. *We Stand as One: The International Ladies Garment Workers Strike, New York, 1909*. Minneapolis, MN: Twenty-First Century Books, 2010.

Schofield, Ann. "The Uprising of the 20,000: The Making of a Labor Legend." In *A Needle, a Bobbin, a Strike: Women Needleworkers in America*, edited by Joan M. Jensen and Sue Davidson, 167–82. Philadelphia: Temple University Press, 1984.

Seller, Maxine Schwartz. "The Uprising of the Twenty Thousand: Sex, Class and Ethnicity in the Shirtwaist Makers' Strike of 1909." In *"Struggle a Hard Battle": Essays on Working-Class Immigrants*, edited by Dirk Hoerder, 254–79. DeKalb: Northern Illinois University Press, 1986.

Stein, Leon. *Out of the Sweatshop: The Struggle for Industrial Democracy*. New York: Quadrangle/New York Times Book Co., 1977.

Tyler, Gus. *Look for the Union Label: A History of the International Ladies Garment Workers' Union*. Armonk, NY: M. E. Sharpe, 1995.

Websites

"Clara Lemlich and the Uprising of the 20,000." American Experience Collection, PBS. https://www.pbs.org/wgbh/americanexperience/features/biography-clara-lemlich/.

Dwyer, Jim. "One Woman Who Changed the Rules." *New York Times*, March 23, 2011. https://archive.nytimes.com/query.nytimes.com/gst/fullpage-9807E0D91231F930A15750C0A9679D8B63.html.

Lewis, Jone Johnson. "1909 Uprising and 1910 Cloakmakers Strike." *ThoughtCo*, 2019. https://www.thoughtco.com/1910-cloakmakers-strike-4024739.

Michels, Tony. "Uprising of 20,000 (1909)." *The Shalvi/Hyman Encyclopedia of Jewish Women*. Jewish Women's Archive, 1999. https://jwa.org/encyclopedia/article/uprising-of-20000-1909.

Sachar, Howard. "The ILGWU Strike of 1909." *My Jewish Learning*. https://www.myjewishlearning.com/article/the-international-ladies-garment-workers-union-strike/.

Documentaries

1909 N.Y. Shirtwaist Workers Strike. PBS Learning Media. https://indiana.pbslearningmedia.org/resource/amex24.socst.ush.triangle/1909-ny-shirtwaist-workers-strike/.

"INDIAN LAND FOR SALE" POSTER

AUTHOR/CREATOR	IMAGE TYPE
Department of the Interior; De Lancey Walker Gill	FLYERS
DATE	SIGNIFICANCE
1911	Documented the sale of Native American lands to settlers as the United States pushed inexorably westward

Overview

This image is of a broadside that advertised "Indian Land for Sale" in the western states. For more than a century, the United States had been dealing with what white people called the "Indian Problem." The nation's population was growing, and its boundaries were pushing westward. President Thomas Jefferson proposed to solve the problem by forcing Native Americans to become farmers. President Andrew Jackson signed into law the Indian Removal Act of 1830, which relocated eastern tribes from their ancestral lands to locations west of the Mississippi River—resulting in the infamous Trail of Tears, when up to 4,000 Native Americans died of starvation, disease, or exposure on the 5,000-mile trek. Between the Civil War and 1911, the West continued to expand rapidly, with Nebraska, Colorado, North Dakota, South Dakota, Montana, Washington, Idaho, Wyoming, Utah, and Oklahoma joining the Union. Much of this growth came at the expense of the Native American tribes who had been forced off their ancestral lands and onto reservations designated by the U.S. government. Although numerous treaties were signed to secure the status of Native American tribes as self-governing nations and to protect their lands, the United States routinely broke those treaties. In the late nineteenth century, the political consensus was that the "Indian Problem" could be solved only by assimilating Native Americans into mainstream American culture. To that end, the General Allotment Act was passed in 1887 to confiscate reservation lands and divide them among individual tribal members. The goal was to force Native Americans to become individual farmers rather than live communally, but the eventual consequence of the act was the selling off of Native lands.

About the Artist

It is not known who specifically designed and executed the poster. It was issued by the U.S. Department of the Interior, an executive-level department created by an act of Congress in 1849, and it features the names of the secretary of the interior and the commissioner of Indian Affairs. The responsibilities of the Department of the Interior were so various that it was often referred to in jest as the "Department of Everything Else." Its responsibilities included everything from exploration of the western wilderness to management of public parks and public lands, oversight of Indian affairs, patents, and pensions—any matter having to do with the internal development of the nation or the welfare of Americans.

Document Image

"Indian Land for Sale"
(Library of Congress)

In 1911, the secretary of the interior was Walter Lowrie Fisher. Fisher was born in Wheeling, Virginia (now West Virginia), in 1862, although he grew up in Indiana, where he received a bachelor's degree from Hanover College in 1883. He began his career as a lawyer in Chicago, where he was president of a reformist organization, the Municipal Voters League of Chicago, and where he established the National Conservation Association. His friend President William Howard Taft appointed him to the Railroad Securities Commission. Then, from 1911 to 1913, he served as the head of the Department of the Interior. He died in 1935.

Also appearing on the poster is the name of Robert Grosvenor Valentine, who at the time was the nation's commissioner of Indian Affairs. Valentine was born in West Newton, Massachusetts, in 1872. After graduating from Harvard University in 1896, he taught English at the Massachusetts Institute of Technology until 1902. After a stint in the banking industry, he moved to Washington, D.C., where he became the private secretary to Francis E. Leupp, the commissioner of Indian Affairs. Valentine served as an inspector, traveling widely in the western states and supervising Native American schools. In 1908 he was appointed assistant commissioner of Indian Affairs, but after Leupp retired in 1909, President Taft appointed him commissioner, a post he filled until 1912. He died in 1916.

The photograph of the Native American on the poster was taken by De Lancey Walker Gill (1859–1940), an illustrator and photographer in Washington, D.C. He enjoyed a long career with the Smithsonian Institution's Bureau of American Ethnology. In this position he took thousands of portrait photographs of Native Americans and tribal leaders when they visited the capital.

Context

Throughout much of the nineteenth century, violent conflict between European settlers and Native Americans had been increasing. White settlers were pushing westward across North America, and many believed that living in peace with "primitive" and "barbaric" peoples they regarded as "savages" seemed impossible. To mitigate the violence, the reservation system was created in 1851; this system would remove Native Americans from land that European Americans wanted to settle and minimize contact between seem-

ingly incompatible cultures. The reservation system was only partially successful. A number of tribes resisted confinement to reservations, leading to the so-called Indian Wars, a series of conflicts between the U.S. Army and Native tribes. In the late nineteenth century, the most famous of these conflicts was the Battle of Little Bighorn in 1876 and the massacre at Wounded Knee in 1890. Ultimately, the Army prevailed, and by the early twentieth century, the wars had essentially ended.

By the time of the 1910 U.S. census, the population of Native Americans had fallen to about 250,000 (some sources say 237,000), the lowest number in history. Many western settlers and government officials in Washington, D.C., believed that the only hope for the survival of the Native tribes was assimilation into mainstream American society. They often couched this view in religious terms, arguing that Native tribes had to abandon their spiritual traditions and become Christianized. As part of the assimilation process, a number of boarding schools for Native American youth were established. The most famous of these was the Carlisle Indian Industrial School in Pennsylvania, founded by found in 1879 by Richard Henry Pratt, an Army officer who famously stated, "Kill the Indian, save the man."

The political consensus for assimilation led to the passage of the 1887 General Allotment Act, sometimes called the Dawes Severalty Act or simply the Dawes Act, named after its congressional sponsor, Senator Henry Dawes of Massachusetts. The goal of the act was to assimilate Native Americans into mainstream society by eradicating their social and cultural traditions and convert them into sedentary farmers. The act authorized the president to confiscate reservation lands and divide them among individual tribal members; these parcels were called allotments. Allotments were to consist of 80- or 160-acre sections to be used for farming or grazing by individual tribal members. Any Native American who accepted an allotment was allowed to become a U.S. citizen. Any land remaining after the distribution of the allotments was to be sold and homesteaded by white settlers. The allotments were to be held in trust for up to twenty-five years, after which time the tribal member would attain full ownership. The problem was that nearly two-thirds of the trust allotments passed into non-Native ownership. The western states at the time were still sparsely populated. In the 1910 census, for example, Wyoming claimed just 145,000 souls, Idaho 325,000. To put these figures into perspective, thirty-one states at that time had populations in excess of one million. Vast swathes of land seemed to lie there for the taking, so it was sold off to white settlers.

Compounding the problem was that when a Native American died, his or her interest in the allotment was divided among heirs, but the land itself was not divided. In time, the same allotment could have numerous owners across generations. This "fractionation" made it difficult, if not impossible, for the many owners to use or derive income from the land. Accordingly, they sold it. The result was a patchwork of land ownership, which reduced tribal authority, eliminated what remained of tribal culture and society, and raised complicated questions of ownership.

Initially, the Dawes Act did not apply to the so-called Five Civilized Tribes: the Cherokee, Chickasaw, Choctaw, Creek, and Seminole tribes. Their tribal lands were presumably protected by treaty. However, the members of the tribe refused to accept individual allotments, resulting in the Curtis Act of 1898, an amendment to the Dawes Act making the latter applicable to the Five Civilized Tribes. Their tribal governments were eliminated, and 90 million acres of their tribal lands were confiscated and sold to white settlers. The allotment system ended in 1934 with the passage of the Indian Reorganization Act during the administration of President Franklin Roosevelt.

Explanation and Analysis of the Document

This poster draws the potential buyer in with promises that the buyer can "get a home of your own" with "easy payments." The poster reassures potential buyers that title to the property can be "perfect" (that is, it cannot be disputed) and that the buyer can take possession within thirty days. The sales pitch continues with the phrase "Fine Lands in the West" and assurance that the lands are irrigated or irrigable and can be used for grazing or farming. The poster indicates that 350,000 acres would be sold in 1911. In smaller print, the poster specifies the amount of such land that had been purchased in 1910 in Colorado, Idaho, Kansas, Montana, Nebraska, North Dakota, Oklahoma, Oregon, South Dakota, Washington, Wisconsin, and Wyoming. The average sales price per acre ranged from $7.27 per acre in Colorado to $41.37 per acre in Washington (about $281 to about $1,244 in 2021 dollars). Anyone interested in making a purchase is invited to write for booklet titled "Indian Lands for Sale" to "the Superintendent U.S. Indian School" in the listed states. Visual appeal is added to the poster by a photo of Padani-Kokipa-Sni ("Not Afraid of Pawnee"), a member of the Yankton tribe. He is garbed in Native dress and wears a two-eagle-feather hair charm.

The poster illustrates the extent to which the U.S. Department of the Interior and the Bureau of Indian Affairs maintained control over western lands that in previous generations had been occupied by Native tribes. The poster highlights the efforts of the federal government to entice settlers to these sparsely populated states, primarily for agricultural purposes to feed the nation's growing population in the East.

—Michael J. O'Neal

Questions for Further Study

1. Was the Dawes Act intended to help or harm Native Americans?

2. What effects did the Dawes Act and the sale of Native American lands have on Native American cultural beliefs and traditions?

3. What were the major differences between Native American and European American views of land and property ownership?

Further Reading

Books

Black, Jason Edward. *American Indians and the Rhetoric of Removal and Allotment.* Jackson: University Press of Mississippi, 2015.

Genetin-Pilawa, C. Joseph. *Crooked Paths to Allotment: The Fight over Federal Indian Policy after the Civil War.* Chapel Hill: University of North Carolina Press, 2012.

Justice, Daniel Heath, and Jean M. O'Brien, eds. *Allotment Stories: Indigenous Land Relations under Settler Siege.* Minneapolis: University of Minnesota Press, 2022.

Otis, D. S. *The Dawes Act and the Allotment of Indian Land,* edited by Francis Paul Prucha. Norman: University of Oklahoma Press, 1973.

Ruppel, Kristin T. *Unearthing Indian Land: Living with the Legacies of Allotment.* Tucson: University of Arizona Press, 2008.

Articles

Carlson, Leonard. "Federal Policy and Indian Land: Economic Interests and the Sale of Indian Allotments, 1900–1934." *Agricultural History* 57, no. 1 (January 1983): 33–45.

Websites

Kidwell, Clara Sue. "Allotment." *Encyclopedia of Oklahoma History and Culture.* https://www.okhistory.org/publications/enc/entry.php?entry=AL011.

"Tribal Land and Ownership Statuses: Overview and Selected Issues for Congress." Congressional Research Service, July 21, 2021. https://crsreports.congress.gov/product/pdf/R/R46647.

"The Tribes Sell Off More Land: The 1905 Agreement." WyoHistory.org, December 10, 2018. https://www.wyohistory.org/encyclopedia/tribes-sell-more-land-1905-agreement.

Documentaries

The "Indian Problem." National Museum of the American Indian, Smithsonian, 2015. https://www.si.edu/object/indian-problem%3Ayt_if-BOZgWZPE.

Photograph Of Health Inspection Of New Immigrants, Ellis Island

AUTHOR/CREATOR
Unknown

DATE
1914

IMAGE TYPE
PHOTOGRAPHS

SIGNIFICANCE
Documents one of the chief hurdles that immigrants to the United States passing through Ellis Island in the early twentieth century had to clear: the medical inspection

Overview

In the late nineteenth and early twentieth centuries, U.S. immigration officials faced an onslaught of immigrants arriving at disembarkation points such as Ellis Island in the United States. In previous decades, most immigrants to the United States had come from northern European countries: England, Germany, the Netherlands, Scandinavia, and others. The bulk of the "new" immigrants were from the countries of eastern and southern Europe: Italy, Russia, Greece, the Baltic states, and the Slavic countries. Others were from non-European countries such as Turkey, Armenia, and Syria. Virtually all were fleeing drought, famine, oppression, war, or religious persecution. These immigrants, however, faced considerable prejudice in the United States. Many Americans believed that the new immigrants brought with them crime, subversion, dirt, and disease. One step that immigration officials took to prevent people with infectious diseases from entering the United States was to require each newly arrived immigrant to submit to a brief health inspection before passing through Ellis Island. This photograph shows two medical inspectors at work as they examine the eyes of the men before them. The goal was to bar admission to anyone who, because of ill health, was likely to become a "public charge" by being unable to work and support him or herself.

About the Artist

It is unknown who, specifically, took the photograph. It is likely that the photographer was an immigration official or someone hired by the immigration authorities to document the history of Ellis Island. Ellis Island, situated between New York and New Jersey in New York Harbor at the mouth of the Hudson River, opened in 1892 as an immigration station. It operated as such until it closed in 1954. Estimates are that from 1892 until 1914, the year the photograph was taken, 12 million immigrants passed through Ellis Island. At its peak, from 1900 to 1914, an average of about 1,900 people each day passed through on their way to a new life in the United States. An all-time daily high of 11,747 immigrants was reached on April 17, 1907, and that year, Ellis Island welcomed 1,004,756 arrivals, the highest number for a single year. So many immigrants passed through the station that it is estimated that nearly 40 percent of American citizens can trace at least one ancestor to an Ellis Island immigrant. The island began

Document Image

Health Inspection of New Immigrants, Ellis Island
(Shawshots / Alamy)

as just three acres, but landfill was brought in to expand its size to twenty-seven acres, to include two hospitals and a ward for the mentally ill. Although Ellis Island no longer functions as an immigration station, the very name survives to symbolize the promise of a better life in the New World.

Context

In the early 1900s, millions of immigrants from the countries of Europe paid roughly $30 (about $860 dollars in 2022) for a steerage ticket to make the arduous steamship voyage across the Atlantic and make a new life for themselves in the United States. Between 1892, when Ellis Island opened, and 1914, the year this photo was taken, some 12 million immigrants, or 70 percent of the immigrants who arrived in the United States, passed through Ellis Island.

In the twenty-first century, an American can only try to imagine the excitement and anticipation felt by steamship passengers, many of whom had likely never traveled out of their village, as the skyline of New York City came into view, as they passed the Statue of Liberty, and as the end of the voyage was in sight. That excitement likely turned to a measure of frustration as immigrants had to negotiate a bureaucratic maze to attain their landing card authorizing them to enter the country. A key part of the maze was the health inspection, conducted by doctors of the U.S. Public Health Service (PHS), who in 1891 were assigned the task of inspecting all immigrants to the United States. Those involved in the medical inspections referred colloquially to the "line," which consisted of a number of techniques and procedures the officers used to quickly examine the thousands of immigrants who arrived.

First, an arriving ship had to pass a quarantine inspection in New York Harbor. The Immigration Service and PHS inspectors boarded the ship and examined all first- and second-class passengers—generally the more affluent passengers—as the ship steamed into the harbor. The inspectors identified steerage passengers—those who were likely poor—by means of a piece of paper pinned to their clothes. The paper indicated the ship manifest on which their names could be found. The steerage passengers, along with their luggage, were then loaded into barges and taken to Ellis Island. There, attendants ushered them to the main building, making sure that they walked in single file through the door. After they entered the building, they walked toward a U.S. Public Health Service physician in a military-style uniform. The physician made a quick, systematic observation of the person, starting with the feet and moving upward to the face. These physicians were in effect undergoing training in medical diagnosis, and the training was a challenge, for the physician was expected to recognize, in about six seconds, any physical or mental defect that might have afflicted every man, woman, and child who passed before him. Any such defect was grounds for making the immigrant inadmissible to the United States. Part of the process was turning back their eyelids to check for trachoma, a form of conjunctivitis, often referred to as "pink eye," that could lead to blindness.

The emphasis was on what was called the doctor's "gaze." At the time, it was believed that the presence of disease could readily be determined by simply looking that the body. One Boston doctor, Alfred Nute, stated that "almost no grave organic disease can have a hold on an individual without stamping some evidence of its presence upon the appearance of the patient evident to the eye or hand of the trained observer." According to PHS regulations, officers were to place a chalk mark on the clothing of immigrants needing further attention as they passed through the line. "EX" signified that the person should be examined further because the officer suspected the presence of disease. "C" was an indication that the officer suspected an eye condition. "S" was used to indicate suspicion of senility, and "X" was marked for suspicion of insanity. It is estimated that some 120,000 arrivals were turned away and sent back to their home countries based on the belief that they would potentially become public charges. Most new arrivals were sent upstairs, where they anxiously waited for their landing card and were typically given it within a few hours. The unlucky few with chalk marks had to undergo delay. Those with acute conditions were sent to the island's hospital for treatment. After several expansions, the Ellis Island Immigrant Hospital had 750 beds, including 450 in the Contagious Disease Hospital and 300 in the General Hospital. Meanwhile, those who had caught the attention of the physicians were detained and given a more thorough examination.

The questions might arise: What prompted the Immigration Service to institute medical examinations when it did? Why were such examinations regarded as necessary and appropriate? Until 1891, immigration had fallen under the jurisdiction of the states, with New York as the largest port of entry. But the Immigration Act of 1891 placed immigration under the authority of the federal government and strengthened the Immigration Act of 1882, which excluded immigrants who were "likely to become a public charge." These included convicts, those who had been convicted of political offenses, or those who were "idiots, psychopathics, or afflicted with a loathsome infectious or contagious disease." Of particular concern were those who fell into the latter category. That concern represented a sea change in American medicine brought about by the discoveries of Joseph Lister (1827–1912), a British surgeon, and Louis Pasteur (1822–1895), a French chemist and microbiologist. The research of these men led to the development of the "germ theory" of disease. Until their work gained traction, the view that invisible germs could cause disease seemed implausible, but numerous American doctors spent time at European clinics during the 1870s and 1880s and returned to the United States to become ardent proponents of the germ theory. In 1882 Robert Koch identified the bacterium that caused tuberculosis. An 1886 edition of a standard medical textbook contained a chapter on bacteriology. Quickly, the germ theory became part of medical orthodoxy. The U.S. Public Health Service particularly championed the germ theory, and it was likely because of this new recognition of the etiology and transmission of disease

that medical inspections at the nation's ports of entry were required.

Explanation and Analysis of the Document

The photograph is relatively simple. It shows a number of men standing in line to be given a health inspection by two uniformed immigration physicians. Both of the inspectors appear to be examining a man's eyes, a procedure commonly used at immigration ports to check for trachoma. All of the immigrants in this photo are men. All are dressed in suits and ties, and all appear to be carrying a suitcase—containing the sum of their belongings as they arrived in the United States. The photo makes clear that admission to the United States was not a given; a person could be denied admittance and shipped back to his or her home country because of a medical condition that made the person "undesirable." The question arises as to whether the emphasis on medical examinations might have had a tinge of bigotry to it, given the widespread distrust of the "new" immigrants from less highly regarded countries.

—Michael J. O'Neal

Questions for Further Study

1. What was the purpose of the health inspections given to new immigrants at Ellis Island?

2. Is it surprising that men fleeing the countries of their birth and embarking on an arduous voyage to the New World are dressed as well as they are? How might this have come about?

3. Was it fair and equitable to subject immigrants to a health inspection on their arrival?

Further Reading

Books

Bayor, Ronald H. *Encountering Ellis Island: How European Immigrants Entered America.* Baltimore, MD: Johns Hopkins University Press, 2014.

Cannato, Vincent J. *American Passage: The History of Ellis Island.* New York: Harper Perennial, 2010.

Moreno, Barry. *Encyclopedia of Ellis Island.* Westport, CT: Greenwood Press, 2004.

Articles

Bateman-House, Alison, and Amy Fairchild. "Medical Examination of Immigrants at Ellis Island." *AMA Journal of Ethics*, April 2008. https://journalofethics.ama-assn.org/article/medical-examination-immigrants-ellis-island/2008-04.

Yew, Elizabeth. "Medical Inspection of Immigrants at Ellis Island, 1891–1924." *Bulletin of the New York Academy of Medicine* 56, no. 5 (June 1980): 488–510. https://www.ncbi.nlm.nih.gov/pmc/articles/PMC1805119/pdf/bullnya-cadmed00114-0060.pdf.

Websites

"Ellis Island/Angel Island: A Tale of Two Islands." Angel Island Immigration Museum. https://www.aiisf.org/ellis-an-gel#:~:text=Dr.,hand%20of%20the%20trained%20observer.%E2%80%9D.

Markel, Howard. "Before Ebola, Ellis Island's Terrifying Medical Inspections." *PBS Newshour*, October 15, 2014. https://www.pbs.org/newshour/health/october-15-1965-remembering-ellis-island.

Documentaries

"Ellis Island Expedition Series." National Park Service. https://www.nps.gov/elis/learn/education/eie-series.htm.

Woman's Party Campaign Billboard

Author/Creator Smith-Brooks Co. **Date** 1916 **Image Type** Illustrations	**Significance** Evidence of a national campaign to urge voters, particularly women, to vote against Woodrow Wilson and the Democratic Party because of the president's and the party's apparent opposition to women's suffrage

Overview

By 1916, the women's suffrage movement had been gathering momentum for decades, starting with the Seneca Falls (N.Y.) Convention in 1848. With the election of Woodrow Wilson to the presidency in 1912, women's groups, including the National American Woman Suffrage Association (NAWSA) and the National Woman's Party (NWP), were hopeful that the U.S. Constitution could be amended to grant women the right to vote. Wilson, however, despite his generally progressive tendencies, appeared to be lukewarm on the issue of woman suffrage, much to the chagrin of suffragists. Accordingly, in 1916, when the president was up for reelection, the Woman's Party campaigned in opposition to him and to Democratic congressional representatives who failed to support their goals. In 1893, a referendum was passed by both women and men in Colorado giving women the right to vote "in the same manner in all respects as male persons are." By 1916, the year in which this billboard appeared, Colorado was one of a number of western states, including Wyoming, Utah, Idaho, Washington, Oregon, California, Kansas, Arizona, Nevada, and Montana, that had granted voting rights to women. Work still needed to be done at the national level, however. To that end, the Woman's Party put up billboards such as this one in opposition to Democratic opponents.

About the Artist

Smith-Brooks Co. Engravers Printers in Denver, Colorado, produced the billboard. The company billed itself as a "Complete Service" for "Printing Lithographing Engraving and Commercial Art." The company's brochure stated that it provided "The right method for the purpose" and that it had a "Creative Department Co-operating with sound ideas, copy, plans, sketches, layouts, dummies, information."

Context

Sometimes people change their minds. A noteworthy example of a reversal of opinion was provided by President Woodrow Wilson, who occupied the White House from 1913 to 1921. Wilson was in many respects a progressive, concerned about issues of social justice and equal rights. But in earlier years, before he became president, his views were not particularly forward

Document Image

Billboard put up by the Woman's Party in 1916
(Library of Congress)

looking. In 1884, in describing a Woman's Congress meeting of the Association for the Advancement of Women in Baltimore, he wrote in a letter to the woman he would marry: "Barring the chilled, scandalized feeling that always overcomes me when I see and hear women speak in public, I derived a good deal of whimsical delight . . . from the proceedings." He went on to comment on one speaker, "a severely dressed person from Boston, an old maid," whom he believed was "a living example—a lively commentary—of what might be done by giving men's places and duties to women."

Yet by 1918, Wilson had taken a very different stance. The Nineteenth Amendment to the Constitution, which would extend voting rights to women, had (barely) passed in the U.S. House of Representatives. It was up for debate in the U.S. Senate. On September 30, 1918, Wilson addressed the Senate in support of the amendment: "The women of America are too noble and too intelligent and too devoted to be slackers, whether you give or withhold this thing that is mere justice; but I know the magic it will work in their thoughts and spirits if you give it them. I propose it as I would propose to admit soldiers to the suffrage, the men fighting in the field for our liberties and the liberties of the world, were they excluded. The tasks of the women lie at the very heart of the war; and I know how much stronger that heart will beat if you do this just thing and show our women that you trust them as much as you in fact and of necessity depend upon them."

What changed Wilson's mind? Scholarship has generally portrayed Wilson as having obstructed the passage of a women's suffrage amendment, but some have conceded that in the mid-1910s Wilson faced the immense distraction of World War I and the need to mobilize the citizenry. By late 1918, however, he had seen the extraordinary contributions of women to the war effort, both overseas and on the home front. The war in his view was fought "to make the world safe for democracy," so it is not entirely inconsistent for him to have finally come around to the view that women should have a voice in the nation's governance.

Wilson was also under considerable pressure from women's groups. In 1890, the National Woman Suffrage Association and the American Woman Suffrage Association merged to form the National American Woman Suffrage Association under the leadership of prominent suffragist Elizabeth Cady Stanton. Its chief goal was to back a constitutional amendment to give women the right to vote. In 1913, on the day before Wilson's first inauguration, the NAWSA led 5,000 women in a march on the White House. The NAWSA modeled its actions on those of prominent British suffragists Emmeline Pankhurst and her sisters, whose chief strategy was to hold the feet of whichever political party was in power to the fire on suffrage and other issues involving the rights of women.

Alice Paul and Lucy Burns, both prominent—and fiery—suffragists and members of the NAWSA, in time became disenchanted with the NAWSA, believing that it was too cautious in its methods. Accordingly, in 1913 they broke away and formed the Congressional Union for Woman Suffrage (CU). Paul and Burns proved to be masters of theatrical publicity. They led protests, marches, and demonstrations. They published a newspaper, *The Suffragist*. They sent representatives to the states, including Colorado, to campaign against Democrats who were not doing their part on women's issues, including the right to vote. Then in 1916, Paul, Burns, and their CU allies formed the Woman's Party, the nation's first political party for women. That year, the party, backed by other women in the western states, convened in Colorado. There they made plans to ensure that the upcoming national election campaigns placed issues affecting women, including suffrage, high on their agendas. During the election season, the party aggressively organized women against the Democratic leadership nationwide. The poster is indicative of that campaign.

The following year, Paul and Burns forged an alliance between the CU and the Woman's Party to form the National Woman's Party (NWP), with Paul as its first chairperson. The NWP attracted women from all walks of life, among them union workers, doctors, lawyers, philanthropists, and homemakers. In early 1917, the pressure on Wilson continued. Paul and her supporters began to picket the White House. A rotating group of women who called themselves the Silent Sentinels carried signs challenging the president, whose initial attitude toward the picketers was one of amused condescension. Then in June 1917, six were arrested. A second group was arrested on July 4, and a third group was arrested ten days later. The protesters were sentenced to sixty days in the workhouse, where they endured beatings, unsanitary conditions, and forced feeding. In August, melees broke out in front of the White House. Picketers were dragged, punched, and choked by angry crowds as the police looked on and did nothing.

Wilson was no supporter of the picketers, whose methods he despised, but he could see the handwriting on the wall. It was only after Carrie Chapman Catt, president of the less-militant NAWSA, aligned her organization with the war effort and made a personal appeal to Wilson that he expressed his support of women's suffrage to the U.S. Senate. On August 18, 1920, the Tennessee House of Representatives voted to ratify the Nineteenth Amendment by a vote of 50 to 49; the one determining vote was cast by twenty-four-year-old Harry Burn, a Republican, who stated that he voted in favor of ratification after receiving a stern note from his mother telling him to vote "yes." With Tennessee's ratification, the amendment became part of the Constitution. The amendment simply read: "The right of citizens of the United States to vote shall not be denied or abridged by the United States or by any State on account of sex."

Explanation and Analysis of the Document

The photograph depicts an unidentified woman using a bucket and a broom to put up a billboard in Denver, Colorado. The billboard features a figure of a hatless woman in a dress, striking a pose of determination with her fists on her hips. Her feathered hat is on the ground before her inside a ring. Above the ring are the words "Our hat's in the ring." The chief message of the billboard states "Women of Colorado, you have the vote." The message goes on to state: "Get it for women of the nation by voting against" (and then in smaller print) "Woodrow Wilson and the Democratic candidate for Congress." The absence of the names of those Democratic candidates—Benjamin Hilliard, Edward Keating, and Edward T. Taylor—suggests that the billboard may have been prepared well in advance of the election, ready for use no matter who the candidate was. The billboard continues: "Their party opposes national woman suffrage." At the bottom is the "signature" of the National Woman's Party. The billboard reminded the women of Colorado—and men as well—that women in the state already had the right to vote but that women in many other states were denied that right. The billboard would appear not to have had the desired effect, for in Colorado, Wilson defeated his Republican opponent, Charles Evans Hughes, by a margin of 61 percent to 35 percent. Further, all three Democratic congressional representatives in Colorado were reelected.

—Michael J. O'Neal

Questions for Further Study

1. What motivated the National Woman's Party to put up this and other billboards?

2. How effective would a billboard such as this have been in swaying voters?

3. Why was the National Woman's Party opposed to President Woodrow Wilson?

Further Reading

Books

Buhle, Mari Jo, and Paul Buhle. *The Concise History of Woman Suffrage: Selections from History of Woman Suffrage*. Urbana: University of Illinois Press, 2005.

Cassidy, Tina. *Mr. President, How Long Must We Wait? Alice Paul, Woodrow Wilson, and the Fight for the Right to Vote*. New York: 37Ink, 2019.

Catt, Carrie Chapman, and Nettie Rogers Shuler. *Woman Suffrage and Politics: The Inner Story of the Suffrage Movement*. Mineola, NY: Dover Publications, 2020.

DuBois, Ellen Carol. *Suffrage: Women's Long Battle for the Vote*. New York: Simon & Schuster, 2020.

Gibson, Katie L., and Amy L. Heyse. "Suppression of the Suffrage Movement." In *Silencing the Opposition: How the U.S. Government Suppressed Freedom of Expression during Major Crises*, edited by Craig R. Smith, 151–74. 2nd edition. Albany: State University of New York Press, 2011.

Irwin, Inez Haynes. *The Story of the National Woman's Party*. New York: Harcourt, Brace, 1921.

Spruill, Marjorie J., ed. *One Woman, One Vote: Rediscovering the Woman Suffrage Movement*. Tillamook, OR: NewSage Press, 2021.

Steinson, Barbara J. "Wilson and Woman Suffrage." In *A Companion to Woodrow Wilson*, edited by Ross A. Kennedy, 343–63. Malden, MA: Wiley-Blackwell, 2013.

Ware, Susan, ed. *American Women's Suffrage: Voices from the Long Struggle for the Vote, 1776–1965*. New York: Library of America, 2020.

Articles

Cott, Nancy. "Feminist Politics in the 1920's: The National Woman's Party." *Journal of American History* 71 (June 1984): 43–68.

Graham, Sally Hunter. "Woodrow Wilson, Alice Paul, and the Woman Suffrage Movement." *Political Science Quarterly* 98, no. 4 (Winter 1983–84): 665–79.

Lunardini, Christine A., and Thomas J. Knock. "Woodrow Wilson and Woman Suffrage: A New Look." *Political Science Quarterly* 95, no. 4 (Winter 1980–81): 655–71.

Websites

"Address of President Woodrow Wilson on Equal Suffrage, September 30, 1918." United States Senate. https://www.senate.gov/artandhistory/history/resources/pdf/WilsonSpeech1918.pdf.

"The 19th Amendment: Women's Suffrage." President Wilson House. https://www.woodrowwilsonhouse.org/wilson-topics/the-19-amendment-2/.

Documentaries

"The Vote," *American Experience*, PBS, July 7, 2020. https://www.pbs.org/wgbh/americanexperience/films/vote/.

"GEE! I WISH I WERE A MAN": NAVY RECRUITING POSTER

AUTHOR/CREATOR	IMAGE TYPE
Howard Chandler Christy	FLYERS
DATE	SIGNIFICANCE
1917	A patriotic poster urging men to join the U.S. Navy during World War I

Overview

After the guns of war erupted over Europe in the summer of 1914, U.S. president Woodrow Wilson pledged to keep the United States out of the war. That state of affairs changed on April 6, 1917, when Congress voted to support the president's declaration of war against the Central Powers, primarily Germany. Recruitment of troops became a pressing concern. So too was marshaling support for the war effort among the civilian population, particularly at a time when many Americans were steadfastly opposed to the war. To support the war effort, the federal government mounted a massive propaganda campaign designed to convince Americans that war was the only option and that it had to be fought, as Wilson put it, "to make the world safe for democracy." Most Americans pitched in: They supported "Wheatless Mondays" and "Meatless Tuesdays" to conserve food supplies for the troops. Boy Scouts planted backyard vegetable gardens. Chicago homemakers were so successful in using leftovers that the volume of trash in the city fell by a third. Americans did their patriotic duty. For many, that meant serving in the military, including the Navy, and posters such as this one helped persuade them.

About the Artist

Howard Chandler Christy was noteworthy for documenting the Spanish-American War, creating the "Christy Girl," and designing patriotic posters during World War I. Christy, born in 1872, was trained in art in New York City at the Art Students League and the National Academy of Design. When the Spanish-American War broke out in 1898, he traveled with U.S. troops to Cuba, where he used his skills to document events with pen-and-ink drawings that were published by *Scribner's Magazine, Harper's, Century Magazine*, and *Leslie's Weekly*. After the war, he went to work for *Scribner's Magazine*, where he created the famous Christy Girl, images of a woman regarded as an embodiment of the ideal American women because of her grace, elegance, and beauty. Christy became such a trendsetter that he would be selected as the only judge for the first Miss America pageant in 1921.

After the United States entered World War I in 1917, Christy again offered his services, designing posters in support of the Red Cross and of the war effort. His "Gee! I Wish I Were a Man" poster, along with one called "I Want You for the Navy," were iconic World War I posters that contributed to successful Navy recruitment drives.

Document Image

"Gee! I Wish I Were a Man"
(Library of Congress)

After World War I, Christy became a portraitist, painting portraits of numerous celebrities and political figures: Presidents Franklin Delano Roosevelt, Herbert Hoover, Calvin Coolidge and his wife, Grace, Crown Prince Umberto of Italy, Amelia Earhart, General Douglas MacArthur, Mrs. William Randolph Hearst, and Benito Mussolini, among others. Then in the 1930s he shifted his focus to mural painting. Perhaps his most famous mural was *The Signing of the Constitution*, completed in 1940 for the Capitol rotunda in Washington, D.C. He died at the age of eighty in New York City in 1952.

Context

World War I officially began when Austria-Hungary declared war on Serbia on July 28, 1914. Within days, numerous European nations, including France, England, Germany, Russia, and others, were drawn into war, primarily because of webs of interlocking alliances but also out of fear of a resurgent and militarized Germany. The initial position of the United States was one of neutrality; it was a European war that did not concern the United States, although ultimately it did: Germany resumed a policy of unrestricted submarine warfare, sinking any ships, including American ships, in the Atlantic; a particular outrage was the sinking of the *Lusitania*, a British ocean liner, in 1915, resulting in the deaths of nearly 1,200 civilians, including 128 Americans. Public opinion in the United States was inflamed in February 1917 by revelation of the so-called Zimmermann Telegram, a coded message from German foreign minister Arthur Zimmermann to the German ambassador in Mexico instructing the ambassador to propose an alliance between the Central Powers and Mexico.

America's position may have been one of neutrality, but it was an armed neutrality to ensure that the United States was prepared for war, both on land and on the high seas, if it came. At the end of 1909, the country had 187 active naval vessels. On August 29, 1916, Congress passed the Naval Act, which authorized an expenditure of $500 million for new warships of various types, including fifty destroyers. By the end of 1916, the number of vessels had risen to 245, and over the course of American participation in the war, the number grew to 774. These battleships, cruisers, destroyers, submarines, and other vessels had to be staffed, so naval recruitment became a priority. In late 1916, the number of men in the Navy totaled about 59,000. By the end of the war in late 1918, the number had swollen to 530,000.

With the U.S. declaration of war, mobilization had to take place with dispatch. Americans had to be convinced to take part in a war "Over There," the name of a popular song of the era written by George M. Cohan. One of the chief ways of marshaling public support was posters, many of which were so well designed and powerful in their message that they were hung in art galleries. Posters had visual appeal, and they could be easily reproduced to be put up in workplaces, on the sides of buildings, in post offices, schools, libraries, and even in the windows of homes. Many were downsized to appear in magazines or in cable car windows. To carry out the advertising—many would say "propaganda"—campaign, the U.S. government's Public Information Committee formed the Division of Pictorial Publicity in 1917, often called the Creel Committee after the name of its chairman, George Creel. Creel asked Charles Dana Gibson, one of the nation's most famous illustrators, to join him in the effort. Gibson was the president of the Society of Illustrators, so he had the ear of most of the nation's best-known illustrators. He encouraged them to donate their creativity to the war effort.

The number of posters created was legion. Patriotic images abounded: U.S. flags, Lady Liberty, men in uniform marching off with smiles on their faces. Bold graphics, strong imagery, and sharp commands made it nearly impossible for the citizen to turn away. The posters roused nationalism and inspired citizens to support the troops, buy war bonds, fund international aid projects, conserve food, enlist for military service, and take other steps in support of the war effort. Good and evil were clearly distinguished. "The Huns" (a pejorative terms for Germans) were depicted as brutes and as dark, evil-looking monsters, sometimes as apes; sunny American servicemen (along with the women who sold war bonds and served on the home front in other capacities) were representative of all that was democratic and civilized.

Messages on the posters included "Buy U.S. Government Bonds: Remember! The Flag of Liberty," "Join the Navy: The Service for Fighting Men," "Beat Back the Hun with Liberty Bonds," "Will You Supply Eyes for the Navy?" (an appeal to the public to donate binoculars and spyglasses), "Wake Up, America! Civilization Calls Every Man, Woman and Child," "Help Uncle Sam Stamp Out the Kaiser," and "Are you 100% American?

Prove it! Buy U.S. Government Bonds." Perhaps the most famous poster, and the most iconic one, was the "I Want YOU for U.S. Army" poster created by James Montgomery Flagg. The poster features a chiseled, stern figure of Uncle Sam pointing a menacing finger at the viewer—a figure inspired by British artist Alfred Leete's image of Lord Kitchener, the British secretary of state for war. This image also appeared on a Navy recruitment poster whose legend read: "First Call: I Need You in the Navy this Minute! Our Country will always be proudest of those who answered the FIRST CALL."

In connection with a World War I poster exhibit, the curator of graphic arts and social history at the Huntington Library in California, David H. Mihaly, summed up the value of posters like this one during World War I: "Posters sold the war. These posters inspired you to enlist, to pick up the flag and support your country. They made you in some cases fear an enemy or created a fear you didn't know you had. Nations needed to convince their citizens that this war was just, and we needed to participate and not sit and watch."

Explanation and Analysis of the Document

The poster features a cheerful young woman dressed in a blue Navy uniform and wearing a white sailor's cap. The woman has a beguiling smile on her face. Her collars and a bandana appear to be blowing in the wind. The rank insignia on the uniform is that of a First-Class Petty Officer. She is stating, "Gee! If I were a man, I'd join the Navy." Underneath the signature of the artist are the words: "Be a man and do it." Men are then encouraged to visit a "United States Navy Recruiting Station." The color scheme of the poster is primarily navy blue, with touches of red and a white background; red, white, and blue, the colors of the nation's flag, make a subtle appeal to patriotism. Overall, the poster is an appeal to masculine pride. A "true man," it implies, would join the Navy and fight for his country—and perhaps fight to defend and win the heart of the pretty girl depicted in the poster.

—Michael J. O'Neal

Questions for Further Study

1. How effective might this poster have been in persuading men to join the Navy?

2. Why did the artist use the figure of a woman to make the appeal?

3. How did the poster appeal to male pride?

Further Reading

Books

Hardie, Martin, and Arthur K. Sabin. *War Posters: The Historical Role of Wartime Poster Art 1914–1919*. Mineola, NY: Dover Publications, 2016.

Historical US Navy Recruitment Posters: USA Naval History Recruiting Art Images: Pre 1900 to World War I & II. Libero Photo Books, 2012.

James, Pearl, ed. *Picture This: World War I Posters and Visual Culture*. Lincoln: University of Nebraska Press, 2010.

Kingsbury, Celia M. *For Home and Country: World War I Propaganda on the Home Front*. Lincoln: University of Nebraska Press, 2010.

Linder, Ann P. *World War I in 40 Posters*. Mechanicsburg, PA: Stackpole Books, 2016.

Ward, Arthur. *A Guide to War Publications of the First & Second World War: From Training Guides to Propaganda Posters*. Barnsley, England: Pen and Sword Books, 2015.

World War One Posters: An Anniversary Collection. Mineola, NY: Calla Editions, 2018.

Websites

Cook, Jia-Rui. "The Posters That Sold World War I to the American Public." *Smithsonian Magazine*, July 28, 2014. https://www.smithsonianmag.com/history/posters-sold-world-war-i-american-public-180952179/.

Cull, Nicholas J. "Master of American Propaganda: How George Creel Sold the Great War to America, and America to the World." *American Experience*, PBS. Accessed August 17, 2022. https://www.pbs.org/wgbh/americanexperience/features/the-great-war-master-of-american-propaganda/.

"The Poster: Visual Persuasion in WWI." National World War I Museum and Memorial. Accessed August 17, 2022. https://www.theworldwar.org/exhibitions/poster-visual-persuasion-wwi.

"World War I Posters." Library of Congress. Accessed August 17, 2022. https://www.loc.gov/collections/world-war-i-posters/about-this-collection/.

Documentaries

Kulig, Camille. *Propaganda Posters and WWI*. WWI Changed Us Webinar Series, National World War I Museum and Memorial, January 5, 2021. https://www.youtube.com/watch?v=C9Hc1dxjaLE.

Photograph Of Harlem Hellfighters Regiment

AUTHOR/CREATOR
Uncredited/U.S. Department of War

DATE
1919

IMAGE TYPE
PHOTOGRAPHS

SIGNIFICANCE
One of many photographs authorized by the U.S. Department of War (now Department of Defense) to inform the general public of the country's progress in the struggle, and a testament to the service of African Americans in World War I

Overview

They were known as the Harlem Hellfighters, though the origin of the term is a matter of debate. Some say that their German enemies gave them the name, but there is no conclusive proof to back this up. The unit was originally called the 15th New York National Guard. It was put together in 1913 and reconstituted as the 369th Infantry Regiment after the United States' entry into World War I on April 6, 1917. This photo of some of the medal of honor recipients from the 369th was among a great number of images put out by various branches of government to highlight positive aspects of America's involvement in the conflict on the side of the Allies. The intent was to sustain morale and support on the home front and to foster a sense of pride as the soldiers returned home.

About the Artist

The uncredited artist was probably a U.S. Army serviceman who would have been assigned special duties as a U.S. Army photographer. This photo, like others taken by Army photographers, would have had to pass inspection for approval up the ranks of the military prior to being officially released for publication and distribution.

Context

African Americans had served in all the prior wars in which the United States was involved, up to the twentieth century, in racially segregated units. Through the Civil War, the commissioned officers for these African American units had been exclusively white. This slowly changed after that war; in 1877 Second Lieutenant Henry Ossian Flipper (1856–1940) became the first African American to break into the officer corps. However, by 1917, only one, Charles Young (1864–1922), had attained the rank of colonel. Nonetheless, Black units had demonstrated their effectiveness: the 24th and 25th Infantry, and the 9th and 10th Cavalry—the legendary "Buffalo Soldiers"—had proven themselves in the wars against Native Americans on the frontier, in the Spanish–American War (1898), and in the Philippine–American War (1899–1902), and they would later participate in the 1916 Mexican Expedition against Pancho Villa. However, a great many white citizens at the time viewed African American military personnel with apprehension, and public sentiment was strongly

Document Image

The 369th Infantry Regiment
(National Archives)

supportive of continued segregation, even among service personnel.

The period from roughly the late 1890s to 1921 has been termed by some historians the Progressive Era for campaigns conducted by reformers at the time against the against the corruption and domination of big business over government and society. These were highlighted by such measures as anti-trust legislation, the Pure Food and Drug Act of 1906, the introduction of graduated income tax, the popular election of U.S. senators, conservation measures, and women's suffrage. Other historians, however—notably Rayford Logan and James Loewen—have noted that the progressive reforms did not extend to improving the situation of African Americans but rather was a time when legalized racial prejudice was at its most entrenched and institutionalized stage, and lynching and racially inspired mob violence were at their worst. Logan coined the term "nadir of American race relations" and applied it to the period from 1877 to 1901; subsequent historians such as Loewen extended it into the 1920s and even the mid-1940s.

The military was not exempt from this rampant racism: both Lieutenant Flipper and 9th Cavalry chaplain Henry Vinton Plummer (1844–1905) were court martialed and dishonorably discharged on trumped-up charges (and both were posthumously pardoned). The Brownsville Affair of 1906 was perhaps the most blatant example of racial discrimination against Black servicemen. The 25th Infantry was stationed at Fort Brown, just outside Brownsville, Texas. On August 13, 1906, Black soldiers of the 25th were accused of an attack on a white woman and the shooting of two white men, one of whom died. Though the soldiers had all been in their barracks during the times in question and the case against them was supported only by hearsay allegations and dubious planted evidence, 167 of the men were dishonorably discharged—a decision supported by President Theodore Roosevelt. All those charged were exonerated in 1972, at which time only one of the men was still alive. As the United States entered World War I, there were complaints from white officers over the possibility that they might have to serve under Colonel Young, who would be in line for promotion to brigadier general. Young was, however, placed on the inactive list at the rank of colonel on account a medical examination revealing high blood pressure and kidney problems. This was widely seen as an expedient way to shove Young aside and avoid racial tensions, and the medical diagnosis remained a source of controversy for years thereafter. This was acknowledged over a century later, when on April 29, 2022, Young was posthumously promoted to brigadier general.

As was the case both before and after the United States' entrance into World War I, young African American men joined the service in hopes not only of securing employment but that when the war was over, having proven themselves by defending their country's interests, they would be accorded a more equal measure of rights and opportunity, and institutionalized racism would at least be somewhat reduced.

Explanation and Analysis of the Document

This image of some of the veterans of the 369th who had won the Croix de Guerre, France's medal recognizing exceptional valor and heroism in combat, was taken in 1919, after the hostilities had ended—probably in January or February 1919, just before the soldiers embarked from France to New York for deactivation. The 369th had, by this time, become famous. The photo of these heroes would surely have inspired pride and hope for a brighter future for the African American community. In the front row (left to right) are Private Ed Williams, Private Herbert Taylor, Private Leon Fraitor, and Private Ralph Hawkins. In the back row are Sergeant H. D. Prinas, Sergeant Dan Storms, Private Joe Williams, Private Alfred Hanley, and Corporal T. W. Taylor.

The 369th Infantry was first assigned in 1917 for preliminary training to Fort Whitman in New York, then for more intensive training to Camp Wadsworth in South Carolina, before being deployed to France in January 1918. At first assigned to noncombat labor duty because many of the all-white units refused to fight alongside them, on April 8, 1918, the members of the 369th were transferred to the French army, where they were accepted on equal terms with other units and subject to little or no racism from the French. Under French command and using French equipment, while donning American uniforms, the 369th participated heavily in the Second Battle of the Marne (July 15–18, 1918) and the Meuse-Argonne Offensive (September 26–November 11, 1919). By war's end, the 369th had suffered greater casualties than any other American unit and had likewise logged more time on the front lines than any of the others. It was also the most highly decorated American unit: besides the 170 who won the Croix de Guerre, the 369th received a unit citation, and one soldier, Henry Johnson (1892–1929), was posthumously conferred the Congressional Medal of Honor in 2015. It was not until 2021 that the regiment was awarded the Congressional Gold Medal.

Unfortunately, the new harmonious future between the races that the returning veterans had hoped for did not materialize. Instead, the United States fell into what was probably the lowest ebb of the "nadir" in race relations, the early 1920s. The resurgent Ku Klux Klan became a powerful national political force, openly staging mass rallies in Washington, D.C., and even capturing the government of two northern states, Indiana and Oregon. The pace of lynching and anti-Black riots only accelerated. To make it worse, rumors spread that returning African American soldiers had been motivated by the success of the Bolshevik Revolution in Russia and were carrying home a communist ideology. This was given impetus by an ill-considered remark by President Woodrow Wilson to that effect. Considerable tension was generated by the immediate postwar economic situation. With war production halted, there were fewer jobs, and with soldiers of both races being discharged there were not enough positions of employment to go around, resulting in often violent competition for such positions as there were.

From January 22 to December 27, 1919 (but more frequently during the months of May through August), at least sixty riots broke out in various locations throughout the United States in which white gangs attacked African Americans. This became known as the "Red Summer" of 1919. The exact number of deaths has never been precisely determined, though they likely numbered in the hundreds. Contrary to previous outbreaks of white mob violence, however, there were many instances of African Americans fighting back and even getting the better of their attackers, notably during the riots in Chicago (July 27–August 12) and Washington, D.C. (July 19–24). The Red Summer thus marked a turning point after which African American demands for equal treatment steadily became stronger and more insistent. A sense of pride also manifested itself in the cultural and artistic revival known as the Harlem Renaissance (though it was a nationwide phenomenon and not confined to Harlem, New York). Several veterans of the 369th Infantry, in their civilian roles, would play prominent roles in the Harlem Renaissance as jazz musicians and composers; these included Noble Sissle, Charles Luckyth Roberts, Otis Johnson, and Janes Reese Europe.

The 369th Infantry Regiment was reconstituted in 1942 and saw action in the Pacific Theatre in World War II, including combat in New Guinea and the Philippines.

—Raymond Pierre Hylton

Questions for Further Study

1. What might have motivated young African Americans to join the U.S. military service?

2. What effect might the image of the Harlem Hellfighters have had on an African American audience at the time? What might the photographer have intended the effect to be?

3. What factors and events contributed to making the first decades of the twentieth century a "low point" in civil rights and racial harmony?

Further Reading

Books

Harris, Bill. *The Hellfighters of Harlem: African American Soldiers Who Fought for the Right to Fight for Their Country*. New York: Carroll & Graf, 2003.

Harris, Stephen L. *Harlem's Hell Fighters: The African-American 369th Infantry in World War I*. Washington, DC: Potomac Books, 2003.

Krugler, David F. *1919, the Year of Racial Violence: How African Americans Fought Back*. New York: Cambridge University Press, 2015.

McWhirter, Cameron. *Red Summer: The Summer of 1919 and the Awakening of Black America*. New York: St. Martin's Griffin, 2012.

Nelson, Peter N. *A More Unbending Battle: The Harlem Hellfighters' Struggle for Freedom in WWI and Equality at Home*. New York: Basic Civitas, 2009.

Websites

"Photographs of the 369th Infantry and African Americans during World War I." National Archives, September 23, 2016. https://www.archives.gov/education/lessons/369th-infantry.

Photograph After Raid On IWW Headquarters

AUTHOR/CREATOR Unknown	IMAGE TYPE PHOTOGRAPHS
DATE 1919	SIGNIFICANCE Illustrates the disdain the U.S. government held for labor union like the Industrial Workers of the World during the era of World War I

Overview

The picture symbolizes the disdain that federal government held for radical organizations like the Industrial Workers of the World (IWW) during the World War I era. The federal agents who raided the group's headquarters on November 15, 1919, wanted to find information that could be used to deport the group's leaders. At the very least, they wanted to destroy the IWW's ability to function.

While it is commonly assumed that the government campaign against the IWW did destroy that organization, the group actually persisted. The survival of this photograph demonstrates that it persisted because the IWW kept it to show how much the federal government hated them and to evoke sympathy for their cause.

About the Artist

The photographer is unknown.

Context

The Industrial Workers of the World (IWW), nicknamed the Wobblies, formed in 1905. Unlike most unions at that time, the IWW embraced revolutionary socialism and organizing workers across industries regardless of skill level. Because of their politics, both employers and the United States government kept IWW members under close surveillance, and their labor actions often led to retaliatory violence by right-wing mobs against the group's organizers.

The outbreak of World War I led the federal government to suppress many radical organizations, but especially the IWW. The Espionage Act of 1917, which limited speech that impeded the war effort, led directly to raids against the IWW all over the country since the federal government contended that the group's opposition to the war made its members subject to prosecution under that law. In 1918, in Chicago, the government brought 113 Wobblies to trial at once, each charged with over 100 separate crimes. Every one of them was found guilty. Most defendants got long prison sentences. Other IWW members were locked up in jails across the United States. The organization appeared to be on the brink of collapse, and the raid against the group's headquarters at 115 East 10th

Document Image

The IWW Headquarters following the raid in 1919
(Labadie Photograph Collection, University of Michigan)

Street in New York City was supposed to provide the death blow.

This New York City raid is sometimes counted as one of the so-called Palmer Raids, a series of raids against radical organizations instigated by Attorney General A. Mitchell Palmer in the years following World War I. While this raid does fit the pattern of other raids from this era, it is better to think of the wartime moves against the IWW as a preview of these later raids. With the IWW effectively crippled during the war, rounding up its remaining leaders as part of a broad move against all radicals was practically an afterthought. The way in which the agents treated the IWW headquarters during the 1919 raid demonstrated the federal government's continued contempt for the union. The Sedition Act of 1918 gave the government new powers to suppress speech, which it used in 1919 against the remaining members of the Wobblies.

Despite the government's effort to destroy the Industrial Workers of the World, the organization persists to this day. In 1927, for example, it led a long strike against coal companies in Colorado. While no longer a particularly large union, the IWW has always been good curators of its own history. The picture of its New York City Office after the raid has been used in multiple ways to illustrate the disdain that the government once showed that organization—a disdain that could not destroy a labor organization full of committed radicals.

Explanation and Analysis of the Document

Who took this picture? The name of the photographer has been lost to history, but it is worth considering which side of the labor struggle had the most interest in documenting the destruction of the New York City office of the Industrial Workers of the World. The U.S. government was trying to destroy the Wobblies—to arrest their leaders and many of their members, or at least deport them out of the country. The fact that federal agents destroyed the office while looking for evidence did not help that cause, and neither did this photograph of the destruction.

The IWW wanted to evoke sympathy from the public to attract support in its life-or-death struggle. While it seems possible that this photo may have been taken as evidence in the case against IWW members, the union

itself is the reason that the photo has been preserved and popularized. This particular copy, for example, came from the files of the Sacco and Vanzetti Defense Committee, which formed to protect to anarchists accused of robbery who were executed by the State of Massachusetts in 1927. Another copy is in the files of Emma Goldman, a radical whom the federal government deported to Russia about the same time as the government moved against the IWW. Regardless of who exactly took the picture, seeing what the government did to the headquarters helps paint the IWW in a sympathetic light by making the government appear oppressive.

This picture also fits the story of the raid that the IWW promulgated after it happened. The IWW members contended that armed agents who raided their headquarters on November 15, 1919, burst in and then beat fifty defenseless trade unionists who were just sitting around reading, talking, and playing checkers. Allegedly, the group huddled together to protect each other from the beatings, but they were all eventually expelled out onto the street so that the search for evidence could proceed. The next evening, the Wobblies' story went, all of those members who weren't hospitalized returned to the headquarters to resume their previous nonthreatening activities. When they first arrived, one of them might have taken this picture. Certainly, government agents who were determined to destroy the IWW were unlikely to have picked up after themselves before leaving.

The agents who sacked the office were looking for evidence that could be used to try members of the union organization for sedition. While the signs that remain in the picture are for union rallies, not every sign or piece of paper in a headquarters would have revealed the labor union's politics. That left plenty of paper that the government would have felt free to leave strewn on the floor. At the same time, IWW members were more than willing to explain their politics to anybody willing to listen. Therefore, signs such as the one in the back that read "Don't Mourn, Organize!!," a quote from the IWW martyr Joe Hill, didn't really tell agents anything that they didn't already know. Perhaps the most persuasive explanation for why the government sacked the offices of a labor organization that already appeared to be on its last legs was to intimidate its members even further.

If IWW members really did return the next day, then this photograph served as evidence that the Wobblies would not be intimidated. The persistence of the group beyond this raid into the present day only reinforces this attitude. The use of the picture to evoke sympathy for the organization after the IWW had supposedly been destroyed testified to its continued existence. While the IWW is not nearly as strong as it once was, the continued use of the Espionage Act against groups with unpopular political opinions makes the way that the IWW was once treated historically important.

—Jonathan Rees

Questions for Further Study

1. Do you think the raid against IWW headquarters was justified? Why or why not?

2. Do you think the IWW is a reliable historical source? Why or why not?

3. Why does it matter who took this picture?

Further Reading

Books

Dubofsky, Melvyn. *We Shall Be All: A History of the IWW*. New York: Quadrangle, 1969.

McCartin, Joseph A. *Labor's Great War: The Struggle for Industrial Democracy and the Origins of Modern Labor Relations, 1912–1921*. Chapel Hill: University of North Carolina Press, 1998.

Websites

Evans, Hew. "An East Village Raid on the 'Wobblies' Hobbles, but Doesn't Destroy, the I.W.W." *Off the Grid: Village Preservation Blog*, November 15, 2021. https://www.villagepreservation.org/2021/11/15/the-1919-iww-raid/.

Parfitt, Steven. "The Justice Department Campaign against the IWW, 1917–1920," IWW History Project, University of Washington, 2016. https://depts.washington.edu/iww/justice_dept.shtml.

"The Only Way To Handle It" Cartoon

Author/Creator Hallahan	**Image Type** Cartoons
Date 1921	**Significance** Illustrated a common opinion about a recently passed congressional bill that restricted immigration from Europe by means of a quota system

Overview

This cartoon addresses public anxiety about the influx of immigrants from eastern and southern Europe. In the aftermath of World War I, the Russian Revolution of 1917, and the spread of radicalism throughout much of Europe and anarchism in America, Congress was under pressure to severely restrict immigration, particularly from the "less desirable" countries of eastern and southern Europe. The 1921 Emergency Quota Law, also called the Immigration Restriction Act and the Emergency Immigration Act, imposed quotas on immigration based on the potential immigrant's country of birth. An annual quota for each country was established at 3 percent of the number of persons from that country as recorded in the 1910 census. This act would be entrenched in 1924 with the passage of the National Origins Act.

About the Artist

The cartoon identifies the artist as a person named Hallahan, but no information about such a person is available. The cartoon appeared in the May 7, 1921, issue of the *Literary Digest*, a general interest weekly magazine that had been published since 1890. The magazine was founded by Isaac Kaufmann Funk, one of the cofounders of Funk & Wagnalls, which published the magazine. The *Literary Digest* later merged with two other magazines, *Public Opinion* and *Current Opinion*. The magazine lost credibility and ceased publication in 1938 after it made a highly off-target prediction about the outcome of the 1936 presidential election.

Context

A pressing issue that faced the presidential administrations of Warren G. Harding and Calvin Coolidge in the 1920s was immigration. That the United States was and is a nation of immigrants is an oft-repeated truism, but the immigrants who arrived on American shores tended to do so in waves. Throughout much of the nineteenth century, most of the nation's "old immigrants," the first wave, were from the countries of northern Europe: England, Ireland, Germany, France, and the Scandinavian countries, although the immigrant population of the West Coast was dominated by people from China. In the 1890s, however, when the second wave began, the ethnic composition of immigrants began to change. Many of the "new immigrants"

Document Image

"The Only Way to Handle It"
(Library of Congress)

were from Italy, Greece, and the Slavic countries, along with many Russian Jews. From 1892 until 1914 (when immigration came to a virtual halt because of the outbreak of World War I), about 17 million immigrants passed through Ellis Island, the New York City point of entry less than a mile from the Statue of Liberty in New York Harbor. Most of the immigrants in this wave were from eastern and southern Europe. It is noteworthy that by 1910, between 40 and 50 percent of the U.S. population consisted for foreign-born immigrants and their children.

The "new immigrants" were not always greeted with open arms. It was not long before "nativist" Americans who traced their ancestry to the old immigrant countries began to see the new immigrants from presumably less-desirable countries as the source of dirt, disease, and crime. Many of them looked odd to native-born Americans and dressed in fashions the Americans considered strange. They had unfamiliar habits and ate unfamiliar foods, and it was believed that they could not become part of the American melting pot. In 1924, for example, the magazine *Current Opinion* wrote: "There is no blinking the fact that certain races do not fuse with us, and have no intention of trying to become Americans. The Poles, for example, are determined to remain Polish." (At the time, the word *race* was often used to mean *ethnicity*.) In response to this wave of immigration, the Immigration Restriction League, which had been formed in 1894, campaigned for limits on immigration based on its members' belief in the genetic superiority of Nordic (i.e., northern European) peoples. Their efforts gained support during World War I, when foreigners in general were looked on with suspicion. In the aftermath of the war, many Americans were frightened by the influx of immigrants who were fleeing the poverty and starvation of postwar Europe. Organizations such as the Ku Klux Klan fueled this fear.

Another source of fear was the so-called Red Scare of the postwar years. (Red is the color typically associated with communism.) In the wake of the Russian Revolution of 1917, many Americans came to see eastern European immigrants as Bolsheviks, referring to the Communist political party that had seized power in Russia. These people were regarded as a threat to American security, and their views were confirmed by a number of events. One was a massive strike against the steel industry in 1919; many eastern European workers took part in the strike. Race riots in many cities rocked the country, and anarchists and commu-

nists were threatening to overthrow the U.S. government. On June 3, 1919, a bomb exploded at the home of Attorney General A. Mitchell Palmer in Washington, D.C. Other bombs were mailed to various public figures (although they were never delivered). In late 1919 and into 1920, police rounded up and arrested 10,000 people in the "Palmer raids," and many of these people were deported. On September 16, 1920, a bomb thought to be the work of foreign anarchists exploded on Wall Street in New York City. One of the most controversial criminal cases of the era was the trial of Nicola Sacco and Bartolomeo Vanzetti, Italian immigrants accused of a daring holdup in Massachusetts. They were found guilty in 1921 and eventually executed in an atmosphere of Red hysteria. For a century, historians have debated the question of their guilt, with some believing that they were the victims of prejudice against Italians.

Meanwhile, Congress had been trying to forge a consensus on steps to restrict immigration from Europe, particularly eastern and southern Europe. To this end, in 1907, Congress authorized the formation of the Dillingham Commission, named for Senator William Paul Dillingham of Vermont, to investigate the causes and impact of recent immigration. Following the lead of the Immigration Restriction League and drawing on eugenics theories of racial hierarchies, the commission endeavored to show "scientifically" that eastern and southern European immigrants were unable to assimilate and were degrading the quality of American life. In 1911 the commission issued a forty-one-volume report containing its conclusions. Among other recommendations, it called for literacy tests for new immigrants (which Congress authorized in 1917) and immigration quotas—that is, "limitation of the number of each race arriving each year to a certain percentage of that race arriving during a given period of years."

Eventually, all of these factors coalesced in the passage of the National Origins Act of 1924, but in the meantime, Congress passed a stopgap measure in 1921, the Emergency Quota Law, also called the Immigration Restriction Act or the Emergency Immigration Act. This act limited the number of immigrants to 3 percent of the foreign-born of each nationality already living in the United States as of the 1910 census. The 1924 act entrenched this system. Thus, for example, 51,000 immigrants would be admitted each year from Germany, 34,000 from Great Britain and Northern Ireland, and 9,500 from Sweden, but just 5,900 from Poland, 3,800 from Italy, and 671 from Yugoslavia. The total number of immigrants was to be just under 165,000, less than a fifth of the pre–World War I annual average. By selecting the 1890 census rather than a more recent one, immigrants from the countries of the "old immigrants" would be favored over those from the less-favored countries. Meanwhile, however, the 1921 act relied on the 1910 census.

The 1921 act, which formed the basis of the widely reproduced *Literary Digest* cartoon, was called "An Act to limit the immigration of aliens into the United States." The act stated: "That the number of aliens of any nationality who may be admitted under the immigration laws to the United States in any fiscal year shall be limited to 3 per centum of the number of foreign-born persons of such nationality resident in the United States as determined by the United States census of 1910 . . . (b) For the purposes of this Act nationality shall be determined by country of birth, treating as separate countries the colonies or dependencies for which separate enumeration was made in the United States census of 1910. . . ."

Explanation and Analysis of the Document

The cartoon accompanied an article titled "An Alien Antidumping Bill." In the upper left-hand corner is a legend consisting of the word "Europe." A large funnel extends across the Atlantic Ocean, with the small end of the funnel reaching land identified as the "U.S.A." At the top, large end of the funnel, an immense number of people are shown trying to enter the funnel and pass through it to the United States. Standing watch over the small end is the figure of Uncle Sam. He is holding in one hand a copy of the 1921 law; in the other he holds a sign that says "Gate" with another sign that says "3%." The signs are inserted into the funnel to cut off the flow of immigration. A small number of people, the 3 percent, are emerging onto U.S. soil from the small end of the funnel. It was thought by the *Literary Digest* that with regard to immigration, the 1921 law was "the only way to handle it." The cartoon is indicative of the widespread sentiment that immigration to the United States had to be restricted.

—Michael J. O'Neal

Questions for Further Study

1. What was the purpose of the Emergency Quota Law?

2. How did the editorial cartoon illustrate the immigration problem as it was perceived at the time?

3. In what ways, if any, did the cartoon play on the fears of many Americans about immigration?

Further Reading

Books

Anderson, Kristen L. *Immigration in American History.* New York: Routledge, 2021.

Benton-Cohen, Katherine. *Inventing the Immigration Problem: The Dillingham Commission and Its Legacy.* Cambridge, MA: Harvard University Press, 2018.

Bon Tempo, Carl J., and Hasia R. Diner. *Immigration: An American History.* New Haven, CT: Yale University Press, 2022.

Daniels, Roger. *Coming to America: A History of Immigration and Ethnicity in American Life,* 2nd ed. New York: Harper-Collins, 2002.

Douglas, Karen Manges. "National Origins Systems." In *Encyclopedia of Race, Ethnicity, and Society,* edited by Richard Schaefer. Thousand Oaks, CA: Sage Publications, 2008.

Pula, James S., ed. *United States Immigration, 1800–1965: A History in Documents.* Peterborough, Ontario, Canada: Broadview Press, 2020.

Yang, Jia Lynn. *One Mighty and Irresistible Tide: The Epic Struggle over American Immigration, 1924–1965.* New York: Norton, 2021.

Websites

"An Alien Antidumping Bill." *Literary Digest,* May 7, 1921. http://www.oldmagazinearticles.com/1921-immigration-restrictions#.YvFWUeDEflU.

Diamond, Anna. "The 1924 Law That Slammed the Door on Immigrants and the Politicians Who Pushed It Back Open." *Smithsonian Magazine,* May 19, 2020. https://www.smithsonianmag.com/history/1924-law-slammed-door-immigrants-and-politicians-who-pushed-it-back-open-180974910/.

"The Immigration Act of 1924 (The Johnson-Reed Act)." U.S. State Department, Office of the Historian. https://history.state.gov/milestones/1921-1936/immigration-act.

"Primary Sources: The 1920s: Immigration." Christian Newport University. https://cnu.libguides.com/1920s/immigration.

"Table of the Quota System Targeting Specific Immigrant Groups." American Social History Project. https://shec.ashp.cuny.edu/items/show/1230.

Zeidel, Robert F. "A 1911 Report Set America on a Path of Screening Out 'Undesirable' Immigrants." *Smithsonian Magazine,* July 16, 2018. https://www.smithsonianmag.com/history/1911-report-set-america-on-path-screening-out-undesirable-immigrants-180969636/.

Assembly Line Photograph

Author/Creator Detroit Publishing Company **Date** 1923 **Image Type** Photographs	**Significance** Portrayal of an early assembly line, the culmination of generations of development in labor-saving devices, management practices, and production methods that, when married with the American values of speed, innovation, and precision, created a production process that would change the world

Overview

The photo depicts two assembly-line workers installing finished components on a rolling automobile frame, probably a Ford Model T, in 1923. During this period, known as the Progressive Era in the United States, businesses and government demonstrated a particular zeal for scientific management. Developed by Frederick Winslow Taylor, scientific management was the intentional study of manufacturing. Taylor studied all aspects of manufacture, from shoveling coal to the necessity for breaks for laborers to restore physical stamina. Taylor argued that hiring, training, and paying the right person for each task was critical to keeping production levels high. Automobile manufacturers, including Henry Ford and his Ford Motor Company, tried several different manufacturing techniques to organize their manufacturing process.

The production of automobiles was well suited to the use of the assembly line. Automobiles are the final form of hundreds, thousands, or tens of thousands of parts. At the turn of the twentieth century, all vehicle manufacturing was completed by bringing parts to one location in a factory. Here a group of workers familiar with many operations would hammer, file, weld, adjust, and bolt components together to achieve a unique assembly that often was troublesome to repair because of the custom-built parts and configuration. As new orders for automobiles increased, manufacturers began to search for methods to increase production efficiency.

Henry Ford took this several steps further. Through intensive study of the tasks required to build an automobile, Ford broke each task down into simple steps requiring little skill or knowledge that took roughly the same amount of time. This reduced or eliminated the need for many skilled workers. Ford hired industrial architect Albert Kahn to design a three-floor reinforced-cement factory design in which parts were assembled on upper floors and delivered by chutes to the factory floor where assemblers needed them and as close to hand level as possible. Ford demanded that all parts and components be delivered to the factory floor with exacting standards so that no further adjustment by the assembly worker was necessary. Then Ford placed his workers with their parts at fixed points where the work would travel in front of them. Ford's assembly line allowed each of his employees to repeatedly conduct a straightforward task, which greatly

Document Image

1923 photograph of an early assembly line
(Library of Congress)

simplified the training required for employees. The assembly line eliminated unproductive employee time traveling from automobile to automobile, gathering parts, or waiting on other employees to finish their tasks.

About the Artist

The Detroit Photographic Company was founded in 1885 by publisher, banker, and investor William A. Livingstone Jr. and photographer Edwin H. Husher. Detroit Photographic Company was a franchisee of a Swiss printing company that had patented a process to colorize black and white negatives realistically. Initially a printer of religious books and calendars, the firm shifted production in 1897 to postcards and high-quality three-dimension stereoview cards. When respected landscape photographer William Henry Jackson joined the company in 1898, the Detroit Photographic Company immediately gained nearly 10,000 negatives, significantly increasing its library.

Livingstone and Husher convinced Jackson to become president of the Detroit Photographic Company. Jackson grew the publication firm by employing over a dozen salespeople and some forty artists to produce sales and catalog products and souvenirs for companies and the popular industrial tourism industry. The Detroit Photographic Company likely would have used images like this to create postcards and souvenirs of Ford's factory for tourists. While the picture is very clear, it is not colorized, as the color printing process used a black and white negative to create a series of overlapping jigs to print color on top of the image. Under Jackson's management, the Detroit Photographic Company grew to hold more than 40,000 photographic negatives and expanded into publishing educational tools and inexpensive wall art. Though business was strong for the Detroit Photographic Company, new printing methods that did not require the Swiss processes to produce quality materials and declining sales brought on in part by the Great Depression resulted in the business closing in 1932.

Context

The photo depicts assembly-line workers installing finished components on an automobile frame, most likely a Ford Model T. Each worker would install only one component before the automobile rolled along to another station. Very likely, neither of these men would know how to complete tasks elsewhere in the factory but knew they were operating as part of a team. If they did not complete their task in the time allotted, the whole factory had to stop. Breaking tasks down to these precisely timed actions required several innovations to be developed before the assembly line could be realized.

Mass-production methods began as early as 750 in Chinese royal workshops and were used extensively in the Venetian Arsenal of the twelfth century; however, mass production did not automatically translate into production speed. Before the Industrial Revolution, manufacturing depended on highly skilled craftspeople who made each component by hand to construct a final product. This form of craft production was slow and required skilled labor. This allowed laborers to control production speed, and it often took years of training to educate a new laborer. This educational process was firmly in the hands of master laborers. These craftsmen often dictated to factory owners who could work where and how the factory would operate.

The meatpacking industry heavily influenced the development of the assembly line. By the 1840s, the Chicago meatpacking industry had pioneered the disassembly of animals through a very efficient process that moved hundreds of animal carcasses by a pully system in front of stationary workers who would each remove a specific meat cut. Because each animal was different, many of these workers were highly skilled butchers. Industrial tourism was a typical vacation activity in the early twentieth century. When William Klann, a Ford machinist, visited the Swift meatpacking plant in Chicago in 1913, he returned to Detroit with an idea to reverse the process.

The development of machine tools and control jigs made quality interchangeable parts functional and relatively reliable. However, these required the standardization of material (wood roughly cut to size, for example, or a specific thickness of an iron sheet) and skilled craftspeople to operate effectively. Many of the earliest machine tools were powered by water wheels, windmills, or steam engines. This required that factories be constructed near water or windy prominences. Machinery was powered through thick shafts and leather belts that physically connected the machinery to the power source, limiting how factories could be arranged. The adoption of electricity as a source of power meant that factories were able to be built away from water or windy outcroppings and allowed machine tools to be placed where laborers needed them on the factory floor. Albert Kahn's ingenuous design and construction methods provided Ford, and later other manufacturers, an open floor factory that was as strong as steel manufacture, but for a fraction of the price or time to construct.

The assembly line is a balancing process in which a defined order of operation is translated to a series of simple tasks that unskilled workers—aided by specialized tools, fixtures, and jigs—can complete in a standardized cycle of time. This reduced the amount of skilled labor needed and lowered the costs of production while placing managers, not craftspeople, in charge of production. Through continued experimentation with layout, tasks, and tools, by the fall of 1913, Ford had reduced the production time for a Model T from twelve hours to an hour and a half while reducing workforce requirements by almost 800 percent. This allowed Ford to continue to reduce the price of his finished product and reduce the number of hours his employees worked while increasing the pay of his assembly-line employees.

Explanation and Analysis of the Document

William A. Livingstone Jr. was an influential politician and businessman in Detroit in the late nineteenth and early twentieth centuries. Owning a steamship transportation company, the *Detroit Evening Journal*, the Detroit Photographic Company, and the president of the Dime Savings Bank of Detroit, Livingstone was a diversified and influential investor. Livingstone's *Detroit Evening Journal* was the first to report on Henry Ford's 1896 invention of the Quadricycle—a gasoline-powered engine mounted to a frame with four bicycle tires. This was terrible timing for Ford, as a lawyer named George Selden had secured a patent in 1895 that created a monopoly on automobile production in the United States. While many companies elected to pay 1.25 percent for each vehicle produced as royalties to Selden, Ford elected to fight the patent in court. The eight-year court battle between Ford and Selden was popular news in the *Detroit Evening Journal*. Livingstone, through the Dime Savings Bank of Detroit, seeing the potential in Ford's products and methods, provided Ford with a line of credit that allowed him to secure a partnership that would become

the Ford Motor Company in 1903. The court battle and its media coverage provided publicity for the fledgling company. The media coverage also created a public image of Ford as the hero of the everyday man fighting an immoral corporate monopoly.

The assembly line was a significant turning point in economic and cultural history. Most commonly associated with Henry Ford and his Model T automobile, the assembly line was not the product of any one person but the combination of several ideas and processes that, for one reason or another, had never been harnessed together before. Since 1913 the assembly line has been constantly adapted, improved, and reorganized to produce food, consumer goods, household appliances, office equipment, tools, and electronics. The assembly line did at least two things very well: it increased efficiencies and lowered costs in production. Because of the increased production of goods at lower prices, manufacturers could make more money by reducing the prices of their goods while increasing wages. This meant that more people could purchase these goods, which increased demand. This piling-on effect made mass production of more goods possible in many more industries and applications. Though many other technologies, ideas, and social institutions unquestionably played a role in its over 100-year existence, the assembly line has done more to rapidly increase the quality of life for more people around the globe than any other development in any similar period.

Ford employed a collection of employees that had experience in other industries and was trusting enough in his staff to allow them to experiment with ideas, methods, and organization—provided that the quality and production of the Ford automobile did not suffer. Progressing quickly from a simple rope tethering axels together to chain-driven cars on elevated rail lines, as pictured, the Ford assembly line quickly matured and continued to find new efficiencies. The continued reduction in price of a new Model T and the five-dollar-a-day pay for Ford employees meant that by 1916, fifteen weeks' pay would buy any employee a brand-new Model T. Ford, like many manufacturers, attracted workers by providing housing for workers and their families as a part of their compensation. Ford also offered English language courses and encouraged employees to join the company temperance society. Ford's methods significantly increased worker safety and greatly reduced workplace injuries.

While this may sound noble, these were essentially practical. Ford attracted many immigrant laborers who had trouble adapting to the rigid schedules of the factory. Ford found that he had to hire nearly one thousand workers to have net retention of one hundred in just a few weeks. Ford was a teetotaler who had a very negative opinion about alcohol consumption; employees who drank on the job or frequented saloons were subject to eviction and loss of pay. Additionally, many workers felt alienated and bored because of the repetitive nature of their work, which was often required to take place in cramped, unergonomic spaces. The relatively high wages, quality housing, English classes, and temperance societies encouraged Americanization, socialization, and retention of Ford employees.

Ford's assembly-line methods allowed the automobile to be accessible to the growing American middle class. Production soared, with the one millionth Model T rolling off the line in 1915 and the twenty-five millionth produced by 1937. Ford rapidly expanded his production methods to Ford production lines in France, Britain, Denmark, Germany, and Japan, causing more than 250 competing companies not using assembly-line methods to close their doors by 1925.

—Bryant Macfarlane

Questions for Further Study

1. Ford is said to have said of the Model T, "A customer can have a car painted any color that he wants, so long as it is black." Why would Ford limit his car models to one color?

2. At the beginning of the twentieth century, many labor unions refused to represent unskilled laborers, minorities, or women. Why would these labor unions adopt policies like this? What do Ford's company policies suggest about his opinions about organized labor?

3. Imagine yourself as an immigrant who has gotten a job on the Ford assembly line. Your supervisor tells you about the classes and societies available to you. Would you want to participate in courses or organizations offered by the company? Which of these sounds more beneficial to you? Why?

Further Reading

Books

Freeman, Joshua B. *Behemoth: A History of the Factory and the Making of the Modern World.* New York: W.W. Norton, 2018.

Hounshell, David A. *From the American System to Mass Production, 1800-1932: The Development of Manufacturing Technology in the United States.* Baltimore: Johns Hopkins University Press, 1985.

Nye, David E. *America's Assembly Line.* Cambridge, Mass: MIT Press, 2013.

Websites

"Henry Ford: Assembly Line." Henry Ford Museum of American Innovation. 2022. https://www.thehenryford.org/collections-and-research/digital-collections/expert-sets/7139/.

"The Moving Assembly Line and the Five-Dollar Workday." Ford Motor Corporation. 2020. https://corporate.ford.com/articles/history/moving-assembly-line.html.

Documentaries/Films

American Experience, Season 25, Episode 4: "Henry Ford." Sarah Colt, director. PBS. Aired January 29, 2013.

Master Hands. Chevrolet Motor Co. and Jam Handy Organization, producers. National Film Preservation Foundation. 1936; 2022. https://www.filmpreservation.org/sponsored-films/screening-room/master-hands-1936.

Modern Marvels, Season 7, Episode 32: "The Evolution of the Assembly Line." Bruce Nash and Don Cambou, producers. History Channel. Aired October 19, 2000.

Modern Times. Charlie Chaplin, director. United Artists. 1936.

Judge Magazine Cover: The Roaring Twenties

Author/Creator John Held Jr.	**Image Type** Illustrations
Date 1925	**Significance** A magazine cover that captures the spirit of the Roaring Twenties

Overview

For its New Year's issue in 1925, *Judge*, a satirical magazine, included this image on its cover. By the middle of the 1920s, the nation was deep into the "Roaring Twenties," with its carefree excess, sense of personal freedom, and rejection of the values of earlier generations. In particular, women—who had earned the vote in 1920—were feeling newly empowered and were rejecting the straitlaced respectability of their mothers and grandmothers. In a few bold strokes and splashes of color, this cover captures much of the spirit of the decade as experienced by young people.

About the Artist

Although the artist who created this cover is not specifically identified, it almost certainly was created by John Held Jr., a cartoonist, printmaker, illustrator, sculptor, and author and one of the best-known illustrators of the 1920s. In many respects, Held was the chronicler of the Roaring Twenties, with cartoons and other drawings that captured the spirit of the age by depicting people dancing, drinking, driving, swimming at the beach, and taking part in other popular activities. Held was born in 1889. During World War I he worked for U.S. Naval Intelligence in Central America as a cartographer and artist. In 1922 he created the cover for F. Scott Fitzgerald's *Tales of the Jazz Age*, and in 1924 he created the cover for Edna Ferber's Pulitzer Prize–winning novel *So Big*. In 1925 a high school friend, Harold Ross, launched *The New Yorker* magazine—a magazine for urban sophisticates—and by 1927 Held's work was appearing in *The New Yorker* as well as in *Life*, *Vanity Fair*, and *Harper's Bazaar*. He also contributed illustrations and covers for *Judge* and *The Smart Set*. His cartoons and covers were immensely popular and defined the stylish image of the flapper and her boyfriend, whom he nicknamed Betty Co-Ed and Joe College; *Vanity Fair* went so far as to assert that he invented the flapper. During the 1930s he lost most of the fortune he had amassed in the 1920s. He died in 1958.

Judge was a weekly satirical magazine. It was first published in 1881 and ran until 1947. The founders of the magazine, cartoonist James Albert Wales, publisher Frank Tousey, and author George H. Jessop, had been defectors from its better-known rival, *Puck*. The magazine achieved considerable success, reaching a circulation of 100,000 by 1912.

Document Image

The New Year's 1925 cover of Judge magazine
(Everett Collection Inc / Alamy)

Context

Mention the 1920s—the "Roaring Twenties"—and a host of trends in fashion, music, entertainment, and personal behavior come to mind. It was the era of speakeasies and bathtub gin and bootleggers, of cosmetics and sheer nylon hosiery, of rising hemlines and falling (by the wayside) corsets. It was the era of the Charleston and the Lindy Hop, of jazz clubs and the Cotton Club, of dance marathons and flagpole sitting, of Prohibition and sexual liberation, of the first Miss America pageant, of bohemians and flappers such as the one depicted on the poster. The Roaring Twenties gave America Eddie Cantor, Florence Ziegfeld, Charles Lindbergh, Louis Armstrong, Duke Ellington, Rudolph Valentino, Houdini, and Al Capone. It produced the Harlem Renaissance, the New York Renaissance basketball team ("the Rens"), Babe Ruth, Charles Atlas, Red Grange (the "Galloping Ghost"), golfer Bobby Jones (and his putter, "Calamity Jane"), the Four Horsemen of Notre Dame, and the birth of the National Football League. In downtown theaters, the "talkies" became all the rage, so much so that by 1930 the number of movie admissions *per week* was more than 100 million. Cars, radios, and refrigerators—wonders of modern technology—were becoming more and more commonplace in American homes. The spread of the automobile, in particular, made Americans more mobile, opening up avenues of entertainment that formerly had been closed by distance. And grandmothers were shocked by the willingness of young women to get into cars and ride off with young men who might have had more on their minds than just driving.

It was an era with its own slang. A person who was cool or trendy was "hip to the jive." Bootleg liquor was often called "coffin varnish" because much of it contained poisonous ingredients. Otherwise it could be called "giggle juice," and a person who was consuming copious amounts of giggle juice at a "juice joint" was "on a toot." Anything that was the "bee's knees," the "cat's meow," or the "cat's pajamas," was excellent. "Get a wiggle on!" was an incentive to "get a move on," "let's get going." "Glad rags" were fancy clothes worn during a night out on the town—and a person out on the town who perhaps needed to use the restroom would announce that he was going to "iron his shoelaces."

In the aftermath of World War I, the people of the United States were weary. They were weary of the war and the privations it created. They were weary of the destruction and loss of life. They were weary of learning about the horror and brutality of the war from young writers and thinkers. They were weary of the curtailments of freedom of speech and the loss of civil liberties as the government tried to clamp down on sedition and treason. They were weary of the flu pandemic of 1918 that claimed the lives of 20 million people—some estimates are as high as 50 and even 100 million—worldwide. Americans were ready for a sea change. Put simply, they were ready to have some fun. Indeed, one of the most popular tunes of the decade was "Ain't We Got Fun."

The Eighteenth Amendment to the Constitution, the Prohibition amendment, added to the allure of drinking on the sly in speakeasies that were often raided by police. The Nineteenth Amendment, extending the right to vote to women, seemed to open the door for a new kind of woman: confident, sophisticated, ready to take her place in society. The 1920s flapper—a term whose origins are disputed but that may have originated as a description of the way the new woman walked, flapping her arms with a self-confident swagger—broke free of her mother's restrictive, modest clothing and concern with respectability. She was determined to express herself, and the flapper survives as one of the most enduring images of the Roaring Twenties. The flapper wore lipstick and rouge, particularly after publications such as the *Saturday Evening Post*, which had condemned makeup early in the decade, started to carry cosmetics advertisements. She cut her hair in a short, blunt style called a bob. She plucked her eyebrows. She drove cars, attended movies, and adopted fads such as ping-pong and mah-jongg. She drank. Her raised hemlines would have scandalized her grandmother, and sheer nylons gave the impression of nude legs, which would have scandalized her grandmother even more. (Ohio and Utah passed laws requiring hem lengths to be no more than seven inches above the floor.) Her dress was lightweight and breezy. Many women, particularly those in the cities, adopted an exotic ancient Egyptian style after the discovery of the tomb of King Tutankhamen ("King Tut") in 1922. She flung aside her restrictive corset. She smoked: cigarette sales increased from about 1.5 billion before the war to 100 billion in 1928 as more women took up smoking. Further liberation was promised when Margaret Sanger opened her first birth control clinics in New York City in the 1920s.

To many Americans, particularly those in rural areas and those with strong religious views, the world seemed upside down, headed toward moral decay. In any case, photojournalists were on hand to document the antics of the flapper. Magazines printed pictures of young women wearing scandalous one-piece bathing suits, dancing the Charleston, or collapsing after dance marathons. They chronicled women's newfound leisure provided by economic growth—the U.S. gross domestic product rose from $688 billion in 1920 to $977 billion in 1929—and labor-saving devices. With stock market values soaring (only to crash in 1929), the party seemed as though it would never end.

Women were not the only ones who adopted the new style. Men, often influenced by "Joe College" types on campus, did as well. Men's fashions became looser and more relaxed. Trousers known as "Oxford bags" began to appear, and sporty men wore sweaters and short trousers called "knickers." A common fashion trend among men was "plus fours," trousers that extended four inches below the knee. Men adopted a wide array of jaunty hats, including the straw boater, the panama, the gambler, the homburg, the newsboy cap, the bowler, the derby, the fedora, and top hats. And of course, men stood ready to accompany their stylish and independent ladyloves on outings of all sorts—to the beach, on a drive in their motorcar, to a movie, or to a jazz club.

It was at the end of the decade that author Preston W. Slosson described the flapper. She was "breezy, slangy, and informal in manner; slim and boyish in form; covered in silk and fur that clung to her as close as an onion skin; with carmined cheeks and lips, plucked eyebrows, and close fitting helmet of hair; gay, plucky, and confident."

Five years after this cover appeared, the Roaring Twenties ceased to roar. The country—indeed, much of the industrialized world—began to endure the worst economic crisis in its history, the Great Depression. People lost fortunes. Poverty and unemployment were rampant. Banks failed. But for a decade after World War I, the world was one of endless possibilities.

Explanation and Analysis of the Document

The magazine cover relies on the bold colors and sharp lines of the Art Deco style of the 1920s. It also has a satirical quality, with stylized images of the two characters who dominate. A young man is driving a car. In the place of the license plate in front is the year, 1925. The man is smoking a cigarette in a cigarette holder. He is extending to the woman next to the car a bottle, mostly likely intended to be seen as a bottle of liquor. The woman, for her part, is representative of the flapper of the era. She is smoking a cigarette, her lower legs are exposed beneath her short (by 1920s standards) dress, she is wearing knee-length nylons, and a hint of petticoat can be seen. At the very bottom, in small print, are the words "They're Off!," suggesting not just that the two are about to take a car ride but that the young people of the decade are setting their own course for the future. In all, the image attempts to capture the spirit of the Roaring Twenties—in particular, the values of the bohemian "bright young things" of the decade.

—Michael J. O'Neal

Questions for Further Study

1. Why was the flapper of the 1920s regarded by some as scandalous?

2. What historical factors led to the excesses of the 1920s?

3. What role did technological developments play in the carefree quality of the Roaring Twenties?

4. Why was the decade of the 1920s called the "Roaring Twenties"?

Further Reading

Books

Bleitner, Thomas. *Women of the 1920s: Style, Glamour, and the Avant-Garde*. New York: Abbeville Press, 2019.

Gourley, Catherine. *Flappers and the New American Woman: Perceptions of Women from 1918 through the 1920s*. Minneapolis, MN: Twenty-First Century Books, 2007.

Henderson, Jake. *Roaring Twenties: A Condensed History of the 1920s in America*. Woodward, OK: Reading Through History, 2016.

Moore, Lucy. *Anything Goes*. London, England: Atlantic Books, 2009.

Ryan, Erica J. *When the World Broke in Two: The Roaring Twenties and the Dawn of America's Culture Wars*. Santa Barbara, CA: Praeger, 2018.

Sagert, Kelly Boyer. *Flappers: A Guide to an American Subculture*. Westport, CT: Greenwood Press, 2010.

Slosson, Preston W. *The Great Crusade and After, 1914–1918*. New York: AMS Press, 1930.

Zeitz, Joshua. *Flapper: A Madcap Story of Sex, Style, Celebrity, and the Women Who Made America Modern*. New York: Three Rivers Press, 2006.

Articles

Chalberg, John C. "The Spirit of the 1920s." *OAH Magazine of History* 20, no. 1 (January 2006): 11–14.

The Roaring '20s (single-issue magazine). *New York Times*, January 3, 2020.

Websites

"The Roaring 20s." *American Experience*, Image Gallery, PBS. https://www.pbs.org/wgbh/americanexperience/features/crash-roaring-20s/#:~:text=Many%20Americans%20spent%20the%201920s,market%20in%20liquor%20after%20Prohibition.

Thulin, Lila. "What Caused the Roaring Twenties? Not the End of a Pandemic (Probably)." *Smithsonian Magazine*, May 3, 2021. https://www.smithsonianmag.com/history/are-we-headed-roaring-2020s-historians-say-its-complicated-180977638/.

Edward Hopper: *Automat* Painting

Author/Creator Edward Hopper	**Image Type** Paintings
Date 1927	**Significance** A classic Edward Hopper painting that illustrates the loneliness of urban life during the 1920s

Overview

Even though the subject of this painting is in an urban and therefore crowded setting, the work illustrates Hopper's typical themes of loneliness and isolation. To achieve this effect, Hopper had to choose a particular angle and manipulate the natural properties of light to suggest that the subject is surrounded by nobody even though there had to be strong evidence of other people all around her. Hopper simply chose not to place most of that evidence in the painting.

The Automat is a highly appropriate place for these themes to be depicted. These restaurants were famous for being coin-operated, which meant no wait staff and no direct contact with anybody who made the food. While some people were amazed by the technology behind these places, others felt that the lack of human contact alienated customers. This kind of critique was common for technologies of all kinds during this period of American history.

About the Artist

The American painter Edward Hopper (1892–1967) was best known for his depiction of loneliness on canvas. Many of his painting depict single individuals in larger landscapes and often no individuals at all. While his work shares some similarity with the painters of the Ashcan School, who were known for their urban scenes that depicted popular culture, in particular among poor people, Hopper's paintings depict both urban and rural scenes and do not have the same focus on people from the working class.

Hopper was always reluctant to talk about himself or his work. Nevertheless, looking across any range of his paintings, the sadness in them is obvious. It seems like no coincidence, then, that Hopper rose to prominence during the 1930s, the decade of the Great Depression, even while many other artists struggled. Both his subject matter and his approach to lighting (especially since many of his urban paintings are set at night) suggest general attitudes about broader subjects like individuality, technology, and cities.

Hopper's best-known works include *Nighthawks* (1941), *Chop Suey* (1929), and *Early Sunday Morning* (1930). All of them share the same realist, lonely aesthetic as *Automat*. The mood in Hopper's urban paintings greatly influenced the filmmakers who cre-

Document Image

Edward Hopper's Automat
(© 2022 Heirs of Josephine N. Hopper / Licensed by Artists Rights Society, NY)

ated the so-called *film noir* detective movies of the 1940s and 1950s. His rural scenes influenced the looks of other scary movies as well, such as Alfred Hitchcock's *Psycho*.

Context

The Automat was a kind of cafeteria in which individual pieces of food were placed in separate compartments in banks of coin-operated vending machines. The first one appeared in Berlin, Germany, in 1895. Restaurateurs Joseph Horn and Frank Hardart licensed this technology, which they quickly improved upon after opening the first American Automat in Philadelphia in 1902. They brought the chain to New York City in 1912. In New York, people referred to the restaurant as the Automat, while in Philadelphia it was always Horn & Hardart's. Nevertheless, both names were on the signs in both locations.

While the restaurant grew significantly, especially during the post–World War II years, it never went beyond these two East Coast markets. By the 1950s, there were more than 100 Automats in New York City alone, and more than 800,000 people ate in an Automat each day. Even though they were confined to just two cities, at its height the size of the New York and Philadelphia markets made the Automat the most popular restaurant in the world. While the chain was restricted to just two markets, it was well known across the country because of its appearance in movies and because it was also a major tourist attraction.

Automats were famous for the low prices. Their cup of coffee was only a nickel, and it remained that way for decades even though the firm eventually lost money on every cup it sold. As depicted in Hopper's painting, Horn & Hardart's coffee offered patrons a low-cost item that they could sit and sip indefinitely, even if they didn't order food. The policy at Horn & Hardart was to let anyone sit indefinitely in the dining room, which symbolized their efforts to democratize dining in America. The fact that diners didn't have to interact with anyone to get their food made the restaurant appealing to immigrants who didn't speak English.

The coin-operated technology prevented customers from seeing the people who made most of the food or those who refilled the empty compartments that held the food until customers put their nickels in the machines to open the doors. While this made it seem as if the food came out of nowhere, there was an elaborate commissary system where baked goods and other products were manufactured for all the stores in that city. The only public-facing jobs at an Automat were the women stationed in glass booths who made change for people who needed to exchange dollar bills for nickels to insert in the food compartments. The separation of the server from the customer made the Automat much less social than any other restaurant. Labor unions became outspoken critics of Automats because of the threat they posed to workers at traditional restaurants.

The lack of waiting time before customers got their food made the Automat a forerunner of the fast-food revolution, which began during the 1950s with McDonalds. While people could easily visit most McDonald's restaurants in their cars, Automats, being located in urban settings, depended on customers walking in, which limited their ability to expand. While they were never particularly widespread, they received lots of attention in popular culture because the technology behind them was so sensational and because of their strong presence in New York City. The last Automat closed in 1991.

Explanation and Analysis of the Document

The only indication that this painting depicts an Automat is its title. By choosing an angle that looks out the front window, Hopper avoids the need to depict the banks of coin-operated compartments where customers got their food or, indeed, any other customers at all. The only hint of the size of the place is the row of lights reflected in the front window. At the same time, in an urban setting after dark, there must have been some light outside the window that would have shined into the restaurant. However, Hopper keeps the window dark in order to highlight the loneliness of this individual patron. While the style of the painting can be described as realism, it is worth remembering that a realist painting does not necessarily reflect real life. Artists like Hopper manipulated their work to evoke the feelings they wanted their pictures to raise.

Throughout his career, Hopper's primary objective was to paint loneliness. While the subject of the painting is alone and apparently thinking, it is worth noting that Automats were busy places, even at night. Because she is near the front door, the noise from the street would have been inescapable, and people would have passed her coming in and out of the restaurant. In this way, the painting illustrates the feelings of loneliness that city dwellers can have even in the most crowded urban settings.

The only visual hint that this restaurant is an Automat is the subject's decision to take off only one glove. Had she been there for a whole meal, she likely would have taken both off. The empty plate next to the saucer suggests that she stopped for a small snack and is quickly finishing her cup of coffee before she leaves again. This kind of speed was the advantage of an Automat over a full-service restaurant. The fact that she is unaccompanied suggests that she is getting a quick bite while working some nocturnal job rather than being out looking for a good time. There was no reason that this picture had to take place in an Automat as opposed to any other kind of restaurant. By setting it in one, Hopper is implying that people can be lonely in places that are invariably crowded, even late at night.

The view of the female customer's legs makes this painting slightly risqué for this time. While she is not dressed the same way as the legendary flappers of the 1920s, the fact that her skirt is short enough to show that much leg while seated does illustrate the rising hemlines that are often associated with the first stage of modern women's fashion. The ability to dine alone, especially at night, was a symbol of new freedom for women in this era. In this way, she illustrates what observers in that decade called the "new woman," someone who embodied a few of the new gender freedoms of the era without being completely out of step with previous traditions.

We can learn a bit more from her clothes and her pose. The thickness of her coat suggests that it's cold outside. Therefore, the heater in the corner is probably operating, especially at night. The way she has both hands on the cup and saucer suggests that she has had a trying day. However, as is the case with so many of Hopper's lone, isolated figures, the exact story of the scene is never fully told in a single picture. The viewer may empathize with the lone figure, but paintings designed to invoke loneliness never offer full explanations of how their subjects got that way.

—Jonathan Rees

Questions for Further Study

1. Why would an artist name their painting after a kind of restaurant if that kind of restaurant isn't visible in the painting itself?

2. What are the visual clues that *Automat* was painted during the 1920s rather than any time before or after?

3. Does the scene depicted here look sad to you? Why or why not?

4. Do you think Automats might work if they were revived today? Why or why not?

Further Reading

Books

Hardart, Marianne, and Lorraine Diehl. *The Automat: The History, Recipes, and Allure of Horn & Hardart's Masterpiece.* New York: Clarkson Potter, 2002.

Levin, Gail. *Edward Hopper: An Intimate Biography.* New York: Rizzoli, 2007.

Websites

Carlton, Genevieve. "How The Automat Paved the Way for Fast Food in the Early 1900s." *All That's Interesting,* May 6, 2020. https://allthatsinteresting.com/automat.

Documentaries

The Automat. Lisa Hurwitz, director. A Slice of Pie Productions, 2021.

FAZIL MOVIE POSTER

AUTHOR/CREATOR
H.C. Miner Lithograph Company

DATE
1928

IMAGE TYPE
FLYERS

SIGNIFICANCE
Symbolic example of the rise of Hollywood movies as a challenge to traditional Christian-centered moral standards and as a promise of vicarious experience for the audience

Overview

This is one of several posters advertising the movie *Fazil* (1928), a typical Hollywood romantic drama of the late silent era. The poster promises "Desire under the Palms and along Parisian Boulevards," an appeal to the audience's desire to be removed from their average American lives in the 1920s to a world of sex and spectacle. Hollywood movies like *Fazil* and the promotional materials attached to them, like this poster, presented a level of both popular entertainment and moral scandal unlike any previously experienced by American audiences.

About the Artist

This poster was produced by the H.C. Miner Lithography Company, a father-and-son operation working out of New York City. The company's artists drew posters for numerous popular entertainment theaters and events from 1896 until 1934: burlesque theaters, plays, vaudeville shows. The Miners gave up the presidency of their company to one Hugo Ziegfield, who extended their clientele to new cinema production companies, then located mostly in New Jersey and New York City. By the 1920s, the company was owned by Walter J. Moore, who obtained regular contracts for H.C. Miner from United Artists and Fox Film Corporation to produce movie posters. The content of their posters changed dramatically with the new contract. Once exhibiting a comic sensibility in their lithographs, the Miner company's movie posters incorporated elements of Art Nouveau, in keeping with the spirit of the productions they advertised. The Great Depression hit the company hard, and Moore had to file bankruptcy in 1934; when he revived his contracts a year later, he formed a new lithographic company, and H.C. Miner Lithography Company was not revived.

Context

From the beginning of the cinema as a form of entertainment, the goal was to provide escapism for the audience. At first, from the 1890s to 1915, the very novelty of watching people on a screen for fifteen to thirty minutes was enough. Following the release of *The Birth of a Nation* (1915), a three-hour epic, movies became more of a spectacle—longer, with bigger budgets, and featuring racier content to attract larger audiences to pay for those budgets. The actress Theda Bara was the

Document Image

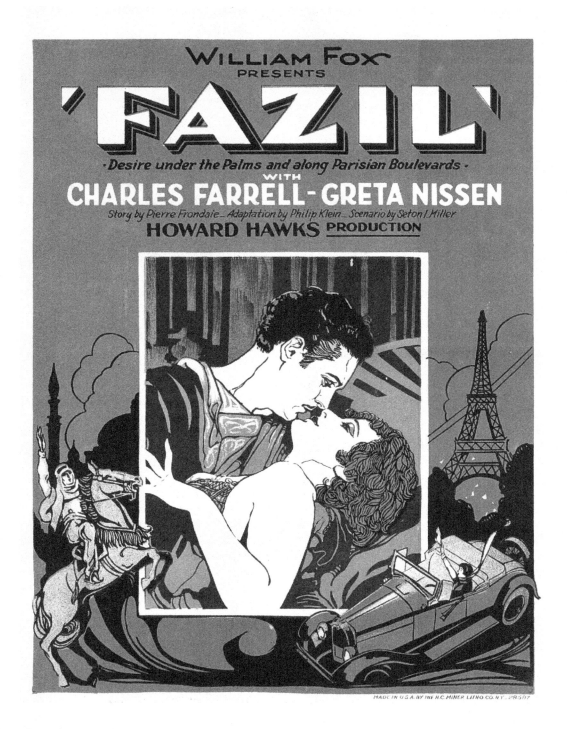

***Fazil* movie poster**
(Wikimedia Commons)

movie industry's first sex symbol, and her appeal was in her exoticism, dressing in barely-there costumes and portraying vampires and the ancient Egyptian queen Cleopatra.

By the 1920s, the world's capital of moviemaking had become the Los Angeles district called Hollywood. Because movies were still silent, it was easier for European and other countries to produce films that made large profits in the United States; all that was necessary was to change the dialogue cards. Nonetheless, Hollywood was such a center for film production that it would simply poach actors and actresses from around the world, bringing even more exoticism to the screen with actors like Rudolph Valentino (from Italy) and Greta Garbo (from Sweden). The atmosphere surrounding Hollywood movies and their content was suffused with sex, glamor, sin, and hedonism. The cinema was a place for people to go to escape their humdrum daily lives, and the 1920s was when that experience became truly widespread throughout the United States. Fifty million people on average attended at least one movie a week—a little less than half of the U.S. population—paying about seven cents for the privilege of being transported out of their presumably dull existences. In the nation's cities, movie houses themselves were decked out in florid decorations, including statues, vast curtains, plush seating, and orchestra pits for musicians to play a score to accompany the movie.

The loose and decadent morality of Hollywood spectacles was only enhanced by their exoticism, with many films set in Arabia, ancient Rome or Babylon, the Islamic empires, and Europe. There was a general fascination with all things far away in either time or geography, and going to a movie made the attainment of such exoticism cheap. Usually, such "orientalism"—fascination with the East in particular—could be introduced in a film simply by having a character wear silk, dress in strips of revealing fabric, and be surrounded by vaguely Eastern art and décor. It was enough to keep people coming and paying their seven cents, which was all that counted to Hollywood studios.

However, the loose atmosphere in Hollywood itself—where mysterious deaths and sex scandals abounded in the 1920s—was believed to be related to the product that Hollywood churned out. Fear of the movies' exoticism, glamor, and sexual license led to the establishment of a set of censorship rules called the Hays Code, after the former postmaster general who leant his name to enforcing it. Just as sound was being introduced to theaters, so was morality, and the escapism that movies represented would become more circumspect in the 1930s.

Explanation and Analysis of the Document

Several posters were created by H.C. Miner for the movie *Fazil*, all of them based on the same theme: of lovers intertwined, the man controlling the woman in his embrace, above her and about to kiss her. In each of them, the couple is surrounded with symbols of vicarious wealth and exotic locations—horses, sleek cars, and silhouettes of the Eiffel Tower and Istanbul's Hagia Sophia mosque in this one, other eastern architectural towers in the background of others, along with sun, sand, and tents. The colors are mostly warm oranges and yellows, hinting of the heat of the desert, not to mention the heat of passion. This poster promises "desire under the palms and along Parisian boulevards; another sings the praises of gondoliers in Venice as well. The obvious idea in going to see a movie like *Fazil*, as far as its poster is concerned, is to lose oneself in a story of romance and exotic travel—for women to imagine themselves being swept off their feet by roguish Arab Bedouins, and for men to imagine the control they wished to have over women at a time when flappers and the vote made it clear that old versions of male domination of women would no longer be tolerated in Western society in the 1920s.

Like many posters of its time, this poster was influenced by the Art Nouveau style of the previous era. Art Nouveau was employed in advertisements in the pre–World War I era, and the audience's comfort with its organic look allowed it to last as a symbol of beauty, freedom, and decadence in movie posters. *Fazil*'s florid font was meant to look like Arabic or Persian calligraphy. The garish colors, wavy and natural-looking background lines, and the detail in its characters' bodies and faces all suggest the influence of Art Nouveau. Any movie patron looking on this poster would respond immediately to the symbolism in it to understand the movie it advertised: a torrid romance played out across an international setting, promising to carry the watcher out of their own world and into one of luxurious living and dramatic love.

—David Simonelli

Questions for Further Study

1. How can one see movie posters as a reflection of their times? In other words, what in this poster makes you realize that the movie it advertises would be taking place in the 1920s?

2. Nearly half of all Americans attended a movie once a week, meaning—in an era where radio was in its infancy and there was no television—that they often must have shown up at theaters without knowing what movie was showing. What in this poster would make them choose (or not choose) this one to watch?

3. What might a Christian moralist find objectionable about this poster, if anything? The 1920s was as much an era of rising Christian fundamentalism as it was an era of loosening morals and relaxed social standards. What about *Fazil* and its poster would lead to the development of the Hays Code in the 1930s?

Further Reading

Books

Cleveland, Dwight M. *Cinema on Paper: The Graphic Genius of Movie Posters*. New York: Assouline, 2019.

Döring, Jürgen. *The Poster: 200 Years of Art and History*. New York: Prestel, 2020.

Fertig, Mark. *Hang 'Em High: 110 Years of Western Movie Posters, 1911–2020*. Seattle, WA: Fantagraphics Books, 2021.

Websites

Buckmaster, Luke. "The Greatest Decade in Cinema History?" BBC.com, June 1, 2020. https://www.bbc.com/culture/article/20200601-the-greatest-decade-in-cinema-history.

Dubitsky, Meghan. "The History of Movie Posters." Central Casting, December 20, 2021. https://www.centralcasting.com/history-of-movie-posters/.

Podcasts

Longworth, Karina. *You Must Remember This: The Secret and/or Forgotten History of Hollywood's First Century*. Podcast Audio. 2015–present. http://www.youmustrememberthispodcast.com/. Accessed March 24, 2022.

Photograph Of Bread Line, New York City

Author/Creator Unknown	**Image Type** Photographs
Date 1930	**Significance** Documentation of bread lines in New York City in the face of widespread poverty and hunger during the Great Depression

Overview

After the rollicking excesses of the 1920s—the "Roaring Twenties"—the United States was shocked back to reality by the advent of the Great Depression, the worst economic crisis in the nation's history. Seemingly overnight, banks failed, unemployment soared, and people were going hungry. In cities and towns across the country, people queued up in bread lines or outside charity soup kitchens just to get something to eat because they could not afford to buy food on their own. Municipalities, charitable organizations, and even celebrities labored to provide food for those in need. This photograph shows a bread line in New York City in 1930.

About the Artist

It is not known who took this photograph.

Context

The Great Depression began in late 1929 and persisted until 1941 and the outbreak of World War II, but economic conditions were at their worst from 1929 through 1933. During these years, some 90,000 U.S. businesses failed, and factories across the nation were closing. Steel production, for example, fell to about 12 percent of the industry's capacity. The gross national product—the value of all goods and services produced in the country—fell by almost half. The number of unemployed people rose steadily: In 1929, a mere 3.2 percent of the labor force was unemployed. In 1930 that figure rose to 8.7 percent; in 1931, 16 percent; in 1932, 23 percent; and in 1933, 25 percent. In 1930, the year in which this photo was taken, more than 4.3 million Americans were unemployed, and at its peak, the number of unemployed reached 13 to 15 million people. Many people were unemployed for the first time in their lives, and most were finding it difficult to feed themselves, let alone their families.

Although the stock market crash of October 1929 did not cause the Great Depression, it was clearly a symptom of a precarious economy. During the late 1920s, a kind of mania had taken over as investors were realizing dizzyingly high returns on stock market investments. The stock price of companies such as the

Document Image

A bread line in New York City in 1930
(Everett Collection Historical / Alamy)

Radio Corporation of America (RCA), General Electric, and U.S. Steel was in many cases doubling or even tripling as more and more investors poured money into the stock market. The market peaked on September 3, 1929, but the bubble was about to burst. Throughout September and October, the market was volatile, and on October 29, stock prices collapsed, wiping out the fortunes of numerous investors in the worst one-day market decline in history to that time.

The crash exposed underlying weaknesses in the economy. One was overproduction. Industry was churning out cars, radios, refrigerators, and other goods, but wages and farm profits were low, so many people could not afford the fruits of American industry. Those who did buy did so on credit, but when employers started laying off workers, many could no longer pay their debts. Banks that had loaned money to consumers then failed, taking with them the savings of their customers, who now could not pay off *their* debts. In 1929, 659 banks failed. The number increased to 1,352 in 1930, to 1,456 in 1931, to 2,294 in 1932, and to 5,190 in 1933.

The other underlying weakness was the uneven distribution of wealth. The Roaring Twenties were roaring for some Americans but not for others. Factory production had gone up 43 percent during the decade, but factory wages increased hardly at all. Throughout the decade, farm prices were falling at the same time as farmers were having to buy expensive machinery, so they were caught in a cycle of debt that they could not get out of. Billions of dollars were going into stock market speculation rather than into increasing wages. Economists believe that had wealth been more evenly distributed, Americans would have been able to absorb the output of industry; with production and purchasing more in balance, the nation might have averted the worst effects of the Depression.

African Americans, Native Americans, and Hispanics were among the hardest hit by the onset of the Depression. Many African Americans, for example, had migrated to the northern industrial states to find employment and to escape the racism and segregation of the South. These men, as the latest hired, were usually the first ones to be laid off. Mexican immigrants faced the same problem, and Native Americans who had moved to the cities during the construction boom of the 1920s were suddenly laid off when construction skidded to a halt. Nearly everyone, however, was affected in some way. College students had to drop out because their families could no longer afford tuition. Middle-class families that had lost everything stopped seeking medical care because they had no money, so doctors and dentists fell on hard times. Military veterans were often reduced to selling apples and pencils on street corners. The irony is that many people were subsisting on watery soups and beans while produce was rotting in the fields because prices were so low that harvesting was not worthwhile. Youngsters scavenged the cities for stray bits of coal to heat their homes while idle mining equipment stood nearby. The anthem of the Great Depression was the 1932 song, "Brother, Can You Spare a Dime?"

People were hungry. An oft-repeated story tells of a West Virginia schoolgirl who was told by her teacher to go home and get something to eat. The girl replied, "I can't. It's my sister's turn to eat today." The people of New York were just as hungry. Many were unemployed. Those who were fortunate enough to have a job saw their wages cut or were forced to accept part-time employment. These people were often unable to buy food. The result was that they went to soup kitchens, where they could get a meal, or stood in bread lines such as the one depicted here. Because of the large number of people who were standing in these lines, the city joined with private investors to provide fresh bread, often to thousands of people each day. Many bread lines were run by private charities such as the Red Cross. In Chicago, gangster Al Capone opened a bread line.

The New York City bread line, however, did not originate during the Great Depression. Shortly after the Civil War, Charles and Maximilian Fleischmann immigrated to the United States from Austria. Initially, they settled in Cincinnati, where they sold compressed yeast; still today, grocery shoppers can readily find Fleischmann's yeast on the shelves. Later, one of the brothers moved to New York City to open the Fleischmann's Vienna Model Café at the corner of 10th Street and Broadway in lower Manhattan. (The name of the café referred to the Viennese practice of cafés selling only their own baked goods.) By the late 1890s, the café's bread line was virtually an institution in the city: each night at midnight, homeless men would line up at a side door of the café. The door would open, and each man, often as many as 500 hundred during the economic downturn of 1893–94, would be given a half a loaf of bread, and anyone with a mug could get coffee. The Fleischmann enterprise even offered a "labor bureau," that is, information about available jobs. In time, photographers were taking pictures of this and other bread lines, and writers such as Theodore Dreiser were providing descriptions of them. In this way the bread line, with its images of silent, stolid men, their heads down, standing in orderly lines, was becoming an iconic symbol of hardship, poverty, homelessness, and hunger. It remains so to this day, although in the twenty-first century people who need food assistance are more likely to go to food pantries, food banks, or similar facilities.

What might seem odd to modern viewers of the many photos of people in bread lines is that most of them are men, and most of them are nicely dressed, often in suits and hats, not in torn or soiled clothing, as one might expect an indigent person to be dressed. The reason for this was pride. Many men needing food assistance felt in some obscure way that it was their fault they needed a "handout," and they were too proud, or too ashamed, to appear needy to their neighbors. They often felt they had failed their family. Accordingly, they often dressed as if they were heading for work, but instead they headed for an early-morning bread line.

Explanation and Analysis of the Document

This photo was taken on 25th Street in New York City. The location was near the East River, so the view in the photograph was to the west. The street is virtually empty of cars. Instead, a long line of men, four or five abreast, extends along the sidewalk into the distance. A few policemen are in evidence, but the orderliness of the bread line suggests that the police did not have to deal with any disorder, such as took place during the food riots that sometimes erupted in the cities. Most of the men appear to be reasonably well dressed. To the left is a boarded-up construction site that was likely curtailed after the Depression hit. The photo serves as a reminder of the widespread poverty and hunger of the Great Depression, the worst economic crisis in the nation's history.

—Michael J. O'Neal

Questions for Further Study

1. Why might the street shown in this photograph have been virtually empty of cars?

2. What, if anything, seems unusual about the line of people waiting in this photograph?

3. What steps did governments and private citizens take to alleviate hunger during the Great Depression?

Further Reading

Books

Henderson, Aileen Kilgore. *When the Wolf Camped at Our Door: My Childhood in the Great Depression.* Tuscaloosa: University of Alabama Press, 2022.

Miller, Dorothy Laager. *New York City in the Great Depression: Sheltering the Homeless.* Mount Pleasant, SC: Arcadia Publishing, 2009.

Poppendieck, Janet. *Breadlines Knee-Deep in Wheat: Food Assistance in the Great Depression.* New Brunswick, NJ: Rutgers University Press, 1986.

Roth, Benjamin. *The Great Depression: A Diary,* edited by James Ledbetter and Daniel B. Roth. New York: PublicAffairs, 2009.

Shlaes, Amity. *The Forgotten Man: A New History of the Great Depression.* New York: Harper 2007.

Terkel, Studs. *Hard Times: An Oral History of the Great Depression.* New York: New Press, 2000.

White, Ann Folino. *Plowed Under: Food Policy Protests and Performance in New Deal America.* Bloomington: Indiana University Press, 2015.

Articles

Pizer, Donald. "The Bread Line: An American Icon of Hard Times." *Studies in American Naturalism* 2, no. 2 (Winter 2007): 103–28.

Websites

Sculpture depicting a Great Depression bread line at the Franklin Delano Roosevelt Memorial, Washington, D.C., Library of Congress. https://www.loc.gov/item/2011633289/.

Stein, Sadie. "The Depression Radically Changed the Way Americans Ate" (review of *A Culinary History of the Great Depression* by Jane Ziegelman and Andrew Coe). *New York Times,* September 9, 2016. https://www.nytimes.com/2016/09/11/books/review/the-depression-radically-changed-the-way-americans-ate.html.

Documentaries

"Breadline: The Great Depression at Home." *People's Century,* PBS, 2000. https://www.keene.edu/academics/cchgs/collections/media/detail/breadline-the-great-depression-at-home/.

JOHN T. MCCUTCHEON: "A WISE ECONOMIST ASKS A QUESTION" CARTOON

AUTHOR/CREATOR	**IMAGE TYPE**
John T. McCutcheon	CARTOONS
DATE	**SIGNIFICANCE**
1932	Called attention to the role of bank failures in extending and worsening the Great Depression

Overview

In the early years of the Great Depression of the 1930s, large swathes of the American public were left virtually destitute. The economic collapse began in 1929, when the U.S. stock market crashed and billions of dollars in investments were lost. In the months that followed, people were trapped by unemployment and debt, in large part through a cycle of bank failures. In the first ten months of 1930, more than 700 banks failed. In 1932, the year of this cartoon by John T. McCutcheon, more than 1,400 banks failed, and the number rose to 4,000 in 1933. In all, some 9,000 banks failed during the decade. At the same time, unemployment was rampant; at the height of the depression, 25 percent of the workforce was unemployed, and those who had jobs often found their wages and hours cut, leaving them with little income to buy the bare necessities, let alone pay off debt—which in turn added to the insolvency of banks, which in turn created more poverty in what seemed at the time like an endless cycle. Thus, as this cartoon suggests, the savings and investment returns people had "squirreled" away during the Roaring Twenties were gone.

About the Artist

This image was created by John T. McCutcheon, a cartoonist who would come to be known as "the Dean of American Cartoonists." McCutcheon was born in Indiana in 1870 and graduated from Purdue University in 1890. His career as an artist began with the *Chicago Morning News*, where he built a dedicated following until he moved to the *Chicago Tribune* in 1903. His cartoons remained a regular feature of the front page of the *Chicago Tribune* for over forty years, until his retirement in 1946 at the age of seventy-six. He died three years later.

While McCutcheon also earned accolades for his written articles, such as his eyewitness account of the German invasion of Belgium at the beginning of World War I, it was his art that earned him the most acclaim. He added layers of human interest and personality into his illustrations that gave depth and importance to his commentary. His characteristic style allowed a deep and lasting connection with his audience. His career spanned some of the most tumultuous events of American history, including the Spanish American War, both world wars, and the Great Depression, all of which he covered with humor, great sensitivity, and uncompromising common sense. He was respected and acknowledged by his peers with multiple awards, including the Pulitzer Prize for this cartoon in 1932.

Document Image

"A Wise Economist Asks a Question"
(Sarin Images / GRANGER)

Context

The United States was riding a wave of optimism, patriotism, and success during the 1920s. In the wake of victory in World War I, the United States was on course to become a world industrial leader. This high came to an end in the summer of 1929. What initially looked like a normal recession rapidly turned into the greatest financial collapse in history.

While many point to the stock market crash of October 28, 1929, as the primary catalyst for the Great Depression, its origins collectively lay in a complicated mix of financial speculation in both the personal and business sectors, debt from World War I, bank failures, a loss of purchasing power, and protectionist policies. Each of these factors played an important role in the near-total meltdown of the U.S. economy.

In the aftermath of World War I, the urge to live well in the wake of so much destruction was enabled by the new ability to borrow on an unprecedented scale. Many people used this borrowed cash to invest in the stock market, which seemed to be a never-ending cash machine. Common stock prices were at an all-time high, and speculators predicted they would go even higher. However, historically, every huge boom comes with an eventual bust. As stock prices began to fall, people began to sell off as much of their holdings as they could before the prices could fall too much. Thus began a so-called panic that culminated in October. In only four days, the stock market lost 40 percent of its total value. In effect, thirty billion dollars disappeared. That thirty billion dollars amounted to ten times the entire federal budget for that year and more than the United States had spent on the entirety of World War I. Thousands of people were left with worthless stocks and millions of dollars in loans to banks all around the country.

With the stock market crash and fears of further economic woes, people across all economic classes stopped purchasing pretty much everything except necessities. This left many companies with a huge stockpile of products, so employers had little choice but to stop production until they could sell all of the product they had. With the fall of production, companies began to lay off workers at an alarming pace. The unemployment rate rose to 25 percent, and the wages for those individuals fortunate enough to have a job fell by over 40 percent. Around 300,000 businesses closed during the next several months. Hundreds of thousands of people could no longer pay their mortgages and suddenly became homeless when their homes were repossessed. The situation was intensified by droughts and dust storms that swept across the Great Plains. Tens of thousands of youths, whose families could no longer support them, left home in search of work and opportunity, but there was nowhere to go, and large villages of homeless, job-seeking people banded together in "Hoovervilles." Named after President Herbert Hoover, who was blamed for failing to support desperate citizens, these shanty towns were composed of dilapidated shacks often constructed from packing crates or any other scraps of materials the legions of homeless could scrape together.

The Great Depression lived up to its name, making poverty, homelessness, and desperation the norm for the United States for years and clearly defined the decade of the 1930s.

Explanation and Analysis of the Document

This is an excellent example of a political cartoon that uses symbolism to explain a larger issue rather than attempt to persuade the general public of a political point of view.

In the picture a man is sitting on a park bench. The worry lines on his face are clear, as is the vaguely rumpled appearance of his clothing. This ubiquitous image came to represent the legions of unemployed men who populated park benches and unemployment lines throughout America. In this case the central figure is clearly labeled as a "victim of bank failure." He is being questioned by a squirrel, a not-so-subtle stand-in for several sectors of the American public at the time, including "wise economists."

The squirrel, an animal known for stockpiling food for the winter, is asking why the man did not simply save his money for emergencies. This question seems like a sensible one to ask of the woeful populace suffering under the economic collapse of the 1930s, and undoubtedly it was asked millions of times by people with a one-dimensional "squirrel's eye view" of the situation. The reality is that the Great Depression had many more consequences besides high unemployment and repossessions.

As the Depression worsened, people began to rely on their savings more and more. However, most banks were suffering under the financial conditions as well, which included deflation. Deflation is defined as a general decrease in the prices of goods and services. While this may look like a good thing initially, major levels of deflation reduce the value of real estate and lead to lower wages. As a result, many people could not afford to pay their debts to banks, leading to widespread repossessions. At the time, many local banks across the nation were dependent on the income from loan payments to do business. When those payments stopped coming in, many backs found themselves unable to pay out enough cash to meet their own obligations.

Imagine going to the bank to withdraw 2,000 dollars, and the bank tells you that it cannot give you that whole amount today. Instead, the bank can give you 1,000 dollars today and the rest of your money tomorrow. You return home and tell your friends what happened, and they, in turn, rush to the bank to get as much of their money as they can. This is called a "run on the bank," and as the panic accelerates, the bank is then forced to close its doors to preserve what little cash they have left. What happens to your money then? Effectively, it is gone, and there is little or nothing to be done to retrieve it.

Between 1930 and 1933 an estimated 9,000 banks shut down for good. The total loss in personal and business savings was an estimated $140 billion in just over three years. This left millions of people with no savings and no hope. So, while the "wise economist" squirrel in

the cartoon seems to be making an effective point on the surface, the reality is that the people asking such questions have no real idea what is going on with the economy as a whole, and people are suffering and destitute through no real fault of their own.

In response to this economic devastation, President Franklin D. Roosevelt proposed the Emergency Banking Act, which passed through the House of Representatives in March 1933 in just 40 minutes. It was quickly followed that same year with a more official set of laws that created the Federal Deposit Insurance Corporation (FDIC), which was designed to maintain the stability of the nation's banking system. Not only does the organization regulate and watch over banks, but it also provides automatic coverage to traditional depositors, guaranteeing a return on their deposit if some disaster were to befall the bank. The FDIC and other agencies now act as safety valves to slow the system and prevent a repeat of the circumstances that led to the Great Depression.

This simple cartoon illustrates some of the larger issues contributing to the Great Depression and prompts the reader to educate themselves about the totality of the situation. It urges the reader to develop some sympathy and understanding for the people suffering through the situation, rather than simply berating them for a lack of foresight, which could neither have prevented their situation nor alleviated their misery.

—David Adkins

Questions for Further Study

1. How would you summarize the image and the issues surrounding it? Do you think it was effective?

2. What were the events and circumstances that led to the Great Depression?

3. What were the major economic and social conditions that the American people faced during the Great Depression?

Further Reading

Books

Bernake, Ben. *Essays on the Great Depression.* Princeton University Press, 2009.

Shales, Amity. *The Forgotten Man: A New History of the Great Depression.* Harper Collins, 2009.

Websites

"History of the FDIC." Federal Deposit Insurance Corporation website, June 6, 2022. https://www.fdic.gov/about/history/.

Documentaries

When the World Breaks. Hans Fjellestad, director. 2010

NAACP: "A MAN WAS LYNCHED YESTERDAY" PHOTOGRAPH

AUTHOR/CREATOR NAACP	**IMAGE TYPE** PHOTOGRAPHS
DATE 1936	**SIGNIFICANCE** Called attention to the frequent lynching of African Americans during the 1920s and 1930s

Overview

From 1920 to 1938, the National Association for the Advancement of Colored People (NAACP) displayed the ten-foot by six-foot flag from a window of its headquarters at 69 Fifth Avenue in New York City whenever a lynching was reported somewhere in the United States. Fifth Avenue was a well-traveled avenue in the Greenwich Village neighborhood of New York City. The flag's purpose was to bring awareness of African American lynchings to city dwellers and tourists, who were often detached from or unmindful of the brutal murders and the frequency with which they occurred. The flag also served as a form of protest and resistance to the violation of African American civil rights.

The NAACP was organized on February 12, 1909. Sixty white and Black activists, appalled by racial violence and civil rights violations occurring around the United States, established the organization. The NAACP focused on upholding and defending the constitutional rights of African Americans. Among its many courageous battles, the anti-lynching movement became one of the NAACP's most significant campaigns. Members of the organization worked tirelessly to motivate anti-lynching activism and garner public and congressional support for federal anti-lynching legislation.

A particularly compelling project materialized in the July 1916 supplement issue of NAACP's magazine *The Crisis*. In this issue, editor W. E. B. Du Bois presented a photo essay titled "The Waco Horror." It displayed photos chronicling the vicious and gruesome lynching, in Waco, Texas, in 1914, of Jesse Washington, a mentally challenged seventeen-year-old who had just been convicted of killing a white woman. The exposé gained national and international attention and invigorated the anti-lynching movement. However, the movement's efforts to gather federal anti-lynching legislative support was sidetracked by the United States' entrance into World War I in 1917. Nonetheless, the circulation of *The Crisis* grew to 50,000 over the next two years. The NAACP raised twenty thousand dollars for the anti-lynching campaign, and the flag "A MAN WAS LYNCHED YESTERDAY" was purchased with some of the funds. By 1919, the NAACP had grown to 300 branch offices and approximately 90,000 card-carrying members throughout the United States. Each office had its own replica of the flag to display.

The number of times the flag was in place reminded New York City dwellers of the frequency of the brutal acts. There is no record confirming the exact number of times the flag was displayed at the New York City

Document Image

"A Man Was Lynched Yesterday"
(Library of Congress)

headquarters, but the NAACP's procedure was to show it every time a lynching was reported in America, and evidence suggests at least 398 incidents occurred over eighteen years. In the late 1930s, the displaying of the flag became an issue between the NAACP and its New York office building's owner. Finally, in 1938, the flag waved outside the NAACP NY headquarters for the last time after the building proprietor threatened not to renew the organization's lease. Soon after, the NAACP gave the NY headquarters flag to the Library of Congress. Later the flag became part of the civil rights exhibit at the Thomas Jefferson Building at the Library of Congress in Washington, DC.

About the Artist

The creator of the flag and the photographer are not known. The flag, announcing a lynching, is being displayed from a window of the NAACP's New York City headquarters on Fifth Avenue.

Context

The Jim Crow era (1877–1960s) not only codified segregation in the southern states, it also marked a time of increasing racial terrorism, including lynching. The term "lynching" originated in 1780 during the American Revolution. It came to be associated with Charles Lynch, a Virginia plantation owner, politician, and Continental Army colonel. He and some fellow militia officers conducted extralegal arrests and trials and handed out sentences against British loyalists and enslaved people. Alleged criminals were whipped, their property was seized, and they might be drafted into the militia or forced to take loyalty oaths. Death was not associated with lynching at this time.

Thereafter, the term evolved in scope and meaning, depending on the region and time period. For some, lynching was a remedy for eroded trust in legal justice. By the 1830s, lynchings ending in death became a customary penalty in the North American West, where legal justice institutions were sporadic. As a result, in the absence of formal law enforcement, self-appointed punishers burned, hung, shot, or tortured victims.

For others, lynching was an effective way to reinforce traditional white supremacy. In the South, anxiety over uprisings of the enslaved and the rise of abolition movements in the country led many white suprema-

cists to adopt lynching as redress. African Americans, both enslaved and free, who were perceived by whites to have stepped out of line, as well as white abolitionists traveling in pro-slavery counties, often became lynching victims.

At the onset of the Civil War and for decades after, the term transformed to a more predominantly racial meaning. It was commonly associated with lawless killing by groups and sometimes mobs who supported white supremacy and the subjugation of African Americans. From 1877 to 1950, more than 4,000 documented lynchings occurred in the United States. At least 73 percent of lynchings involved African Americans—mostly men, but sometimes women and children as well. Lynchings occurred in thirty-seven states, although southern states accounted for most of the incidents. Circumstances surrounding the attacks varied. Some African American lynchings were clandestine acts carried out by vigilantes, but many more lynchings occurred at the hands of white mobs in public spaces as hundreds of onlookers watched. Sometimes law enforcement officers were complicit, and other times mobs successfully seized the accused despite policing efforts to carry out legal justice. These crimes were rarely investigated by authorities, and few of the executioners were ever brought to justice. As a result, terror swept through African American communities, whose members they could become the victims of racial violence and murder without legal protection. Fear of lynchings greatly contributed to the northern and western migration of millions of African Americans out of the South.

Lynching served as a means of intimidation to instill horror and suppress African American economic, social, and political equality. In some instances, African American victims were targeted because of economic clashes with white farmers. Land disputes and crop competition regularly became issues that escalated to lynchings. In other instances, victims were accused of minor crimes that did not warrant a death sentence, such as theft, vagrancy, or arson. There was a consistent pattern in which Black victims were accused of sexual offenses against a white woman or of the murder of a white woman. Even simple interracial contact or interactions with white women challenged the accepted social order and notions of the purity of white women. Many victims had no allegations at all against them but simply fell prey to a frenzied crowd looking for a Black person to punish. White supremacists used lynching and threats of lynching to coerce African

Americans not to vote, run for office, or testify in court as well. Displaying symbols associated with lynching, such as a noose in public or at a potential victim's dwelling or workplace, also served as a form of intimidation and a tool to reinforce white supremacy.

Explanation and Analysis of the Document

This photograph is a significant documentation of the lynching of African Americans during the Jim Crow era and the attempts to call attention to and end the heinous and racist practice. A broad observation of the photograph tells a story of New York City, an early twentieth century American metropolis. An American flag is displayed in the background. Viewers see a flourishing city avenue lined with multiple-story buildings, rows of automobiles parked along the sidewalks, and pedestrians walking to work, shopping, or perhaps sightseeing. High above it all and in clearer focus waves the NAACP flag, proclaiming "A MAN WAS LYNCHED YESTERDAY." The focus on the flag reflects how the NAACP communicated the horrors of African American lynching to main-street America and worked to promote collective dissent. The word "man" humanizes the lynching victim. The word "yesterday" aims to draw attention to the recentness of the event. The flag's message challenges the notion of progress in a flourishing American city and makes it clear that lynchings of African Americans are not acts of the historical past but a persistent and chronic ill in modern America. Images of this flag and replicas or variations of it have been utilized throughout the twentieth and twenty-first centuries, making it an icon for activism and protest.

In the early twentieth century, flags and banners with phrases and slogans were popular modes of communicating activist messages. This particular flag coincided with a broad NAACP anti-lynching campaign to urge people to take notice of lynching crimes and take action against them. In addition, the NAACP sponsored anti-lynching art exhibitions, held speaking engagements, conducted educational seminars, and organized fundraisers and protest marches. The association also lobbied Congress, filed lawsuits, and published articles and books. Ending lynching was not socially or culturally desirable to many white Americans who held deeply racist beliefs against African American equality. A major part of the anti-lynching

campaign involved working to debunk lynching myths that depicted African Americans as uncivilized, savage, and deserving of lynching because they assaulted white women. This narrative became stronger after the 1915 film *The Birth of a Nation* portrayed the Ku Klux Klan as patriotic heroes defending white womanhood from the alleged evils of African Americans.

The NAACP was successful in persuading some politicians in Congress. In 1918 Representative Leonidas Dyer of Missouri introduced H.R. 11279, known as the Dyer Bill, which would have made lynching a federal crime. The bill did not muster enough support to pass in the House until 1922. It then failed several years in the Senate because southern senators repeatedly filibustered the bill so it could not be voted upon.

Again in 1934, while the United States was still struggling to emerge from the Great Depression, Senators Edward P. Costigan of Colorado and Robert F. Wagner of New York introduced the Costigan-Wagner Act. This legislation centered on punishing law enforcement officers who failed to prevent a lynching and enacting countywide fines where lynchings occurred. Like the Dyer Bill, Southern opposition played a key role in preventing the bill's passage, first by employing the filibuster to stall, and second by leveraging the issue against supporting the president's economic agenda. President Franklin Roosevelt opposed lynching, but he worried that supporting a bill focused on fines and holding police and sheriffs accountable for lynching would cause him to lose southern congressional votes and support for his New Deal programs. Whether the federal government should pass anti-lynching legislation or leave the decision to individual states was a long-standing obstacle to passage as well. Subsequently, anti-lynching legislation passed the House of Representatives in 1937 and 1940 only to be thwarted again by Senate filibusters. Interestingly, a 1937 Gallup poll showed that 72 percent of adults surveyed thought Congress should pass legislation to federally criminalize lynching.

Up until 2021, both houses of Congress failed to pass more than 200 proposed anti-lynching bills. Finally, in the spring of 2022, the Senate and House of Representatives passed the Emmett Till Antilynching Act, making lynching a federal hate crime.

—Michelle Valletta

Questions for Further Study

1. Identify and explain how the meaning and characteristics of lynching changed over time.

2. For New York City onlookers in the 1920s and 1930s, what reactions and responses do you think the NAACP's flag inspired?

3. Identify and explain the political challenges of passing federal anti-lynching legislation.

Further Reading

Books

Blackmon, Douglas A. *Slavery by Another Name: The Re-Enslavement of Black Americans from the Civil War to World War II*. Duxford: Icon Books, 2012.

National Association for the Advancement of Colored People. *Thirty Years of Lynching in the United States, 1889–1918*. New York: National Association for the Advancement of Colored People. New York, 1967.

Articles

Lewis, Danny. "How an Anti-Lynching Banner from the 1920s and '30s Is Being Updated to Protest Modern-Day Violence." *Smithsonian Magazine*, July 11, 2016. https://www.smithsonianmag.com/smart-news/how-an-anti-lynching-banner-from-1920s-30s-being-updated-to-protest-modern-day-violence-180959752/.

Perloff, Richard M. "The Press and Lynchings of African Americans." *Journal of Black Studies* 30, no. 3 (2000): 315–30. http://www.jstor.org/stable/2645940.

Websites

Arrington, Benjamin T. "The History of American Anti-Lynching Legislation." February 5, 2019. We're History: America Then for Americans Now. http://werehistory.org/the-history-of-american-anti-lynching-legislation/.

Coleburn, Christina. "Issue Explainer: The Filibuster." Equal Democracy Project at Harvard Law School. March 21, 2021. https://orgs.law.harvard.edu/equaldemocracy/2021/03/21/issue-explainer-the-filibuster/

Lynching in America: Confronting the Legacy of Racial Terror, Third Edition. Equal Justice Initiative. 2017. https://lynchinginamerica.eji.org/report/.

"NAACP: A Century in the Fight for Freedom; The New Negro Movement." Library of Congress. https://www.loc.gov/exhibits/naacp/the-new-negro-movement.html.

Photograph Of Cab Calloway And Dancing Couples

Author/Creator Unknown	**Image Type** Photographs
Date 1937	**Significance** Memorializes the famed Cotton Club in Harlem, band leader Cab Calloway, and in a larger sense, the Harlem Renaissance of the 1920s and 1930s

Overview

The 1920s—the "Roaring Twenties"—launched the "Jazz Age," but the 1930s continued the revitalization of popular music with the popularity of big bands, which played largely in big-city nightclubs and similar venues One of the most prominent nightspots in New York City was the Cotton Club in Harlem, where numerous Black entertainers got their start in the business. One of the names closely associated with the Cotton Club is that of Cab Calloway, seen here directing his orchestra as a crowd of New Year's Eve revelers dance.

About the Artist

It is not known who took this photograph.

Context

The context of this photograph involves four cultural trends of the 1930s. The first is the rise to prominence of Cab Calloway, one of the most famous and popular singers and bandleaders of the big band era of the 1930s. He was born Cabell Calloway III on Christmas Day, 1907, in Rochester, New York, although he grew up in Baltimore, where he first started singing. Later he moved to Chicago, where he began to study law at what was then called Crane College, now Malcolm X University—but he never lost his love for music. He performed at the Sunset Club in Chicago, where he met Louis ("Satchmo") Armstrong, who taught him "scat" singing, the use of nonsense sounds and syllables to improvise melodies. In 1928 Calloway became the leader of his own band, the Alabamians.

It would be in New York City, the "Big Apple," however, that Calloway's music career—and later, his acting career—would flourish. In 1930 he began performing at the Cotton Club in Harlem, and quickly, as the leader of Cab Calloway and His Orchestra, he became a regular performer at the popular nightspot. In 1931 he hit it big with his number-one bestselling song "Minnie the Moocher," which sold more than a million copies. The song relies on a call-and-response pattern, and its famous "hi-de-hi-de-ho" chorus, which Calloway first improvised when he forgot the words, became the signature phrase that would follow him throughout his career.

Document Image

Cab Calloway at the Cotton Club in Harlem in 1937
(Bettmann / Getty)

Calloway had other hits, including "Moon Glow" (1934), "The Jumpin' Jive" (1939), and "Blues in the Night" (1941). His 1937 songs included "Wake up and Live," "Congo," "Peckin'," "She's Tall, She's Tan, She's Terrific," "Moon at Sea," and "Mama, I Want to Make Rhythm." He also took part in radio broadcasts and appeared in a number of films, including *The Big Broadcast* (1932), *The Singing Kid* (1936), and *Stormy Weather* (1943). In addition to music, Calloway had an impact on the reading culture with books such as 1944's *The New Cab Calloway's Hepster's Dictionary: Language of Jive*, which contained definitions for terms like "in the groove" and "zoot suit."

Calloway and his orchestra had successful tours in Canada and throughout the United States, but they skirted controversy by occupying private train cars when they traveled in the segregated South. He was known for his appealing voice, his energetic moves onstage, and his dapper dress, which often consisted of white tie and tails. As the big band era was drawing to a close in the late 1940s, Calloway turned to performing with a six-member group. He also struck out in a new direction on stage. Starting in 1952 he began a two-year run in the cast of a revival of *Porgy and Bess*, and he later had the male lead in a 1967 all-Black production of *Hello Dolly!* He reintroduced himself to younger fans by appearing on *Sesame Street* and in a 1990 Janet Jackson music video. In the 1980 movie *The Blues Brothers*, he donned his signature white tie and tails and performed "Minnie the Moocher." In 1993, President Bill Clinton presented him with a National Medal of the Arts. He died of complications of a stroke in 1994.

The second cultural trend was the big band era, which originated in the 1910s but reached the peak of its popularity between roughly the mid-1930s and mid-1940s. A "big band" typically was an orchestra of ten or more musicians, generally including saxophones, trumpets, trombones, and percussion, sometimes a clarinet. Very often a vocalist performed with the band. Big bands were particularly noteworthy for popularizing "swing" music, a type of dance music with a driving beat that practically compelled people onto the dance floor. Big band music evolved naturally from the jazz and blues music of New Orleans, Chicago, and Kansas City and began to incorporate elements of ragtime blues and Black spirituals. Among the most famous big band leaders of the era were Duke Ellington, Benny Goodman, Glenn Miller, Buddie Rich, Count Basie, and of course Cab Calloway. Songs that became major hits

and that can still be heard today include "In the Mood" (Glenn Miller), "Song of India" (Tommy Dorsey), "Don't Be That Way" (Benny Goodman), "Moonglow" (Artie Shaw) . . . such a list could go on and on. The growing popularity of the radio, and later of jukeboxes, boosted the fortunes of many big band artists.

The third cultural trend relevant to the context of this photo was the emergence and growing popularity of the Cotton Club in Harlem. For years, the Cotton Club featured prominent Black entertainers, although in a striking irony, it admitted only white audiences, usually wealthy whites who used the Cotton Club as an opportunity to experience the sights and sounds of "exotic" Harlem. The Cotton Club provided a springboard not only for Cab Calloway but for Duke Ellington and numerous other performers. In 1920 the nightspot was opened as the Club Deluxe at the corner of 142nd Street and Lenox Avenue by Jack Johnson, the first Black heavyweight boxing champion. In 1922 it was taken over by Owen Madden, well known as an underworld figure in Manhattan, who renamed it the Cotton Club. He remodeled the interior, limited audiences to whites only, and turned the Cotton Club into one of the most popular entertainment venues in Harlem, with weekly revues and weekly radio broadcasts.

Among the musicians who performed at the Cotton Club, in addition to Cab Calloway, was Duke Ellington, whose orchestra was hired as the house orchestra in 1927. It is thought that the primitive style of the club's décor inspired the "jungle style" of Ellington's music, found in such famous tunes as "Mood Indigo," "Black and Tan Fantasy," "Creole Love Call," and "Rockin' in Rhythm." Cab Calloway and His Orchestra took over as the house orchestra in 1931. Other prominent performers included Louis Armstrong, Ethel Waters, Lena Horne, Bill "Bojangles" Robinson, Billie Holliday, and the Nicholas Brothers. The Cotton Club also became a "hip" meeting spot for various celebrities; among those who could be spotted were Jimmy Durante, George Gershwin, Sophie Tucker, Paul Robeson, Al Jolson, Mae West, Richard Rodgers, Irving Berlin, Eddie Cantor, Fanny Brice, and Langston Hughes. The Cotton Club's peak years were from 1922 to 1935, but in 1935, Harlem was rocked by a race riot, and the Cotton Club moved to the Midtown theater district on West 46th Street before closing under financial pressure in 1940.

A final cultural development relevant to the photo was the Harlem Renaissance of the 1920s and 1930s. During those decades, African American artists, writers, and musicians were creating an explosion of important and highly regarded work. Much of this work emanated from the Harlem district, where the Black population had doubled during the 1920s. The Harlem Renaissance created a new Black identity, summed up by Alain Locke in *The New Negro* (1925). He wrote: "Negro life is seizing its first chances for group expression and self-determination." He saw the renaissance as an opportunity for Black artists to transform "social disillusionment into race pride." In his 1922 *Book of American Negro Poetry*, James Weldon Johnson wrote that Harlem was "the Mecca for the sightseer, the pleasure seeker, the curious, the adventurous, the . . . ambitious, and the talented of the entire Negro world."

The Harlem Renaissance is often associated with writers, among them Langston Hughes, Countee Cullen, Zora Neale Hurston, Claude McKay, Jean Toomer, Jessie Redmon Fauset, Arna Bontemps, Richard Wright, and numerous others. The renaissance, however, made itself felt in all artistic endeavors. Among visual artists were such names as Aaron Douglas, Lois Mailou Jones, Jacob Lawrence, Augusta Savage, and photographer James Van Der Zee. In the musical arts, the period saw the rise not only of big band musicians but also of such figures as Josephine Baker, Ethel Waters, and Bessie Smith.

All in all, the 1930s, along with the preceding years, was a period that saw a resurgence in the arts among Black musicians, performers, painters, and writers. The work of most of these figures, including the music of Cab Calloway, survives as a record of a time of renewed hope and aspiration in the African American community.

Explanation and Analysis of the Document

The photo bears little explanation. It shows a crowd of New Year's Eve revelers dancing at the Cotton Club in 1937. The dancers, all of whom are white, pack the dance floor. Many are wearing party hats. The dancers are elegantly dressed, with men in suits or tuxedos, the women in formal party dresses. At the lower right-hand corner of the photo, a smiling Cab Calloway, baton in hand, can be seen directing his orchestra. The photo memorializes the immense popularity of Harlem's Cotton Club during the 1930s and reminds viewers that despite the ongoing economic hardships of the Great Depression, people were still able to get out and have fun.

—Michael J. O'Neal

Questions for Further Study

1. What was the appeal of the Cotton Club to audiences and dancers?

2. Why did the Cotton Club, whose performers were Black, limit audiences to whites only?

3. What impact did the Cotton Club and musicians such as Cab Calloway have on American popular culture?

Further Reading

Books

Coverdale, George R., Jr. *Cab Calloway, Me, and Minnie the Moocher*. Pittsburgh: Dorrance Publishing, 2017.

Farebrother, Rachel, and Miriam Thaggert, eds. *A History of the Harlem Renaissance*. Cambridge, England: Cambridge University Press, 2021.

Floyd, Samuel A., Jr., ed. *Black Music: Harlem Renaissance*. Knoxville: University of Tennessee Press, 1993.

Haskins, James. *The Cotton Club*. New York: Random House, 1977.

Lewis, David L. *When Harlem Was in Vogue*. New York: Knopf, 1981.

Mallory, Noreen. *Harlem in the Twentieth Century*. Charleston, SC: History Press, 2011.

Rayburn, John. *The Remarkable Big Band Era*. Mechanicsburg, PA: Sunbury Press, 2020.

Shipton, Alyn. *Hi-De-Ho: The Life of Cab Calloway*. New York: Oxford University Press, 2010.

Tumpak, John R. *When Swing Was the Thing: Personality Profiles of the Big Band Era*. Milwaukee: Marquette University Press, 2009.

Wall, Cheryl A. *The Harlem Renaissance: A Very Short Introduction*. New York: Oxford University Press, 2016.

Articles

Jerving, Ryan. "The Cotton Club." In *Encyclopedia of the Harlem Renaissance*, edited by Cary D. Wintz and Paul Finkelman. New York: Routledge, 2004.

Wilber, Bob. "The Cotton Club." In *Music Was Not Enough*, 177–88. London: Palgrave Macmillan.

Websites

Calloway, Cab. "The Hepster's Dictionary." New York Public Library, 1938. https://dancesafari.com/wp-content/uploads/2018/12/The-Hepster%E2%80%99s-Dictionary.pdf.

Kelly, Erin. "Glamour, Gangsters, and Racism: 30 Photos Inside Harlem's Infamous Cotton Club." *All That's Interesting*, March 6, 2019. https://allthatsinteresting.com/cotton-club.

King, Samantha. "Cotton Club: The Staple of Black Talent in the Harlem Renaissance." *NYS Music*, June 8, 2021. https://nysmusic.com/2021/06/08/the-cotton-club-the-staple-of-black-talent-in-the-harlem-renaissance/.

"The Legendary Cotton Club in Harlem 1923 to 1935." *Harlem World*. https://www.harlemworldmagazine.com/harlem-history-the-cotton-club/.

"A New African American Identity: The Harlem Renaissance." *Our American Story*, National Museum of African American History and Culture, Smithsonian. https://nmaahc.si.edu/explore/stories/new-african-american-identity-harlem-renaissance.

Documentaries

Minnie the Moocher and Many, Many More, narrated by Cab Calloway, edited by Melanie Gilman and Jacques Bégin, 1983. https://www.youtube.com/watch?v=DRRr1YaNsQA.

Jacob Lawrence: *The Great Migration* Painting

AUTHOR/CREATOR Jacob Lawrence	**IMAGE TYPE** PAINTINGS
DATE 1940	**SIGNIFICANCE** Draws attention to the Great Migration of African Americans from the South to the North in the early decades of the twentieth century

Overview

This image is one of sixty panels created by African American artist Jacob Lawrence in his extended work *The Migration Series*. The paintings were done with casein tempera (a type of water-soluble paint with a milk base) on hardboard. Taken together, the paintings document the Great Migration, the term that refers to the mass movement of African Americans from the rural South to the urban North that took place largely between the two world wars. During those years, Black southerners were fleeing the segregation and racial oppression of the South in search of better jobs and a better life. This panel is the first of the series and indicates that the destination cities for many migrating Blacks were Chicago, New York, and St. Louis.

About the Artist

Jacob Lawrence was one of the most widely acclaimed African American artists of the twentieth century. His work chronicles the lives and struggles of African Americans, usually in an abstract, colorful style. He was born in 1917 in Atlantic City, New Jersey. After his parents separated, he moved with his mother to Harlem when he was twelve years old. Already as a child he was showing artistic talent at the Utopia Children's Center, an after-school program in arts and crafts. During the Great Depression of the 1930s, he joined the Civilian Conservation Corps. After he returned to Harlem, he was associated with the Harlem Community Art Center and began painting early work depicting Harlem scenes. He decided to produce paintings in various series of panels when he decided to depict the life of Toussaint L'Ouverture, the revolutionary leader who founded Haiti. Most of his subsequent work consisted of panels that, taken together, tell a story about the subject, including his collection *The Migration of the Negro*, later known as *The Migration Series*. Other subjects include Frederick Douglass, Harriet Tubman, John Brown, Harlem, war, the hospital (inspired by his own hospital stay), and the South. In 1941 *The Migration Series* was exhibited in a New York City gallery, making Lawrence, at age twenty-four, the first Black artist to be represented in a mainstream U.S. gallery. That same month, *Fortune* magazine published an article about Lawrence that included illustrations of twenty-six of the panels.

During World War II, Lawrence served in the U.S. Coast Guard. After the war, he returned to painting. He also taught at Black Mountain College in North Car-

Document Image

***The Great Migration* by Jacob Lawrence**
(© 2022 The Jacob and Gwendolyn Knight Lawrence Foundation, Seattle / Artists Rights Society, New York)

olina. He continued to paint through the 1950s, and in 1960 he was honored with a retrospective exhibition by the American Federation of Arts. He later taught at New York's Art Students League and at Brandeis University, the New School for Social Research, California State College at Hayward, the Pratt Institute, and the University of Washington. In 1983 he was elected to the American Academy of Arts and Letters. He died in 2000.

Context

In the 1910s, African Americans living in the rural South began to defect to cities in the North in what became known as the Great Migration. They were fleeing the repressive Jim Crow laws of the southern states as well as the menial jobs and humiliations they were forced to endure, often in conditions that were little better than the slavery their ancestors had endured. They were also fleeing the lynch mobs: the Tuskegee Institute recorded 3,446 lynchings of Blacks from 1882 to 1968, although the peak years had been the 1890s. The Great Migration began in about 1916 and would eventually result in six million people leaving their homes and communities for the North. When the Great Migration began, 90 percent of the nation's Blacks were living in the South. By the time the Great Migration ended, 47 percent were living in the North or the West.

The result of this population movement was a major shift in the culture, the economy, and American politics. What had been almost entirely a rural population rapidly became more urbanized. The Black population of central Harlem, for example, was about 33 percent in 1920. By 1930 the figure was 70 percent. It is safe to surmise that the Harlem Renaissance—the flowering of arts and culture in Harlem in the 1920s and 1930s—would likely not have taken place, at least to the extent it did, without the Great Migration. Similarly, in Chicago, Blacks made up less than 2 percent of the population in 1910. Between 1916 and 1919, 50,000 Blacks moved to Chicago's South Side in what became known as the Black Belt. By 1940, when Lawrence was producing his *Migration Series*, the figure had quadrupled, and by 1960, 25 percent of the city's population was Black.

One of the chief draws for southern Blacks was economic opportunity. In the early years, large numbers of men were serving in the armed forces during World War I. Black people initially were able to get decent-paying jobs in the industrialized North as the nation was churning out the weapons of war. Additionally, employers in such industries as steel, meat packing, and the railroads were actively recruiting Black workers. The *Chicago Defender* newspaper, which was dropped off in southern towns by railroad porters as they traveled their routes, provided potential immigrants in the South with information about the city, including job opportunities.

Most of the immigrants arrived in the cities having absolutely no idea where to go or how to get settled. Organizations such as the Chicago League on Urban Conditions Among Negroes provided information about jobs and other matters of concern to the new migrants. Living conditions were often horrible as newly arrived migrants crowded into ramshackle tenements. Often, they slept in shifts in a single bed. Restrictive covenants in deeds to houses in Chicago's white neighborhoods prevented Blacks from owning homes in more than 80 percent of the city. Author Lorraine Hansberry, the author of the semi-autobiographical play *A Raisin in the Sun* about a Black family living in dilapidated housing in south Chicago, recalled being "spat at, cursed and pummeled in the daily trek to and from school. And I also remember my desperate and courageous mother, patrolling our household all night with a loaded German Luger, doggedly guarding her four children."

The roster of people who took part in the Great Migration, or whose parents did, reads almost like a who's who of prominent Black Americans. Novelist Richard Wright had been the son of a southern sharecropper before migrating. Other prominent figures, from all walks of life, include jazz musician John Coltrane, NBA star Bill Russell, actor James Earl Jones, and folklorist Zora Neale Hurston. The children of migrants include, among countless others, musicians Miles Davis and Muddy Waters; authors Ralph Ellison, Toni Morrison, and August Wilson; singers Diana Ross, Tupac Shakur, Prince, and Michael Jackson; television producer Shonda Rhimes; athletes Venus and Serena Williams, Althea Gibson, and Jackie Robinson; Los Angeles mayor Tom Bradley; and countless others, including Jacob Lawrence. The migrants would become the ancestors of most African Americans born in the North and West.

Essentially, three different routes were followed. Those leaving from such states as Florida, Georgia, the Carolinas, and Virginia tended to remain to the east and arrived in New York City and other cities along the east coast. Those from such states as Alabama, Mississippi, Arkansas, and Tennessee headed north to arrive in Chicago and St. Louis, along with other cities in the middle section of the country. Those from Texas and Louisiana tended to head toward California and other western states. Blacks making the trip by train usually had to ride in segregated Jim Crow train cars, meaning that they were put into the front cars so that they would be the first to absorb the brunt of any collision. They were not allowed into dining cars, so they brought along their own food.

Escaping the Jim Crow South, however, did not solve all of the problems African Americans faced. In many ways, the migration actually heightened racial divisions. As African Americans congregated in the cities of the North, their disproportionate incarceration began to take root, along with disparities in health care, employment, and education. In the summer of 1919 alone, the "Red Summer," there were thirty-eight race riots in cities across the country, including Chicago, New York City, Syracuse (New York), Wilmington (Delaware), Philadelphia, New London (Connecticut), and Baltimore. White union workers in the North came to view Black workers as competitors for jobs rather than fellow workers, particularly during World War I. In the South, resistance to the loss of cheap labor meant that recruiters of Black labor often faced crushing fines and even imprisonment; Macon, Georgia, required a recruiter to have a license that cost

$25,000, plus letters of recommendation from twenty-five local businessmen, ten ministers, and ten manufacturers—a virtual impossibility. Some southern authorities tried to stem the flow of Black workers to the North by arresting them on railway platforms, charging them with "vagrancy." Meanwhile, some towns in the North became known as "sundown towns," meaning that Blacks could not be out and about after dark. In many places, "whites only" signs in shop windows were the norm. Clearly, the new migrants were not always welcome.

Explanation and Analysis of the Document

Lawrence's painting is highly abstract and stylized. It relies on distinct patches of color, including blue, black, yellow, burnt orange, and teal, using the colors to make each figure in the crowd distinct. It depicts crowds of African Americans, their backs to the viewer, heading toward three gates, labeled Chicago, New York, and St. Louis. Latticework divides the three gates. The faces of the figures in the painting are for the most part not visible. The painting tells a simple story. Blacks were abandoning the South and heading toward the cities of the North during the Great Migration, which was ongoing when Lawrence created the painting.

—Michael J. O'Neal

Questions for Further Study

1. Why might Lawrence have adopted the artistic style he used in this painting?

2. In what way does this panel of Lawrence's work tell a story?

3. In what fundamental ways did the Great Migration change the United States?

Further Reading

Books

Arnesen, Eric. *Black Protest and the Great Migration: A Brief History with Documents*. Boston: Bedford/St. Martin's 2002.

Brown, Jessica Bell, and Ryan N. Dennis, eds. *A Movement in Every Direction: A Great Migration Critical Reader*. New Haven, CT: Yale University Press, 2022.

Gregory, James N. *The Southern Diaspora: How the Great Migrations of Black and White Southerners Transformed America*. Chapel Hill: University of North Carolina Press, 2005.

Harrison, Alferdteen. *Black Exodus: The Great Migration from the American South*. Jackson: University Press of Mississippi, 1992.

Lawrence, Jacob. *The Great Migration: An American Story*. New York: HarperCollins, 1995.

Lemann, Nicholas. *The Promised Land: The Great Black Migration and How It Changed America*. New York: Vintage, 1992.

Rhodes-Pitts, Sharifa. *Jake Makes a World: Jacob Lawrence, A Young Artist in Harlem*. New York: Museum of Modern Art, 2015.

Wilkerson, Isabel. *The Warmth of Other Suns: The Epic Story of America's Great Migration*. New York: Random House, 2011.

Articles

Tolnay, Stewart E. "The African American 'Great Migration' and Beyond." *Annual Review of Sociology* 29 (2003): 209–32.

Websites

"The Great Migration (1910–1970)." African American Heritage, National Archives. https://www.archives.gov/research/african-americans/migrations/great-migration#:~:text=The%20Great%20Migration%20was%20one,the%201910s%20until%20the%201970s.

"Great Migration: The African-American Exodus North" (interview with Isabel Wilkerson). *Fresh Air*, NPR, September 13, 2013. https://www.npr.org/2010/09/13/129827444/great-migration-the-african-american-exodus-north.

Grossman, James. "Great Migration." *Encyclopedia of Chicago*, 2004. http://www.encyclopedia.chicagohistory.org/pages/545.html.

"Jacob Lawrence: The Migration Series." Museum of Modern Art. https://www.moma.org/calendar/exhibitions/444.

"Jacob Lawrence: The Migration Series." Phillips Collection. https://lawrencemigration.phillipscollection.org/.

Wilkerson, Isabel. "The Long-Lasting Legacy of the Great Migration." *Smithsonian Magazine*, September 2016. https://www.smithsonianmag.com/history/long-lasting-legacy-great-migration-180960118/.

Documentaries

The Great Migration: From Mississippi to Chicago. PBS, 2003. https://www.tpt.org/american-experience/video/american-experience-great-migration-mississippi-chicago/.